The Jews of
KHAZARIA

The Jews of
KHAZARIA

KEVIN ALAN BROOK

JASON ARONSON INC.
Northvale, New Jersey
Jerusalem

First softcover printing 2002

This book was set in 11 pt. New Baskerville by Hightech Data Inc.

Copyright © 2002, 1999 by Jason Aronson Inc.

Library of Congress Cataloging-in-Publication Data

Brook, Kevin Alan.
   The Jews of Khazaria / Kevin Alan Brook.
      p. cm.
   Includes bibliographical references and index.
      ISBN 0–7657–6032–0 (hardcover)
      ISBN 0–7657–6212–9 (softcover)
      1. Khazars. 2. Jews   Russia   History. 3. Russia   Ethnic
   relations. I. Title.
   DK34.K45.B76 1999
   947'.01'088296—dc21   98-38767

Printed in the United States of America on acid-free paper. For information and catalog write to Jason Aronson Inc., 230 Livingston Street, Northvale, NJ 07647-1726, or visit our website: http://www.aronson.com

This book is dedicated to:

VICTOR BALABAN

JULIAN SIEGMUND BIELICKI

LESLIE MAYO EVENCHICK

GREGORY A. KOSARIN

DAVID ARI KRASSENSTEIN

S. MATS L. PHILIP

DAVID M. RAZLER

BENJAMIN R. ROSENTHAL

and

ALAN J. WOLKOWER

*All of whom graciously shared with me
their families' oral traditions of
Jewish Khazar ancestry.*

Contents

ACKNOWLEDGMENTS

I am indebted to many people for their assistance and encouragement during the course of my research.

First of all, I would like to express my appreciation to Herbert Guy Zeiden for his guidance and innovative linguistic observations.

For news about archaeological expeditions to Crimea and Russia, in which many Jewish artifacts were found, my thanks go to Alexander Gendler and Michael (Menashe) Goldelman. Much credit is also due to Ehud Ya'ari, the Israeli journalist who broadcast a three-part documentary about the Khazars on Israeli television in March 1997.

For important information about Hungarian-Khazar relations, I offer many thanks to Alfred S. Hámori and Peter I. Hidas.

For information about the Bulgars, my gratitude goes to H. Mark Hubey and Shawn McDermott. S. Mats L. Philip provided information about Khazar artifacts in Sweden. Ken Ottinger reported on a special Turkic Jewish community in

Transylvania. William Abram Aldacushion provided information about the Subbotniki people.

For suggestions on reading materials, my thanks go to Paolo Agostini, Fred Astren, Peter Barta, Anders Berg, David Christian, Bruce G. Conrad-Reingold, Alexander Gendler, Daniel E. Gershenson, Michael Goldelman, Saul Issroff, Arif Kiziltug, Martin N. Kruger, Vladimir Levchenko, Philip E. Miller, S. Mats L. Philip, Edward D. Rockstein, Seth R. Rosenthal, Heidi M. Sherman, Sheila Tanenbaum, Nigel Thomas, Rabbi David A. Wachtel, Shaul Wallach, Steven Weiss, Bozena Werbart, and Herbert Guy Zeiden.

I would also like to thank Peter A. Csángó, Pavel M. Dolukhanov, Alexander Gendler, Michael Goldelman, Jeff H. Horen, Heidi M. Sherman, Steven Weiss, and Herbert Guy Zeiden for obtaining copies of articles that proved to be helpful in my research.

Vassil Karloukovski translated from Bulgarian. Fred Hainbach translated from German. Egbert Assink translated from Hebrew. Paolo Agostini, Peter Barta, and Alfred S. Hámori translated from Hungarian. Philip M. Germansderfer translated from Polish and Russian. Elchin Bagirov, Alexander Boguslawski, and Karlygash Irmukhan Sea translated from Russian. Jan-Erik Naarttijarvi translated from Swedish.

Lawrence J. Epstein, Rabbi Nissan Daniel Korobkin, Seth R. Rosenthal, and István Szűcks deserve recognition for giving me the initial encouragement to publish my work.

Finally, I want to thank the following people for their insights and inspiration: Brian Boeck, Deborah Cavel-Greant, David Chagall, Leslie Mayo Evenchick, Anne Hart, Zinetulla Insepov, Timur Kocaoglu, Helen Liesl Krag, Dennis A. Leventhal, Richard Mendoza, Arlene Blank Rich, John Sloan, Barbara Levy Taverna, Bruce Wedgwood-Oppenheim, Avi Yaari, and countless others.

This book could not have been completed without the generous assistance of these fine people.

INTRODUCTION

This book explores the history and culture of the Khazars, a Turkic people who established a large empire in southern Russia during the early medieval period. The Khazars were politically and militarily powerful, representing a "third force" in Europe and Asia on par with the Byzantine Empire and the Islamic Caliphate. They were known to be excellent traders, farmers, fishermen, warriors, and craftsmen.

Perhaps the most interesting aspect of the Khazars' history is their adoption of the Jewish religion. For centuries, the Khazar territory was a major region of settlement for Jewish refugees escaping persecution. These refugees introduced ethical monotheism to the Khazars, and King Bulan found Judaism to be an attractive choice. Under the leadership of the Jewish kings of Khazaria, the Khazar people adopted Judaism in large numbers. Synagogues and yeshivas were established in Khazaria, and the study of Torah and Talmud became commonplace. The Khazars underscored their allegiance to the Jewish faith by adopting the Hebrew script and Hebrew per-

sonal names such as Joseph, Aaron, and Samuel, even to the
extent of naming their children after Jewish holidays such as
Pesach and Hanukkah. Jews lived in all of the major Khazar
towns.

The Khazars exerted a tremendous influence on world
history. The following chapters discuss important Khazar contributions to the medieval world, including:

1. Their halting of Arab conquests north of the Caucasus,
   similar to the role of the Franks in western Europe.
2. Their founding of the great city of Kiev.
3. Their establishment of a major center for world trade.
4. Their impact on the migration of the Bulgars and
   Magyars out of the Volga region and to their present
   lands in Bulgaria, Tatarstan, Bashkiria, Chuvashia, and
   Hungary.
5. Their influence on the early culture and governmental
   system of the Magyars.
6. Their spread of glassmaking technology, which they
   learned from Middle Eastern Jews.
7. Their contribution to the ethnogenesis of Eastern European Jews and other peoples, as will be demonstrated
   in the text to follow.

This book analyzes a wealth of historical, archaeological,
and linguistic evidence in order to trace the events and migrations of the Khazars and dispel popular misconceptions
about them, such as: (1) the notion that the Khazars did not
manufacture most of the goods they used, but rather imported
them; (2) the premise that the conversion to Judaism was re-
stricted to the Khazar rulers and some of the nobility; and (3)
the theory that the Crimean Karaites are largely descended
from Khazars. Additionally, the Khazar conversion will be compared with the adoption of Judaism by some of the Alans,
Cumans, and various other European, African, and Asian
peoples. This will serve to show that the idea that there were
never many converts to Judaism is a misunderstanding.

I will also put forth my theory of the origins of the Eastern European Jews. I believe that the missing link between the Turkic-speaking Khazars and the Yiddish-speaking Jews of later times were the Slavic-speaking Jews who inhabited Kievan Rus in the period immediately following the demise of the Khazar Empire at the hands of Svyatoslav. In my opinion, these Slavic-speaking Jews were a mixture of Khazars, Slavs, and Middle-Eastern Jews. These Jews eventually intermarried with Yiddish-speaking Jews from Bavaria as well as with Jews from Prague, Vienna, the Iberian peninsula, and other communities. Thus, the Ashkenazic ethnogenesis, having been formed by migrations from the East (Khazaria), West (e.g., Germany, Austria, Bohemia), and South (e.g., Greece, Mesopotamia, Khorasan), is more complex than previously envisioned.

The Khazars are an important part of the Jewish heritage. The story of the Khazars proves that Judaism was an appealing alternative embraced by many Turks and also shows that medieval Jewish history includes more than merely tragedy and persecution. The Khazar Jews were once masters of the steppes and forests of Russia, and Ashkenazic Jewry should take pride in its achievements.

I felt compelled to write this book because I want to make the world of the Khazars more accessible to both the average reader and the scholar. Only a precious few extensive studies on the Khazars have been published in the English language in recent times. I am pleased to present this book in the hope that awareness of the Khazar Empire and our Jewish roots will be heightened.

—Kevin Alan Brook

1

THE ORIGINS
OF THE KHAZARS

*F*or millennia, wandering bands of nomads lived in the
*steppes of central Asia and southern Russia. Yet, contrary
to popular belief, these nomads possessed culture and
other traits of civilized life. Some of the most spectacu-
lar archaeological finds in the world have been discovered in the grasslands of Ukraine and Russia. The
Scythians, of Iranian origin, were one of the earliest societies in the steppe (seventh to third centuries B.C.E.),
and their rich treasures are still being explored. In the
summer of 1996, the tomb of a Scythian military commander was found near the village of Ryzhanivka in
Ukraine that contained a gold-handled sword, a head-
dress decorated with gold, wine jars, and silver decora-
tions. Another exciting discovery, from Tolstaya Mogila
along the Dnieper River, was a Scythian gold pectoral
that contained detailed engravings of animals and*

1

*people.¹ At other gravesites, Scythians were buried along
with large quantities of gold bracelets, rings, and tiaras.*

*Centuries after the Scythian society disappeared,
other societies made their mark in the steppes, including the Sarmatians, Huns, and Khazars. The Khazars
emerged on the world scene as Turkic horsemen who
believed in shamanism and lived a nomadic lifestyle.
Over the course of many centuries, the Khazars adopted
a more settled way of life and replaced their former
Tengri beliefs with Judaism, Islam, and Christianity. This
chapter explores the evolution of the Khazars into a
tribe and the earliest development of their kingdom.*

THE TURKIC HERITAGE

The Khazars were predominantly Turkic. The Greek historian
Theophanes (b. about 725, d. about 818) wrote that the
Khazars were "Turks from the East."² Turkic genealogical
myths identified Khazar as the "brother" of other Turkic tribes,
such as the Bulgar, Sabir, Avar, and Oghuz.³ Syriac legends
said that the ancestor of the Khazars was named "Khazarig,"
the brother of "Bulgarios."⁴ Most scholars believe that these
legends have a historical basis, and that the Khazars were indeed closely related to Turkic tribes such as the Bulgars and
Bashkirs. Thus, the Khazars probably originated in the steppes
of central Asia, or perhaps the Ural Mountains or the Caucasus
Mountains. The details of their origins are still somewhat obscure.

According to Turkic legend, as preserved in Chinese
chronicles,⁵ the original Turks lived beside a large swamp.
Enemies killed them off, with the exception of one boy, whose
feet they cut off and whom they threw into a marsh. The boy
was rescued by a female wolf. Years later, the boy impregnated
the wolf. When the leader of his enemies hired someone to
kill the boy, the boy and the wolf fled to a cave in a moun-

tain north of the Turfan Depression (in eastern Turkestan, which today is in northwest China). The wolf gave birth to ten sons in the cave. One of the ten sons was named A-shih-na, and his tribe became powerful and greatly expanded in size. All ten sons settled along the southern slope of the Altai Mountains, came under the control of the Juan-Juan, and became blacksmiths. The A-shih-na adopted the name "Turk." The legend indicates that the wolf is the totem ancestor of the Turks.[6]

As was the case with most nomadic Turks, the Khazars were racially and ethnically mixed. Among them were black-haired peoples with dark brown eyes, red-haired peoples with green or hazel eyes, and fair-haired peoples with blue eyes. Some had high cheekbones, wide faces, and narrow eyes, resembling the peoples of East Asia. Many others resembled Europeans or Middle Easterners. The diversity of the Turks is also made apparent by the fact that the term "Turk" is not a racial term, but rather was applied to a variety of different nomadic tribes that shared a common vocabulary and culture. Some have suggested that the Turks were a mixture of Iranians and Mongols.[7] The heterogeneity of the Turks is still apparent today, since the disparate modern Turkic peoples often look strikingly dissimilar. For example, the Gagauz people of Europe differ from the Kazakhs and Yakuts of Asia, just as Azeris differ from Uyghurs. In certain instances, this diversity can be explained by the frequent process by which diverse peoples originally of non-Turkic origin were "Turkicized" and adopted Turkic as their language.[8]

The Khazars were described by ibn-Said al-Maghribi as having blue eyes, light skin, and reddish hair.[9] Many other early Turkic tribes also had red hair. Chinese and Muslim sources indicated that the ancient Qirghiz (Kyrgyz) people living north of the Sayan Mountains along the upper Yenisei River had red hair, blue eyes, and white skin. For example, Gardizi reported a legend of the origin of the Kyrgyz people that stated that a Khazar nobleman named Bashqird befriended the "Saqlabs"

(Slavs) and called another group of people whom he led the "Khirkhiz." He added that it was said that the Saqlabs mixed with the Khirkhiz and that this explains the incidence of red hair and white skin among the Khirkhiz.[10] The *T'ang-shu* chronicle said that the Kyrgyz people were ". . . tall, with red-hair, ruddy-faced and blue-eyed. Black hair is considered a bad omen."[11] The red hair of the Kyrgyz may mean that they were partly of some non-Turkic origin. A Hsiung-nu ruler in the early fourth century had a red beard, and the *Shih-ku* chronicle said that the Hu people, descended from the Wu-sun (neighbors of the Hsiung-nu), had red beards and blue eyes.[12]

On the other hand, al-Istakhri said that Khazars had black hair.[13] Al-Istakhri added that there were "Black Khazars" and "White Khazars," alleging that the latter were light-skinned and handsome, while the former were dark-skinned. However, scholars agree that this was not a racial distinction, but rather a social one. The Black (*Kara*) Khazars were the lower classes, while the White (*Ak*) Khazars were the nobility and royalty.

When Soviet archaeologists excavated Khazarian kurgans (burial mounds) near the fortress of Sarkel dating from the tenth to the twelfth centuries, they discovered the physical remains of Khazars. Some of these Khazars belonged to a Slavic type, while others were short-skulled Europeans. Only a few Mongolian types were found.[14]

Alternative theories have been proposed about the origins of the Khazar people throughout the years. In the nineteenth century, some scholars considered the Khazars to be Turks or Tatars, while others said that they were Finno-Ugrians, related to the Magyars; still others argued that the Khazars were Slavs or related to the Circassians.[15] A large number of possibilities were raised in the twentieth century as well. In his Ph.D. thesis, *Struktur und Gesellschaft des Chazaren-Reiches im Licht der Schriftenlichen Quellen* (1982), Dieter Ludwig suggested that the Khazars were Hephthalites who formed a union with the Sabirs in around the sixth century. Warren B. Walsh claimed that the Khazars were related to the Georgians and the Armenians.[16]

The scholars who have had the easiest access to Khazar documents and artifacts are, naturally, those in Russia and Ukraine. Unfortunately, the Communist conceptualization of history skewed analysis of the ethnogenesis of tribes in the Russian lands during much of the twentieth century, as Bruce Trigger explained:

> The Soviet Union was the first country where archaeological data were interpreted within the framework of Marxist histori-cal materialism. Since the late 1920s, this paradigm has guided all archaeological research done there.[17]

This ideology had drastic consequences for Khazar studies. Under the oppressive regime of Stalin (1929–1953), Soviet historians and archaeologists were forced to adopt the view that the Khazars were not Turkic migrants from the East, but rather natives of the north Caucasus.[18] Mikhail Artamonov therefore alleged, during the 1930s and 1940s, that the Khazars were local natives of the Don valley and the north Caucasus. Lev Gumilev and several other archaeologists ex-pressed the belief that the Khazars were a "Turkified" Daghestani, Sarmatian, or Alanic people. Vladimir Minorsky, too, wrote that the Khazars were a grouping of local nomadic tribes of southern Russia who were brought together under a new Khazar-Turkic leader.[19] The view that the Khazars were mainly a "Turkified" people does not appear to be valid, since it is known for certain that the Khazars were Turks. However, there remains the possibility that some non-Turkic people under the jurisdiction of the Khazar Empire also assumed the name Khazar—especially Jewish immigrants from the Middle East who intermarried with the Khazars.

The meaning of the ethnonym "Khazar" has been much debated. According to some scholars, "Khazar" may be derived from the root words *kaz* (meaning "wanderer") and *er* (mean-ing "man"). On the other hand, Douglas Dunlop believed it was possible to associate the Khazars with the Chinese name of one of the nine ancient Uyghur tribes, "Ko-sa."[20] Some early Chinese writers knew the Khazars by the names K'osa t'u-chüeh ("K'osa Turks") and T'u-chüeh ho-sa pu, and Dunlop's argument is largely based on the close resemblance between the "Ko-sa" and "K'osa." In *Khazar Studies*, Peter Golden disagreed with Dunlop's suggestion, writing that a connection between the Khazars and the Uyghurs cannot be established, and that the real connection existed with the Oghurs.[21] Early Rus'ian sources called the Khazars the "White Ugry" and the Magyars the "Black Ugry."[22] It should be assumed that "Ugry" is equivalent to "Oghur." The Oghurs were a special branch of Turks who spoke a form of Turkic distinct from common Turkic.

More recently, however, scholars have reevaluated the question of whether Khazars can be associated with Uyghurs, since new evidence has been discovered that may connect the Khazars with people of the ancient Uyghur Empire. The reevaluation involves the name "Qasar." Qasar was found in the form "QSR" on the mid-eighth-century Shine-usu, Terkhin, and Tes runic inscriptions from northern Mongolia, all of which were composed in the Old Uyghur language.[23] In one of the runic inscriptions, the Uyghur kagan Bayanchur (el-Etmish Bilgä) (reigned 747–759) wrote that the Qasars were involved in events of the sixth century. T. Senga believed that the Uyghur tribe or surname "Qasar" may be equivalent to the Ko-sa of the Chinese sources.[24] There has been speculation that part of the Qasar group moved west from Mongolia or northern Kazakhstan into Khazaria, but this is far from certain. Károly Czeglédy and Louis Bazin have proposed that the Qasars were the ancestors of the Khazars.[25] Bazin argued that this Uyghur group migrated westward before the year 555 and suggested that *qas-* means "to tyrannize, oppress, terrorize." Czeglédy argued that the westward migration of the Qasars occurred around 463.[26]

It is interesting that the multitribal Chiu-hsing ("Nine Surnames") confederacy, conquered by the Uyghur kagan, included a tribal leader named Ko-sa, according to the Chinese work *Hsin T'ang-shu*.[27] Additionally, it should be noted that the kagan of the Uyghur Empire between 823 and 832 was named Hosa t'e-le (Hazar Tekin). Were these leaders related to the Khazars? Senga postulated that Ko-sa was the surname of the leader of the Ssu-chieh (Sikari) tribe, possibly associated with the T'ieh-le group rather than with Uyghurs, and that it was the T'ieh-le who were the ancestors of the Khazar people. In any case, a Qasar-Khazar connection is still uncertain but should be explored further.

A complete answer about the origins of the Khazars is not yet available. However, it should be emphasized that the evidence indicates the importance of westward migrations in the creation of the Khazar people.

LEGENDS ABOUT THE BEGINNINGS OF THE JEWISH KHAZARS

The Turkic peoples believed that they could trace their descent back to Noah, the legendary ark-builder. One of the most important Khazar kings, Joseph, wrote in his celebrated *Reply to Hasdai ibn Shaprut* that the Khazars were descended from "Kozar," the seventh of Togarmah's ten sons. Medieval Hebrew essays substantiated this claim. For example, the tenth-century Hebrew historical work *Sefer Yosippon*, by Joseph ben Gorion, stated that Togarmah's son Kozar had nine brothers, who represented the ancestry of the Bulgars, Pechenegs, and other Turkic groups. Genesis 10:2 and 10:3, in turn, traced Togarmah's ancestry back several generations (see Table 1–1). It is also worth mentioning that Shem Tov ibn Shem Tov called Khazaria "the country of Togarmah" in his *Sefer ha-Emunot* (early fifteenth century).

Jewish authors often speculated that the Jews in Khazaria were descended from some of the twelve tribes of ancient Israel. For example, the author of the *Schechter Letter* mentioned a tradition among his people that the Khazarian Jews

were descended from the tribe of Simeon.[28] Similarly, Eldad
ben Mahali ha-Dani (Eldad the Danite), a Jew who may have
hailed from eastern Africa or Khazaria, wrote (in the late nineteenth century) that the tribe of Simeon and the half-tribe of
Menasheh lived in "the land of the Khazars" and took tribute
from twenty-five kingdoms, including some Muslim nations.
Eldad brought this to the attention of the Jews of Spain in 883,
and aroused considerable interest in the topic among them.

Several other versions of the Eldad ha-Dani legend exist in
Hebrew literature. A large assortment of these tales, concerning the whereabouts of the remnants of the twelve tribes of
Israel, were collected in the *Chronicles of Jerahmeel* by
Jerahmeel ben Solomon, a twelfth-century Italian Jew. One of
the documents in Jerahmeel's collection is the *Chronicle of
Elchanan the Merchant*, which was written by Elchanan ben
Joseph, a seafaring merchant from the land where the tribe
of Dan dwelled. This chronicle, as preserved by Jerahmeel, is
more detailed than Eldad's tale and provides valuable additional information. Elchanan's chronicle indicated that the
tribe of Judah and half of the tribe of Simeon lived in tents
in "the land of the Khasdim." They collected tribute from
twenty-five kingdoms, including Muslims and descendants of
Keturah, Abraham's second wife.[29] They were described as
proficient archers and swordfighters who warred against non-
Jewish nations and at times went on excursions to Iraq.
Elchanan said that Judah and Simeon spoke Hebrew, Greek,
and the language of Togarmah (Turkic), and that they were
knowledgeable about the Torah, Mishnah, Talmud, and
Agadah.[30] It is obvious that these statements refer to the Jews
living in Khazaria.

Elchanan noted that the tribe of Issachar, living in mountains "behind the land of the Medes and Persians," also received tribute from non-Jewish kingdoms, and had a plentiful
supply of silver and gold. Members of the Issachar tribe spoke
the Hebrew and "Kedar" languages.[31] He also said that they
studied the Talmud and the Torah, had their own judges and

servants, and owned many oxen, camels, and sheep. The meaning of the term "Kedar" is not entirely clear, but Rabbi Petakhiah mentioned it in his travelogue (see Chapter 9), and it seems to refer to the peoples of the Caucasus region. It is conceivable that Elchanan was referring to the Mountain Jews of Daghestan and Azerbaijan, who may have persuaded the Khazars to adopt Judaism.

The other document from the *Chronicles of Jerahmeel* that provides details about the lost tribes in the Caucasus region was titled *The Ten Banishments of the Sanhedrin*. Some of the details in this document contradict those in Elchanan's account. For example, the tribe of Ephraim and the half-tribe of Menasheh, rather than Simeon and Judah, were said to be collecting tribute from twenty-five kingdoms.[32] Ephraim and Menasheh formed a large confederation of hard-working horse riders who lived "opposite the city of Meyuqa." The document also discussed the tribe of Zebulun, which apparently lived in the Middle East near Iraq and Armenia. The tribe of Zebulun spoke "the language of Kedar" and were scholars of the Torah, Mishnah, Talmud, and Agadah. Every Sabbath, lectures were given in Hebrew but then were translated into the Kedar language. The Zebulun tribe bears resemblance to the Issachar tribe of Elchanan's account, since both groups spoke Kedar.

There was also believed to be a connection between the Khazars and Magog, a son of Japheth. The *Life* of Saint Abo of Tbilisi (Tiflis) said that the Khazars were savage "sons of Magog" who had "no religion whatever, although recognizing the being of a sole god."[33] According to *Expositio in Matthaeum Evangelistam*, a commentary on Matthew 24:14 by the monk Druthmar of Aquitaine (864), the Jewish *Gazari* (Khazars) lived "in the lands of Gog and Magog."[34] The Arab traveler ibn Fadlan wrote (in 921 or 922): "Some are of the opinion that Gog and Magog are the Khazars." The Talmud, however, identified Magog with the White Huns and Gog with the Goths.[35] Josephus, writing in the first century, associated Magog with the Scythians.

Druthmar added that Alexander the Great "enclosed" the *Gazari,* but that they escaped. This statement is derived from an ancient legend in which Alexander was seen as a hero for walling up dangerous, unclean peoples. Prester John described the enclosed peoples as cannibals.[36]

The medieval German legend of the "Red Jews" derived from a combination of three of these stories: (1) about Alexander the Great's enclosure of monstrous nations behind a large mountain northeast of the Mediterranean; (2) about Gog and Magog, said to be the destroyers of the world at the end of time; and (3) about the ten lost tribes of Israel.[37] German writers used the "Red Jews" legend to express anti-Jewish sentiments and fears about the anticipated apocalypse.

The term "Red Jews" was chosen because medieval Germans saw red hair and red beards as signs of a dishonest, deceitful individual. Thus, Red Jews were Jews who had red hair and red beards, according to Andrew Gow.[38] This is visually demonstrated in a fifteenth-century German *Historiated Bible,* which depicted the ten lost tribes of Israel (enclosed by Alexander) with red hair and red beards.[39] By contrast, Alexander and his army were shown with blond hair.

The Red Jews made their first appearance in German literature in Albrecht von Scharfenberg's late-thirteenth-century text titled *Der Jüngere Titurel.* According to Albrecht, the Red Jews are enclosed between two tall mountains called Gog and Magog; these Jews are "warlike" and present a military threat to Christians.[40] Another late-thirteenth-century document, *Der Göttweiger Trojanerkrieg,* stated that the Red Jews lived in the land of "Plotzen," a country that "stretched far and wide." It also said that the Red Jews taxed travelers very heavily, and that they looked ugly and frightening.[41] It further said that after twenty thousand Red Jews were killed in battle against Greek soldiers, the remnants of Red Jewry fled into mountains, where they were conquered by Alexander "many years later."

Gottes Zukunft, penned by Heinrich von Neustadt circa 1300, called the enclosed country "Caspia."[42] Heinrich also wrote that the terrifying people of Gog and Magog, descended from Japheth, are the ten tribes of Israel, locked up by Alexander in the "Caspian Mountains" (the Caucasus Mountains are meant). The Caspian Jews are numerous and have large armies.

Buch der Maccabäer by Ludger von Braunschweig (early fourteenth century) expanded upon the meaning of the legend. It said that Alexander's army came to the "Caspian Mountains" and met the ten Israelite tribes, who were also called Red Jews. The Red Jews were already partially enclosed, and thus imprisoned, by the mountains, because God had punished them for worshipping two golden calves made by their king Jeroboam. Alexander further trapped the Red Jews in these mountains by piling boulders to form a great wall. But Alexander and his men were unable to complete the task of walling up the Jews, so he asked God to enclose the mountains entirely. Von Braunschweig wrote that God answered Alexander's prayer. Nevertheless, medieval Christians were concerned that Gog and Magog would break out of the Caucasus Mountains at the end of time and destroy the Christian world.

In *Judenbüchlein* (early sixteenth century), Victor von Carben imagined a dialog between a Christian and a Jew. The Jew described the king of the Red Jews as a descendant of the tribe of Judah—reminiscent of Elchanan the Merchant's comment that Judahites ruled over the land of the Khasdim—and said that the "Caspian Mountains" were located on "the other side of Babylonia," bordering the sea Germans called the "Wild Sea" and Jews called Sambation.[43] The waves of the "Wild Sea" were so fierce that it was impossible to cross it (by ship) during the week. However, the sea rests from Friday at six o'clock P.M. to Saturday at six o'clock P.M. The Red Jews could not cross during this time because they were observing the Sabbath. The fictional Jew in this dialog lamented the perpetual imprisonment of the Red Jews between the sea and the mountains because only Red Jewry could liberate the German Jews.

Salo W. Baron suggested that the Red Jews were the Khazars.[44] Perhaps the stories about the fiercely independent

Red Jews were vague memories of, or rumors about, the powerful Khazar kingdom, transmitted in distorted form to German Christians.

THE KHAZARS AND THE HUNS

The original Hunnic Empire was established in inner Asia in the 3rd century B.C.E. by the military commander T'ou-man. It was greatly strengthened and enlarged during the reign of Mo-tun, son of T'ou-man. Yet, the empire of the Huns separated into northern and southern divisions in the middle of the first century C.E. The northern Huns began moving west after a major defeat inflicted upon them in 93 C.E. by the Hsien-pi (Mongols).[45]

Huns moved westward into southern Russia and Crimea by the 380s, taking possession of the lower Don river valley and the territory surrounding the Sea of Azov. Priscus recorded (circa 448) that the Akatzirs *(Acatiri)* living near the Black Sea were subjects of the Huns.[46] He wrote that Attila, king of the Huns, installed Karidach (Kuridach) as king of the Akatzirs around the middle of the fifth century. The Akatzirs also were in alliance with the Alans around this time. The Akatzirs may be ancestors of the Khazars.

Oghur Turkic tribes—including the Onogurs, Saragurs, and Uturghurs (Utigurs)—crossed the Volga and entered Europe around the year 463. Previously, the Oghurs lived in western Siberia and central Asia, but they suffered a defeat at the hands of the Sabirs and were forced to migrate. The Oghuric Onogurs settled along the Don and Kuban river basins of the north Caucasus, as well as in the steppelands north of the River Kuban up to the River Don. According to Peter Golden, the Oghurs were members of the T'ieh-le tribal union mentioned in Chinese sources.[47] These Oghuric newcomers apparently intermingled with the Akatzirs and the Huns. Indeed, scholars often consider the Onogurs, Utigurs, and Kutigors of the Crimea and Phanagoria to have been Huns.

The Huns still controlled portions of the European steppelands, including the Crimea, during the sixth century. One of the Hunnic kings of the Crimea, named Grod, sought an alliance with the Byzantine emperor Justinian I.[48] Grod adopted Christianity in 528 and melted many pagan idols, converting them to silver and electrum coins. The Crimean Huns were dissatisfied with Grod, so they killed him and installed Mougel, his pagan brother, as their new king.[49] An important consequence of this change in command was that Mougel reversed Grod's pro-Byzantine policies.

Remnants of the Huns remained in the eastern Pontic steppes and the northern Caucasus for many years, and some ventured into Romania. It is interesting that Druthmar of Aquitaine considered the Jewish *Gazari* living in "Gog and Magog" to be Huns.[50]

One of the earliest factual references to the Khazars dates from the year 555, when an anonymous author wrote a supplement attached to the Syriac translation of *Greek Church History of "Zacharias Rhetor."* In this supplement, the Khazars were listed among the nomadic tribes living in tents north of the Caucasus Mountains.[51]

THE WESTERN TURKISH EMPIRE

For over sixty years, the Khazars were ruled by the western Turks.

The western Kök ("Blue") Türk Kaganate was founded in 552 by Ishtemi, the yabghu kagan, who was the brother of the supreme Türk kagan Bumin.[52] Ishtemi and Bumin were members of the Turkic Asena (Ashina) dynastic clan. The headquarters of this vast empire was located near Lake Balkash. In the year 567, hordes of western Turks arrived in the Volga river region. They soon assumed control over the Sabirs,[53] Onogurs, and Alans of the north Caucasus. By circa 570, the Khazars were under the jurisdiction of the western Turkish Empire.[54] The western Turks took possession of the city of

Bosporus from the Byzantine Empire in 576. The North Caucasian Huns also became subjects of the western Turks.

Ishtemi died in 575 or 576. Ishtemi's son Tardu (reigned 576–603) became the next western Turkish yabghu kagan. After Tardu's death, Ch'u-lo (reigned 603–611) became kagan. Ch'u-lo's unsatisfactory performance led to revolts. His successor, Shih Kuei (reigned 611–618 or 619), expanded the western Turkish realm as far east as the Altai Mountains. Shih Kuei also expanded the western frontier of his empire. His younger brother, Tong Yabghu (reigned 618–630), known as Ziebil by the Byzantines and T'ong She-hu by the Chinese, continued the empire's expansion. Tong Yabghu Kagan's capital, called "One Thousand Springs," was located east of the Talas River.[55] Among his most important officials were the *el-tebers*, who governed conquered peoples, and the *tuduns*, who collected taxes. Tong Yabghu, a follower of Buddhism, was dedicated to the spread of the Buddhist faith among his people.[56] The famous Chinese Buddhist monk Hsuan-tsang (600–664) visited Tong Yabghu in 630 while on a pilgrimage.

The Karluks and other tribes revolted against Tong Yabghu, and he was killed by his uncle (known by the Chinese as Mo-ho-tu hou Ch'iu-li Ssu-p'i) in 630. His uncle ruled as the western Turkish kagan during that year. These events led to a civil war, and the western Turkish Empire broke apart during the 630s.

The tribes of the north Caucasus found themselves in the midst of a major transition. After the disintegration of the western Turkish Empire, the Khazars were able to reassert their independence.

THE FORMATION OF AN INDEPENDENT KHAZAR KINGDOM

The independent state of Khazaria was established by Tong Yabghu's son in the 630s and 640s. The whole region between the Volga and the fortress city of Derbent came into the possession of the Khazars. In creating their new state, the Khazars adopted some governmental institutions and customs from their former western Turkish overlords (see Chapter 3).

The Khazar Empire was multiethnic and multireligious throughout its entire existence. Even as early as the seventh century, the Khazars assimilated with other tribes and confederations of the Caucasus, such as the Sabirs (Savirs or Suwars), Saragurs, Utigurs, Zabenders (Samandars), and Balanjars (Great Endzhers). These various peoples formed the mosaic of Khazarian life. It appears that the Sabirs living in Khazaria intermarried with a large portion of both the Khazar and Magyar tribes. Indeed, al-Masudi reported that the Khazars were called "Sabir" in Turkic but "Khazaran" in Persian.[57]

THE EFFECTS OF KHAZAR EXPANSION ON THE BULGARS

The Khazars soon became the dominant power in southern Russia. The expansion of Khazaria into new territories displaced other ethnic groups, most notably the Bulgars.

The ethnonym "Bulgar" means "mixed ones" in Turkic and derives from the Turkic word *bulgha* ("to mix"). Thus, the Bulgars were actually a tribal confederation of multiple Hunnic and Turkic groups mixed together. During the winter, Bulgar men wore cone-shaped caps lined with fur, long fur coats belted at the waist, and boots.[58] They had a custom of shaving off much of their hair, except for a portion that was worn in a pigtail. Bulgar women wore wide breeches and girdles with ornaments made from iron, glass, copper, and bone.

The early Bulgars were divided into two groups: the Utigurs and the Kutrigurs. The Utigurs allied with the Byzantines and turned against their Kutrigur brethren. The two groups were engaged in bitter conflict during much of the 550s. While the Kutrigurs were defeated and absorbed by Avar invaders around 560, the Utigurs survived the Avar conquest. In the late sixth and early seventh centuries, the western Turkish kaganate took control over Bulgar lands. The Bulgars fought this takeover unsuccessfully, and many died in battle. However, they established their independence from the western Turks around the same time as the Khazars.

The Bulgars established an independent state (Great Bulgaria) along the Rivers Don, Kuban, and Dnieper by 630. The capital of Great Bulgaria was Phanagoria, on the Taman peninsula. Their top leader was Kubrat, a member of the Dulo clan of western Turks,[59] who belonged to the Bulgar Onoghundur tribe. Khan Kubrat united all of the Bulgar and Hun tribes of the north Caucasus and the Sea of Azov region. Thus, in the seventh century, the major tribes making up the Bulgars included the Onoghundurs, the Duchi, the Kufi, and the Kidarite Huns.[60] During Kubrat's reign, Great Bulgaria maintained commercial and diplomatic ties with Khwarizm and Sogdiana in central Asia, and also had relations with Persia.

Khan Kubrat died in 642. The territory of Great Bulgaria was conquered by the Khazars eight years later. The Khazars took the Bulgars' land and split the Bulgar people into multiple groups. Kubrat's five sons—Bayan (Batbayan), Kotrag, Asparukh, Kuber, and Altsek—each assumed power over a portion of the Bulgars, and thus the unity of the Bulgars came to an end.

Some of the Bulgars were forced to flee to the Danube region in the Balkans. This migration was responsible for the formation of the kingdom of Bulgaria. These Bulgars were led by Kubrat's third son, Asparukh, until his death in 701. An anonymous seventh-century Armenian source recorded that after fleeing the Khazars, Asparukh's Bulgars initially settled on the island of Pevka, located at an estuary of the Danube.[61] The Turkic Bulgars in Bulgaria decorated their yurts with embroidered panels such as hunting scenes. In 679–681, Asparukh and his group of Bulgars crossed the Danube and migrated south of Pevka, founding their new capital at Pliska. When Asparukh died in 701, Tervel became the new khan of Bulgaria. The Bulgars of Bulgaria mixed with Slavs and adopted Orthodox Christianity in 864.[62] Only a few Turkic words remain in the modern Bulgarian language, which is most closely affiliated with Serbo-Croatian and Russian.

Kubrat's fourth son, Kuber, led some of the Bulgars into Pannonia (modern Hungary), submitting to the authority of the Avar kagan. A portion of these Bulgars later settled in Macedonia.

A number of the Bulgars settled in Italy, in the duchy of Benevetto and the Abruzzi region, in the 630s.[63] Their leader was Altsek (Alzeco), the fifth son of Kubrat. They became subjects of the Byzantine Empire. In the midst of a new cultural environment, the Bulgars in Italy replaced their Turkic language with Latin.

Another group of Bulgars, led initially by Kubrat's second son, Kotrag, crossed the Don and resettled east of it. Later, in the eighth and ninth centuries, they settled along the middle Volga river region.[64] Culturally and linguistically, the Volga Bulgars were closely related to the Khazars (on linguistic connections, see Chapter 4). The three Volga Bulgar groups were named Barsula, Eskel, and Bulkar (Bolgar).[65]

The Volga Bulgars established a town along the upper Volga called Bulghar and made it the capital of their land. Their territory soon became a major trading hub. By the end of the tenth century, all of the residents of Bulghar were Muslims, and many thousands of horsemen lived there, always ready to attack the enemy. The Bulgars also had a town called Suwar (Suvar), situated near Bulghar on the Utka River. Other major Bulgar towns were Kashan on the River Kama, and Oshel on the Tetiush.

The rulers of Volga Bulgharia had to pay tribute to the government up until the time of Khazaria's demise. The Khazar domination over the Volga Bulgars was also indicated by al-Muqaddasi's inclusion of Bulghar and Suwar in his list of Khazar towns.[66]

Extensive culture, trading, and scholarship made Volga Bulgharia a highly civilized society. Many literate scholars resided there, including the historian Yakub ibn Noman al-Bulgari (author of a history of the Bulgars, composed in 1112) and the poet Kul Gali (author of *Kyssa-i Yusuf,* A Tale About Yusuf, composed circa 1212). The Bulgars exported furs, leather footwear, timber, and other items to a variety of countries in Europe and Asia. They were also experts at working with gold, silver, bronze, and copper. Bulgar architects were highly skilled, and built public buildings both in their home country and abroad (including Kievan Rus and central Asia).[67] Many Bulgar buildings—including mosques and a Khan's tomb—have been preserved up to the present day in Tatarstan.

A number of Bulgars remained in Great Bulgaria after it became part of the Khazar Empire. These were ruled by Bayan, the first son of Kubrat. They entered into a tribal union with the Khazar tribe.

Table 1–1. *Biblical Genealogy of the Turkic Peoples.*

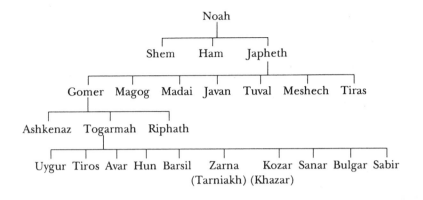

NOTES

1. Mike Edwards, "Searching for the Scythians," *National Geographic* 190:3 (Sept. 1996): 56.

2. Douglas M. Dunlop, *The History of the Jewish Khazars* (New York: Schocken, 1967), p. 5.

3. Peter B. Golden, "Khazaria and Judaism," *Archivum Eurasiae Medii Aevi* 3 (1983): 150.

4. Peter B. Golden, *An Introduction to the History of the Turkic Peoples* (Wiesbaden, Germany: Otto Harrassowitz, 1992), p. 235.

5. Ibid., p. 118; Sev'yan I. Vainshtein, "The Turkic Peoples, Sixth to Twelfth Centuries," in *Nomads of Eurasia*, ed. Vladimir N. Basilov, trans. Mary F. Zirin (Seattle: University of Washington Press, 1989), p. 55.

6. Many other Ural-Altaic groups have similar stories relating their ethnogenesis to animals. The Magyars, for example, believed that Álmos, patriarch of the Árpád dynasty, was born of an eagle.

7. Stuart Legg, *The Heartland* (New York: Capricorn Books, 1971), p. 152.

8. Peter B. Golden, *An Introduction to the History of the Turkic Peoples*, pp. 12–13.

9. Douglas M. Dunlop, *The History of the Jewish Khazars*, p. 11.

10. A. P. Martinez, "Gardizi's Two Chapters on the Turks," *Archivum Eurasiae Medii Aevi* 2 (1982): 125–126.

11. Peter B. Golden, *An Introduction to the History of the Turkic Peoples*, p. 178.

12. J. O. Maenchen-Helfen, *The World of the Huns* (Los Angeles and Berkeley, CA: University of California Press, 1973), pp. 373, 374.

13. Douglas M. Dunlop, *The History of the Jewish Khazars*, p. 96.

14. Itzhak Ben-Zvi, *The Exiled and the Redeemed*, trans. Isaac A. Abbady (Philadelphia: The Jewish Publication Society of America, 1961), p. 207.

15. Dmitrii I. Ilovaiskii, *Razyskaniya o nachale rusi* (Moscow: Miller, 1882), p. 238.

16. Warren B. Walsh, *Readings in Russian History*, vol. 1 (Syracuse, NY: Syracuse University Press, 1963), p. 15.

17. Bruce G. Trigger, *A History of Archaeological Thought* (Cambridge, England: Cambridge University Press, 1989), p. 207.

18. Ibid., p. 226; Neal Ascherson, *Black Sea* (New York: Hill & Wang, 1995), p. 44; Bozena Werbart, "Khazars or 'Saltovo-Majaki Culture'? Prejudices about Archaeology and Ethnicity," *Current Swedish Archaeology* 4 (1996): 200. Similarly, other Soviet scholars assumed that the Volga Tatars were not Turks, but rather were descended from local tribes, and that Crimea always had the same inhabitants, allegedly indigenous to

Crimea, who transformed their identity from Scythian to Goth to Slav.

19. Vladimir F. Minorsky, "A New Book on the Khazars," *Oriens* 11 (1959): 124.

20. Douglas M. Dunlop, *The History of the Jewish Khazars*, pp. 34–35.

21. Peter B. Golden, *Khazar Studies*, vol. 1 (Budapest: Akadémiai, 1980), pp. 55–56.

22. Julius Brutzkus, "The Khazar Origin of Ancient Kiev," *Slavonic and East European Review* 22 (1944): 119. In Turkic, "White Oghurs" were known as *Sara-gurs*.

23. T. Senga, "The Toquz Oghuz Problem and the Origin of the Khazars," *Journal of Asian History* 24:2 (1990): 57.

24. Ibid., pp. 61–62.

25. Károly Czeglédy, "From East to West: The Age of Nomadic Migrations in Eurasia," *Archivum Eurasiae Medii Aevi* 3 (1983): 104; Louis Bazin, "Pour une nouvelle hypothèse sur l'origine des Khazar," *Materialia Turcica* 7/8 (1981–1982): 51–71.

26. Károly Czeglédy, "A Terhin-i ujgur rovásirásos felirat török és magyar történeti és nyelvészeti vonatkozásai," *Magyar Nyelv* 87 (1981): 462.

27. T. Senga, "The Toquz Oghuz Problem and the Origin of the Khazars," p. 59. The Turkic confederations were often named according to the number of tribes they comprised; examples are the ethnic labels *Uturgur* (Thirty Oghur Tribal Groups) and *Onoghur* (Ten Oghur Tribal Groups). In this instance, the Chinese term *Chiu-hsing* (Nine Surnames) is equivalent to the Turkic term *Toquz Oghuz* (Nine Oghuz Tribal Groups). The Hui-ho or Wei-ho (Uyghurs) were among the Chiu-hsing. The Uyghurs were further divided into ten subtribes.

28. Norman Golb and Omeljan Pritsak, *Khazarian Hebrew Documents of the Tenth Century* (Ithaca, NY: Cornell University Press, 1982), p. 113. The author, however, was skeptical about this tradition, saying, "We cannot insist on the truth of this matter."

29. *The Chronicles of Jerahmeel*, ed. Moses Gaster (New York: Ktav, 1971), p. 199.

30. Ibid., p. 200.

31. Ibid., p. 198.

32. Ibid., p. 192.

33. Alexander A. Vasiliev, *The Goths in the Crimea* (Cambridge, MA: The Mediaeval Academy of America, 1936), p. 96.

34. Omeljan Pritsak, "The Khazar Kingdom's Conversion to Judaism," *Harvard Ukrainian Studies* 3:2 (Sept. 1978): 271.

35. J. O. Maenchen-Helfen, *The World of the Huns*, p. 4.

36. Andrew C. Gow, *The Red Jews* (Leiden, Netherlands: E. J. Brill, 1995), pp. 40–41.

37. Ibid., p. 3.

38. Ibid., p. 67.

39. Ibid., p. 69. According to Gow, it was actually quite common for both Christian and Hebrew illustrations on medieval manuscripts to depict typical Jews as those with red hair and red clothing. Jews and red hair were also connected in a pamphlet printed in 1514 or 1515, in which a Jew was alleged to have killed a Christian child in order to extract its blood, but another child—with red hair—was spared. The redheaded child was apparently spared because the alleged Jewish murderer thought it was a Jewish child (see idem., pp. 138–139).

40. Ibid., p. 191.

41. Ibid., pp. 194–195.

42. Ibid., p. 202.

43. Ibid., p. 250–251. The Sambation legend has sometimes been applied to the Khazars of the Dnieper valley near Kiev (see Chapter 2).

44. Salo W. Baron, *A Social and Religious History of the Jews*, vol. 3 (New York: Columbia University Press, 1975), p. 204.

45. Evgenii I. Lubo-Lesnichenko, "The Huns, Third Century B.C. to Sixth Century A.D.," in *Nomads of Eurasia*, ed. Vladimir N. Basilov, trans. Mary F. Zirin (Seattle: University of Washington Press, 1989), p. 53.

46. Douglas M. Dunlop, "The Khazars," in *The Dark Ages*, ed. Cecil Roth and I. H. Levine (New Brunswick, NJ: Rutgers University Press, 1966), p. 326.

47. Peter B. Golden, "The Turkic Peoples and Caucasia," in *Transcaucasia*, ed. Ronald G. Suny (Ann Arbor, MI: University of Michigan, 1983), p. 47.

48. Z. J. Kosztolnyik, *Five Eleventh Century Hungarian Kings* (New York: Columbia University Press, 1981), p. xii.

49. David M. Lang, *The Bulgarians* (Boulder, CO: Westview Press, 1976), pp. 35–36.

50. Omeljan Pritsak, "The Khazar Kingdom's Conversion to Judaism," p. 271.

51. See Károly Czeglédy, "Pseudo-Zacharias Rhetor on the Nomads," in *Studia Turcica*, ed. Lajos M. Ligeti (Budapest: Akadémiai, 1971), pp. 133–148.

52. Peter B. Golden, "The question of the Rus' Qağanate," *Archivum Eurasiae Medii Aevi* 2 (1982): 77. Bumin died at the end of 552 or the start of 553 and was succeeded as eastern kagan by his son Muqan (reigned 552 or 553–572).

53. The Sabirs were refugees who had fled to the north Caucasus by around the year 506. The Sabirs became embroiled in the Byzantine-Iranian Wars of 527–565, which were fought in the south Caucasus.

54. Douglas M. Dunlop, "The Khazars," in *The Dark Ages*, p. 327.

55. Peter B. Golden, *An Introduction to the History of the Turkic Peoples*, p. 135.

56. Luc Kwanten, *Imperial Nomads* (Philadelphia: University of Pennsylvania Press, 1979), p. 46.

57. Peter B. Golden, *An Introduction to the History of the Turkic Peoples*, p. 236.

58. David M. Lang, *The Bulgarians*, p. 32.

59. Peter B. Golden, "Imperial Ideology and the Sources of Political Unity Amongst the Pre-Činggisid Nomads of Western Eurasia," *Archivum Eurasiae Medii Aevi* 2 (1982): 57.

60. David M. Lang, *The Bulgarians*, p. 31.

61. Ibid., p. 37.

62. Vladimir F. Minorsky, *Hudud al-'Alam (The Regions of the World)* (London: Luzac & Co., 1937), p. 423.

63. David M. Lang, *The Bulgarians*, p. 35.

64. The modern name of the Volga may itself be derived from "Bolgar." Members of the Balanjar tribe and other tribes from the north Caucasus joined the Oghurs in settling near the middle Volga by the early tenth century (see Peter B. Golden, *Khazar Studies*, vol. 1, pp. 87–88).

65. A. P. Martinez, "Gardizi's Two Chapters on the Turks," p. 157.

66. Douglas M. Dunlop, *The History of the Jewish Khazars*, p. 187.

67. Azade-Ayşe Rorlich, *The Volga Tatars* (Stanford, CA: Hoover Institution Press, 1986), p. 14.

2

THE CITIES AND TOWNS
OF THE KHAZARS

*K*hazaria was a vast land with many large Jewish settlements (see Figure 2–1). Its towns had scenic vistas and were centers of commerce (especially Atil, Tmutorokan, and Samandar). The author of the ninth-century Bavarian Geographer said that the "Caziri" (Khazars) had a hundred cities or clans. Important Khazarian settlements were located in the Don and Volga river valleys, on the Crimean peninsula (see Figure 2–2), in the plains of present-day Ukraine, and north of the Caucasian mountain range.

The heartland of the Khazar Empire comprised the regions of what are now Astrakhan, Kalmykia, Daghestan, Volgograd, Rostov, Ingushetia, Kabardino-Balkarsk, North Ossetia, and Chechnya. The empire greatly expanded in size from the sixth to the ninth centuries. From the sixth to the ninth centuries, Khazaria included

lands northeast of the Caspian Sea that are now part of
western Kazakhstan and northwestern Uzbekistan. By
650, the eastern boundary of the empire consisted of the
Aral Sea and the Amu Darya (Oxus River), near
Gurganj, and the Khazars controlled the steppes between
the Aral and the Manghishlaq peninsula. During the
seventh and eighth centuries, the Khazars also expanded
their empire west of the Don river valley into parts of
the Crimea and modern-day Ukraine, and the western
boundary of the empire became the Dnieper. The northern and southwestern sections of the Crimea came under the control of the Khazars, while some of the southern coastal towns (such as Cherson) generally remained
under Byzantine authority.

Thus, at its maximum extent (in the ninth century),
Khazaria not only encompassed the northern Caucasus
and the Volga delta, but also extended as far east as the
steppes of Khwarizm (Khorezm) and as far west as Kiev.
However, beginning in the tenth century, the Khazar
Empire contracted and eventually disintegrated.

THE CAPITAL CITIES OF KHAZARIA

There were three Khazarian capitals: first Balanjar, then
Samandar, and finally Atil.

In the earliest period, the central Khazar territory was south
of the Kuma River with its capital at Balanjar.[1] In the 720s,[2]
the Khazars moved their capital to Samandar after the Arabs
invaded the Khazar territory (see Chapter 7). Sometime between 730 and 750, Khazaran-Atil became the capital of the
Khazar Empire.

ATIL AND KHAZARAN

Khazaran-Atil was a "twin city" on the lower Volga near the
Caspian Sea, in eastern Khazaria. Its two sections were con-

nected by a pontoon bridge. It was the most important trading center of the Khazar Empire and also served as the center of government and religion. Khazaran-Atil had many markets and baths.[3] Jews, Christians, and Muslims resided in the capital city in relative harmony.

The eastern half of the city was known as Khazaran.[4] Khazaran was populated by many Muslim merchants and crafters, who originally came from Khwarizm and eastern Iran. About thirty mosques existed in the capital in the 920s, according to the Arab historian Ibrahim ibn Muhammad al-Istakhri, who wrote sometime between 930 and 953. Pagans also lived in Khazaran.[5] In the 920s, according to the Arab traveler Ahmad ibn Fadlan, Khazaran was ruled by Khaz, a Muslim who handled lawsuits and issues of concern to merchants. Around 943, the Muslims in the Khazar capital were served by a vizier named Ahmad ibn Kuya.

The western half of the city was known as Atil (also spelled Itil).[6] Atil became the Khazar capital around 740, according to Peter Golden.[7] Inhabitants of Atil included the kagan, the bek, members of the army, four thousand attendants, and "pure-bred Khazars," and Atil was surrounded by a fortified brick wall.[8] There were four gates in the wall surrounding Atil, three of them opening onto the steppe and one opening onto the river. Al-Istakhri stated that the royal palace, constructed from brick, was "at a distance from the river-bank."[9] Al-Masudi wrote that the palace was located on an island in Atil that was adjacent to the western shore. According to al-Istakhri, the Khazar kagan had a golden throne and canopy. Golden gates decorated the kagan's island palace. The bek also resided in the kagan's castle.[10]

The account of the Persian historian Muhammad ibn Rustah, *Kitab A'laq an-Nafisa*, compiled around the year 903 based on earlier sources, provides details about Khazaran-Atil's earlier history. According to ibn Rustah, Muslims lived in the capital with their "mosques, imams, muezzins, and schools."[11] Furthermore, ibn Rustah indicated that, at this early period, only the kings, leaders, and members of the upper class were Jewish. Judaism later spread to the general Khazar populace (see Chapter 6). People remained in the capital city during the winter, but went out onto the steppe in the spring and summer.

Ibn Rustah called the Khazar capital Sarighshin (Sarighsin), with an associated city allegedly named Khanbaligh, which perhaps meant "city of the Khan." *Sarighshin* meant "White City," and its Arabic equivalent appears to have been Al-Bayda, which also meant "White City." An even earlier account, that of ibn Khordadbeh (ninth century), gave the name of the riverside Khazar capital as Khamlikh. Most authorities agree that *Khamlikh* is a contraction of a longer toponym. It is likely, though not certain, that Khamlikh-Sarighshin was equivalent to the twin city Khazaran-Atil, in which case Khamlikh probably represented the eastern half (Khazaran). Supporting this thesis is the fact that the Jewish Radhanite and Rus'ian traders visited Khamlikh, which coincides with our knowledge of Khazaran as a trading hub.

The theory that the remains of Atil are currently underwater has been supported by the Japanese archaeologist Hoichi Irokawa, as well as by the Russian historian Lev Gumilev. By the late tenth century, the level of the Caspian Sea began to rise, flooding the Khazars' coastal gardens, fisheries, and buildings.[12] Historical reports explained that the Caspian continued to rise during the fourteenth century.[13] Aerial photography, gravitational measurements, and reports from divers appear to indicate that the lost city of Atil—or at least its wall—is located underwater in the Caspian near the Volga delta, just south of Astrakhan, near the islands of Chistanya Banka.[14] On the other hand, a large Khazar settlement found in 1992 at Samosdelka (an arid site southwest of Astrakhan) is also a candidate for being Atil. The German-Russian archaeologist Yevgenia Schneidstein speculates that the royal brick palace is located at Samosdelka. The precise location of Atil still remains to be conclusively established.

BALANJAR

Balanjar may have been the first Khazar town. The toponym Balanjar may derive from *bala* ("great") + *Endzher* (the name of a Khazar tribe in Daghestan).[15] Arab legends, however, said that the town was founded by a man named Balanjar ibn Japheth. Balanjar was equivalent to the northern Caucasian Huns' capital of Varach'an and to the Warsan Mountains noted by Yehudah ha-Levi (see Chapter 6). Balanjar has been identified with the *gorodishche* (hill fort) Verkhneye Chiryurtovskoye, located by the Sulak River, a southern tributary of the Terek, in the Kizilyurtovskii raion of north Daghestan.[16] The town of Balanjar was about 16,000 square meters (i.e., approximately 172,223 square feet) in area.[17] Among the important architectural landmarks in Balanjar were two small roofless Christian churches, dating from around the sixth to eighth centuries, and a white mortar fortress.

Balanjar was the center of a highly developed culture. Potterymaking facilities were located there.[18] Iron smelting also took place. Several cemeteries were discovered in Balanjar, although the latest burials dated only from around the seventh century. These cemeteries contained quite a few weapons, Byzantine coins, harnesses, jewels, belt mounts, and ear pendants. Many items—including belt buckles—were produced from gold. Among other archaeological discoveries in Balanjar were a bone saddle implement bearing an artistic depiction of hunting scenes,[19] coffins woven from reeds, and catacomb burials under *kurgans* (burial mounds). An interesting round decorative rosette with colored glass was buried in a catacomb cemetery. Many of the catacombs with a rich quantity of material remains are believed to be those of Khazar aristocrats. Some of the other burials contain the skeletons of Bulgars, Sabirs, and Alans.

After the dramatic events in the Caucasus in the eighth century (see Chapter 7), Balanjar became a considerably less important part of the Khazar Empire.

CHERNIGOV

Chernigov (Chernihiv) was a major town on the right bank
of the Desna River, founded in the eighth or ninth century.
The Ukrainian historian Omeljan Pritsak considered
Chernigov to have been a Khazarian town.[20] An old legend
stated that its founder was Prince Chorny, whose daughter was
named Cherne. The Severians, an East Slavic tribe, lived in
Chernigov by the ninth century and paid tribute to the
Khazars.

Chernigov was incorporated into Kievan Rus in the tenth
century and became the capital of the Chernigov principality
in 1024. The Mongols destroyed Chernigov in 1239, but it was
later rebuilt, and is today part of Ukraine.

CHERSON

Cherson[21] was located on the Crimean peninsula near present-
day Sevastopol. There was a Jewish settlement in Cherson during the Khazar era, according to Benjamin Pinkus.[22] Cherson
was overseen by a Khazar tudun (provincial governor) in the
early seventh century, although by the mid-seventh century
Cherson was no longer part of the Khazar Empire.[23] Yet
Cherson again had a Khazar tudun around 710.[24]

The Byzantines took possession of Cherson in 834. The city
was ultimately destroyed in 1475.

CHUFUT-KALE

Another settlement in the Khazar realm—in the ninth and
tenth centuries—was the cave town of Chufut-Kale, located
south of Eski-Kermen and present-day Simferopol and northeast of Mangup. It is near the city of Bakhchisarai. Many Jews
lived in Chufut-Kale during medieval times. Indeed, *Chufut-
Kale* means "Jewish fortress" in the Crimean Tatar language.
A Khazar Jewish cemetery exists in Chufut Kale (see Chapter 9).

In 1299, Chufut-Kale was destroyed by Khan Nogai's horde. However, the town was rebuilt years later. The Karaites represented the dominant population of Chufut-Kale until recent times. In the nineteenth and twentieth centuries, Chufut-Kale became depopulated as the Karaites resettled in other towns.

DOROS

Doros, a Gothic town in a mountainous section of southwestern Crimea, was at one time under Khazar jurisdiction. It was founded by the Byzantines around 540 to defend the routes leading to Cherson, but fell into the possession of the Goths and was made the center of the Gothic principality. Doros was also known as Feodoro, Theodoro, and Mangup.

The Khazar kagan captured Doros in around 786 or 787, installing Khazar troops there and subjecting the Gothic ruler to Khazar authority.[25] However, a conspiracy led by Bishop John of Gothia expelled the Khazar garrison from Doros. Certain pro-Khazar residents of Gothia captured the bishop and his rebel supporters, and they were sent to the kagan. The kagan reasserted his control over Doros and imprisoned several people who had participated in John's conspiracy. Although the bishop was himself imprisoned—in Phullai, a city in eastern Crimea—he managed to escape. Khazar tuduns ruled Doros from 786 until around 810.

FEODOSIA

At the height of its power, the Khazar Empire included the town of Feodosia, where a major Jewish community existed. Feodosia was originally the Greek colony Theodosia, founded in the sixth century B.C.E. by Greek settlers from Miletus (Asia Minor). The Genoese ruled over Feodosia (which they renamed Kaffa) from 1266 to 1475. The Turks seized Kaffa in 1475.

KARA TOBE

Kara Tobe is located southeast of Yevpatoria in an open field between the Black Sea and Lake Sasyk, just west of the modern Crimean town of Saki. In early times it served as a Greek outpost, but later was chosen as the site for a medieval Khazarian fort. In the summer of 1997, a team of excavators recovered bones and reddish-colored pottery from Kara Tobe, which are presumably relics of the Khazars.

KERCH

Kerch, also known as Karch and Karch-ev, was a large Khazar town on the eastern edge of the Crimea, located across the Kerch Strait from the Taman peninsula. Kerch is near the site of the ancient Greek colony Pantikapeum. Many early Jewish artifacts have been found there (see Chapter 6).

The Kerch Strait, also known as the Cimmerian Bosporus, connects the Black Sea and the Azov Sea. Kerch, therefore, occupied a strategic location because of its proximity to the Azov Sea, which leads to the River Don. The Genoese took over Kerch in the thirteenth century, and the Turks acquired it in the following century.

KIEV

Kiev, the magnificent "Mother of Rus'ian Cities," is over a millennium old, and in the early days was inhabited by Khazars and Magyars. It is situated on the banks of the Dnieper (Dnipro) and today has a population of over 2.6 million.

Historians of yesteryear claimed that Kiev was founded by the Rus or the Slavs, but this view may not be correct. The *Rus'ian Primary Chronicle* attributed Kiev's founding to three brothers—Kiy, Shchek, and Khoriv—and described Kiev as a Khazar tributary taken later by the Varangians (Rus)[26] after the death of the brothers. While at one point the *Chronicle* made it seem as if the three brothers were Polianians,[27] the

Laurentian, Suprasl, and Semeonovskaya editions of the *Chronicle* associated the three brothers with the Khazar Empire; Julius Brutzkus therefore drew the conclusion that they were ethnic Khazars.[28] As Pritsak has demonstrated, the *Chronicle* at one point explicitly stated that the three brothers were "kin" of the Khazars: ". . . and we [Kievans] are living here and pay tribute to their [Kiy, Shchek, and Khoriv] kin, to the Khazars."[29] Pritsak even suggested that Kiy, the primary founder of Kiev, can be identified as the vizier Kuya, who served the Khazars (see Chapter 3).

Part of Kiev was founded by Khazars in the early ninth century under the name Sambata. The Byzantine emperor Constantine VII Porphyrogenitus wrote that Kiev was also known as Sambatas in his famous *De administrando imperio* (circa 950).[30] Similarly, ibn Rustah, Gardezi, and the *Hudud al-'Alam* all called Kiev Zanbat.[31] The meaning of the toponym Sambata has aroused considerable controversy among scholars. Omeljan Pritsak argued that Sambata meant *Shabbat* (the Hebrew term for the Sabbath).[32] Some other scholars wonder whether Sambata originates in the name of the legendary Sambation River, where the lost tribes of Israel were said to reside. According to a popular Jewish tradition, the mythical Sambation actively flowed and threw up rocks on all days except the Sabbath, when it became stationary. Kiev, situated on the Dnieper on the edge of the Khazar territory, may have been associated with this myth if the Dnieper was indeed considered to be the Sambation. Brutzkus, on the other hand, dismissed the *Shabbat* and Sambation hypotheses as erroneous and suggested that Sambata meant "high fortress," and that Kiev means "riverbank settlement" or "lower settlement."[33] According to Brutzkus, the Turkic prefix *sam-* meant "top, high, main," and *bat* meant "strong" in Turkic. Thus, the combination *Sam + bat* meant "high fortress." He proposed that Kiev means "riverbank settlement," since *küi* meant "a low place, a bank of a river, or a wharf" and *ev* meant "settlement" in the Khazar language.

The Magyars ruled Kiev from 840 to 878.

Kiev consisted of three districts in the tenth century: Gora (a citadel), Kopyrev konets (the inner town, where the "*Kopyr*" people lived), and Podol (an economic hub).[34] Ivan Pantiukhov estimated that in the ninth century Kiev had eight thousand residents and Podol had one thousand residents.[35] In the tenth century, Kiev probably had about fifteen thousand residents and Podol's population increased to about two thousand.

Podol was the commercial center in the Kiev district. It was located on the floodplain below the hills of Kiev astride the Dnieper and the Pochaina stream. Trading activity took place in Podol as early as the seventh or eighth century. Archaeological digs showed that permanent log houses were being built in Podol by 887. The people in Podol in the ninth and tenth centuries were engaged in jewelrymaking, blacksmithing, bone and stone carving, and ironworking.[36] One of the districts in Podol was called Kozare ("the Khazars"). According to the *Rus'ian Primary Chronicle*, in 945 a Christian church, known as the Cathedral of Saint Elias, was located by the Pochaina stream near the Kozare district and the Pasyncha beseda.[37] Pritsak considered the Pasyncha beseda to be a Khazarian customs office.

Pritsak also argued for a Khazarian origin of Kopyrev konets. According to him, the element *Kopyr* in the toponym Kopyrev konets derived from Kabar,[38] a dissident Khazar tribe. Thus, Kopyrev konets may have meant "Kabar ethnic community."

There are several other indications of the Khazarian contribution to Kiev's early history. The culture of early Kiev was based on the Khazarian-Saltovo way of life (see Chapter 4). It is very likely that the Khazars maintained a garrison in Kiev. The *Kievan Letter* (described in Chapter 6) demonstrates the existence of a Jewish community in Kiev during the Khazar era. The Khazar Jews may have lived on the hill in Kiev known as Khorivitsa.[39] A casting mold found at Kiev that was used for making belt ornaments read "Türk" in Arabic letters on its side, and this may also be evidence of Khazar settlement in Kiev.[40] There is no direct evidence that the Khazars used the

Arabic script for writing. Nevertheless, some scholars also believe that the Khazars minted coins with Arabic inscriptions (see Chapter 5).

After several decades of Jewish Khazar rule, the Rus wrested control of Kiev from the Khazars. After taking Smolensk and Lyubech, Prince Igor or Prince Oleg conquered the city of Kiev and killed Askold and Dir, the former rulers of the city. Kiev thereafter became the capital of the Poliane tribe. Based on his analysis of documentary evidence, Constantine Zuckerman has convincingly shown that the Rus took over Kiev between the 910s and the 930s, rather than in the 880s, as is traditionally believed.[41]

In the twelfth century, two separate gates existed in Kiev: the "Podol Gate" and the "Jewish (*Zhidovskye*) Gate." Kopyrev konets was connected to Podol by the Podol Gate, while the Jewish Gate connected Kopyrev konets with "Iaroslav Town" (which became imperial Kiev after 1036). Furthermore, western and southern parts of Kopyrev konets were still referred to as *Zhidove* ("the Jews") during the eleventh and twelfth centuries.[42] Unfortunately, the Jewish section of Podol—apparently dating back to Khazarian times—as well as monasteries in Podol were burned down in 1124.[43]

SAMANDAR

Historians disagree as to who founded the city of Samandar. George Gubaroff suggested that Samandar was founded by the Khazar rulers.[44] It is known that the Khazars built a fortification in Samandar out of white mortar.[45] Svetlana Pletnyova, however, wrote that *Samandar* meant "the farthest gate" in Persian and was built by Persians in the sixth century.[46]

Scholars also have not come to a consensus on where exactly Samandar was located. Medieval Arabic chronicles specified that Samandar was located somewhere between Derbent (Bab al-Abwab) and Atil, near the edge of the Caspian Sea. Several historians have ventured to be more specific. Omeljan Pritsak argued that Samandar became the modern north

Caucasian town of Kizliar.[47] René Grousset, on the other hand, believed that Samandar was located between the Terek River and the fortress city of Derbent and that it later became Tarqu (Tarki), a Caspian coastal city south of the Sulak River.[48] Vladimir Minorsky, too, favored the identification of Samandar with modern-day Tarqu, since Tarqu is located adjacent to the coast, whereas Kizliar is located farther inland.[49] The association of Samandar with Tarqu is bolstered by *Hudud al-'Alam*, which stated that Samandar was located on the seacoast.[50] Indeed, in Tarqu archaeologists found a city from the Khazar era that seems to be Samandar and that had a wall of stones going downhill toward the sea.[51]

Al-Istakhri mentioned that Samandar was governed locally by a Jew and had many gardens and vineyards, and added that Muslims and mosques were plentiful there as well.[52] Merchants frequented Samandar on a regular basis, and the city had many markets. Al-Istakhri described the homes of Samandar's residents: "Their dwellings are made of wood, arranged criss-cross, and their roofs are domed."[53]

Ibn Hauqal, writing in the late 970s, explained that Samandar was a diverse community whose people professed multiple religions: "Its population consisted of Moslems and others; the Moslems had their mosques, the Christians their churches, and the Jews their synagogues."[54]

SARKEL

Around the year 833, the Khazars sent envoys to the court of Emperor Theophilus in Constantinople, requesting the help of Byzantine engineers in establishing a fortress on the lower Don, at the site that became known as Sarkel.[55] The emperor agreed to assist with the project. The construction of a brick fortress on the left bank of the Don, near the modern-day village of Tsimlyanskaya, began in 833 or 834 and was completed sometime between 835 and 838. The fortress was named Sarkel, a Turkic word that translates as "White Fortress" or "White Abode."[56] The East Slavs called it *Byelaya Vyezha*, which also means "White Fortress." Archaeological excavations showed that Sarkel's fortress was rectangular, and had four towers, two gates, and a citadel, all built from sun-dried bricks connected by white limestone.[57]

According to the narrative of Constantine VII Porphyrogenitus, Petronas Kamateros of Byzantium was the chief engineer for the Sarkel construction effort. It appears that both Turks and Greeks participated in Sarkel's construction, but archaeological analysis has tended to emphasize the dominant Turkic role. Turkic clan symbols (*tamgas*) were carved into Sarkel's bricks before they were baked.[58] The tamgas may have served multiple roles: as marks of the ownership of the bricks by certain clans; as indicators of the number of bricks completed thus far; and as a request for magical powers from the shamanist gods to ensure the successful completion of the building project. It has also been shown that the Sarkel bricks were thicker and smaller than Byzantine-style bricks.[59] In addition, the fortress had no underlying foundation, since foundations were not used by the local Turkic tribes.[60] In general, it may be said that the architecture of the fortress of Sarkel was similar to structures from the Turko-Iranian culture of the Saltovo-Mayaki region. On the other hand, the marble columns and capitals were characteristically Byzantine.[61]

Sarkel primarily served as a defensive fortification. Some Hungarian scholars have proposed that Sarkel was built in order to keep out Magyars. Other historians have suggested that Sarkel may have been protection against the Rus. Sarkel's castle guards were Oghuz and Pecheneg warriors from east of the Volga.[62] The Sarkel garrison included three hundred men.

There were about one hundred houses in Sarkel town.[63] Sarkel's population included Asiatic, Slavic, and Mediterranean people. Several scholars have suggested that the town of Sarkel contained synagogues and mosques, but a definite conclusion cannot yet be reached. However, it does appear that Jews lived in Sarkel, since some Jewish symbols—including menorahs— were engraved there (see Chapter 6).

Sarkel was located in an area of extensive trading and industry. Caravans often passed through the town. The remains of two caravanserais were identified in Sarkel, each consisting of rooms for visitors, an area for holding cattle, and a courtyard where the caravans were kept overnight. Near Sarkel were large brick-production kilns and also a blacksmith's shop.[64] Sarkel's residents used Arabic dirhams (coins) for decorative purposes, stringing them alongside beads.

The Rus conquered Sarkel in the year 965 in a dramatic and decisive battle against the Khazars (see Chapter 8).

The Soviet government flooded most of the remains of Sarkel after the completion, in 1952, of the Tsimlyansk Reservoir and Dam, which controls the Don's flow. The Volga-Don Canal was also opened in 1952. The construction of the canal, dam, and reservoir has led to an increase in shipping traffic along the course of the lower Don. This progress has come at the expense of the Sarkel site, most of which is no longer available for further on-site exploration.

SUDAK

Sudak, located on the Crimean coast between Alushta and Feodosia, was founded in the third century, perhaps by Greeks or Sarmatians. In the beginning, Sudak was known as Sugdaia and was generally under the rule of the Greeks. It was a major trading town. Sudak is also notable for its rich vegetation and wildlife.

Archaeological research has revealed that Khazar noblemen lived in Sudak,[65] and at one time there was a full-fledged Khazar settlement in the town, as is indicated by recent discoveries of Khazar jewelry and ceramics beneath an old fortress. Three large pottery-producing kilns were operated within the vicinity of Sudak in the eight and ninth centuries. Unfortunately, no written record of the Khazar settlement in Sudak is known to exist.

In 1365, Sudak became a Genoese possession, but in 1475 it was taken over by the Crimean Tatars.

TMUTOROKAN (SAMKARSH)

Tmutorokan, on the Taman peninsula (east of the Kerch Strait), was another significant Khazar settlement. In premedieval times, Tmutorokan was known as Hermonassa and Phanagoria. Tmutorokan was a trading post established on the site of Phanagoria. It became a Khazar possession by 704, as the Byzantine chronicler Theophanes related in his narrative on Emperor Justinian II's conflicts with the Khazars (see Chapter 7). Tmutorokan was the name given to the town by the *Rus'ian Primary Chronicle*, but Muslim geographers called it Samkarsh al-Yahud ("Samkarsh of the Jews") and Byzantine sources called the town Tamatarxa and Matraxa.[66]

As the toponym Samkarsh al-Yahud attests, Jews were an important component of the population of Tmutorokan. Theophanes recorded that in the year 671 so many Jews lived in and around Tmutorokan, they actually formed the majority of the population in the region.[67] Archaeological relics also confirm the presence of Jews there (see Chapter 6).

Around 986, there was (apparently) a Jewish Khazar prince named David who ruled Tmutorokan and met Rus'ian ambassadors who wanted to consult him about which religion Kievan Rus should adopt, but the Hebrew document that stated this—the *Mandgelis Document*—may or may not be authentic, according to Dunlop.[68] By 988, however, Mstislav established Rus'ian control over Tmutorokan. Tmutorokan remained in Rus'ian hands until 1094.

VERKHNEYE SALTOVO AND OTHER SALTOVO SETTLEMENTS

Verkhneye Saltovo was an important settlement located along the east bank of the upper Donets in eastern Ukraine, approximately twenty-five miles east of modern-day Kharkiv. It was the site of a fortress constructed from white limestone.[69] Archaeologists also discovered a cemetery in Verkhneye Saltovo.[70] Archaeological discoveries indicated that Alan, Magyar, and

Swedish settlements existed there from the sixth to the ninth
centuries.[71] Jewish artifacts have been unearthed there as well
(see Chapter 6). Its residents shared elements of culture with
people living in nearby regions. The culture flourished between circa 700 and circa 950 in numerous settlements in the
Khazar Empire near and along the Don and Donets Rivers.
The general term for this culture, "Saltovo-Mayaki," is named
after Verkhneye Saltovo and the Mayaki *gorodishche* (hill
fort); the latter is located near the River Don. Vladimir
Petrukhin wrote that "the Saltovo culture was the culture of
the population of Khazaria. . . . "[72] The Saltovo-Mayakians were
industrious and creative people.

There were major Saltovo-Mayaki settlements located in the
Verkhneye Saltovo region, the Tsimlyansk area, and around
the Don, and many smaller villages also existed. Twelve small
stone castles were built near the Don in the Saltovo region in
the eighth and ninth centuries. One of the important white
stone fortresses in the Saltovo-Mayaki region was at
Dmitrievsky, in the boundary zone between the forest and the
steppe. Dmitrievsky's fortress may have served as a winter palace for local Khazar chieftains.[73] In total, there were about
twenty military citadels in the Saltovo region. They were situated near the Don, Donets, Severski, and Oskol Rivers, and
many of them were in the land of the Severians.

YEVPATORIA (GŪSLI-EV)

Khazar Jews lived in the Crimean seaport city of Yevpatoria.
Yevpatoria, once part of the Khazar Empire, was also known
by its Turkic name Güsli-ev (meaning "a beautiful settlement").[74]

OTHER KHAZAR SETTLEMENTS

Along the banks of the Dnieper, there was a town named
Borichev, whose name is derived from the Turkic form Berchi-

ev, meaning "Dnieper settlement" and containing the Khazar root for Dnieper (*Bar* or *Var*).[75]

West of the Volga and north of Sarkel, in the Russian guberniya (district) of Penza, there was a village called Kazarki, and the area was called Volost' Kazarskaya ("Khazarian region").[76]

The Khazar town of Semikarakovskoye, located about sixty-two miles south of Sarkel, shared many aspects of Sarkel's society. For example, the typical white mortar construction used at Sarkel was also employed at Semikarakovskoye's hill fort.[77]

The Khazars also had a fort located at Shelkovskaya Stanitsa, in an area later settled by Cossacks.[78] This fort was square-shaped, with walls, gates, and towers, and it was surrounded on all four sides by ditches. Khazarian warriors guarded it from the seventh through the tenth centuries. Gray-colored water vessels made from clay were found there.

According to Brutzkus, the Khazars founded towns named Sambalut, Samiran, Samakha, Samsakhy, Samkalako, and Tetchik-ev in the Caucasus.[79] Like Sambatas, most of these town names contained the Turkic root word *sam*, which, as previously mentioned, referred to the highlands.

Most of the Khazar towns in the plains of Daghestan were surrounded by circular or oval walls, which Svetlana Pletnyova said were constructed for both military defense and protection against floods.[80]

THE PEOPLES OF THE KHAZAR EMPIRE

Khazaria was one of the most diverse nations of medieval Europe. It was a multiethnic society with a population of Slavic, Turkic, Iranian, Arabic, and Caucasian peoples who claimed Judaism, Islam, Christianity, and other faiths.

In the ninth and tenth centuries, Judaism became the most widespread religious influence upon the Khazars (as discussed at length in Chapter 6). Yet other religions also gained in popularity among various tribes in the empire. For example, some Khazars became Muslims from circa 690 to the late tenth century. They lived in Atil and Samandar, and groups of them settled in Azerbaijan (see Chapter 9).

Christianity was also practiced in Khazaria. The Crimean Goths, originally from northern Europe, had been Christians since the third century. An eighth-century Khazarian tarkhan, George, was an Orthodox Christian.[81] The *Life* of Saint Abo said that Christians lived in many Khazar towns in the late eighth century.[82] Bishoprics were established by the Byzantine Empire in strategic parts of Khazaria in an attempt to spread Christianity among the Khazars. There were seven bishoprics in the metropolitan Doros region on the Crimea.[83] A bishop in southeastern Crimea served a community of Khotirs or Khotzirs (Khazars) near Phullai and Kharasiu in the eighth century.[84] Greek Orthodox bishops were also located in Atil and Tmutorokan circa 787.[85] In 861, two hundred Khazars were baptized into Christianity by the Bulgarian-Byzantine missionary Saint Cyril (see Chapter 6). Al-Masudi wrote about Christians living in Atil circa 912 or 913 who participated in a war against the Rus (see Chapter 8).

Figure 2–1. *Map of Khazaria and Neighboring Empires in the Ninth and Tenth Centuries.*

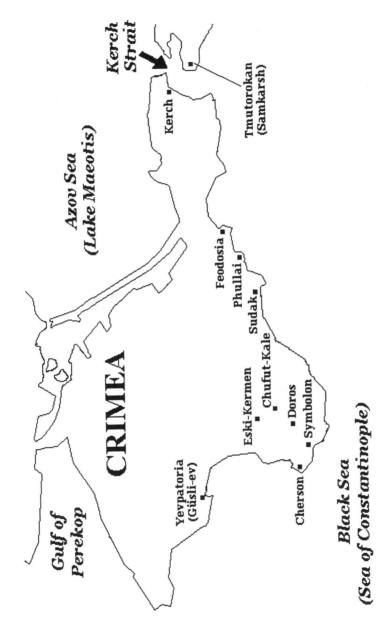

Figure 2-2. Map of the Crimean Peninsula during the Khazar Era.

NOTES

1. Károly Czeglédy, "Khazar Raids in Transcaucasia in 762–764 A.D.," *Acta Orientalia Academiae Scientiarum Hungaricae* 11 (1960): 76.

2. Peter B. Golden, *Khazar Studies*, vol. 1 (Budapest: Akadémiai, 1980), p. 63.

3. Douglas M. Dunlop, *The History of the Jewish Khazars* (New York: Schocken, 1967), p. 92.

4. In Old Rus'ian, Khazaran was known as Khvalisy (see Omeljan Pritsak, "An Arabic Text on the Trade Route of the Corporation of Ar-Rus in the Second Half of the Ninth Century," *Folia Orientalia* 12 (1970): 257).

5. Vladimir F. Minorsky, *Hudud al-'Alam (The Regions of the World)* (London: Luzac & Co., 1937), p. 162.

6. It is clear from the writings of Abraham ibn Daud in *Sefer ha-Qabbalah* and the anonymous authors of the *Schechter Letter* and *Hudud al-'Alam* that "Atil" was also the

Turkic name for the Volga itself, as well as being the name of the city. Interestingly, the Mongols also called the Volga "Idil" (see *Readings in Russian History*, ed. Alexander V. Riasanovsky and William E. Watson, vol. 1 (Dubuque, IA: Kendall/Hunt, 1991), p. 79). Alternative spellings for the river Atil included Itil, Etil, Til, Adil, and other variants. The Chuvashes and Volga Tatars still know the river by this name.

7. Peter B. Golden, "Khazaria and Judaism," *Archivum Eurasiae Medii Aevi* 3 (1983): 139.

8. Douglas M. Dunlop, *The History of the Jewish Khazars*, pp. 91–92.

9. Ibid., p. 92.

10. Vladimir F. Minorsky, *A History of Sharvan and Darband in the 10th-11th Centuries* (Cambridge, England: W. Heffer and Sons, 1958), p. 148.

11. Douglas M. Dunlop, *The History of the Jewish Khazars*, p. 105.

12. Lev N. Gumilev, "New Data on the History of the Khazars," *Acta Archaeologica Academiae Scientiarum Hungaricae* 19 (1967): 80.

13. Ibid., p. 96.

14. István Erdélyi, "Megvan a Kazár Atlantisz!" *Napjaink* (March 17, 1993): 24; Ildikó Hankó "A kazár föváros rejtéje," *Napjaink* (March 17, 1993): 25.

15. Julius Brutzkus, "The Khazar Origin of Ancient Kiev," *Slavonic and East European Review* 22 (1944): 112.

16. Csanád Bálint, "Some Archaeological Addenda to P. Golden's Khazar Studies," *Acta Orientalia Academiae Scientiarum Hungaricae* 35:2–3 (1981): 399; Antal Bartha, *Hungarian Society in the 9th and 10th Centuries*, trans. K. Balazs (Budapest: Akadémiai, 1975), p. 62; Bozena Wyszomirska, "Religion som enande politisk-social länk— exemplet: det Kazariska riket," in *Arkeologi och Religion*, ed.

Lars Larsson and Bozena Wyszomirska (Lund, Sweden: University of Lund, 1989), p. 137.

17. Svetlana A. Pletnyova, *Khazary* (Moscow: Nauka, 1986), p. 25.

18. Csanád Bálint, "Some Archaeological Addenda to P. Golden's Khazar Studies," p. 399.

19. Svetlana A. Pletnyova, *Khazary*, p. 27.

20. Omeljan Pritsak, "The Pre-Ashkenazic Jews of Eastern Europe in Relation to the Khazars, the Rus' and the Lithuanians," in *Ukrainian-Jewish Relations in Historical Perspective*, ed. Howard Aster and Peter J. Potichnyj (Edmonton, Alberta, Canada: Canadian Institute of Ukrainian Studies Press, 1990), p. 7.

21. In ancient times, Cherson was known as Chersonesus and was a vibrant, democratic Hellenistic city-state with a constitution and elected senators. Chersonesus was a major trading port, and received imports from such cities as Athens, Delphi, and Pergamon (see Robert S. MacLennan, "In Search of the Jewish Diaspora: A First-Century Synagogue in Crimea?" *Biblical Archaeology Review* 22:2 (March/April 1996): 47–48). The Khazar Jews called Cherson "Shurshun."

22. Benjamin Pinkus, *The Jews of the Soviet Union* (Cambridge, England: Cambridge University Press, 1988), p. 3.

23. Peter B. Golden, *Khazar Studies*, vol. 1, pp. 60–61.

24. Alexander A. Vasiliev, *The Goths in the Crimea* (Cambridge, MA: The Mediaeval Academy of America, 1936), p. 84.

25. Ibid., pp. 91, 105.

26. *Readings in Russian History*, eds. Alexander V. Riasanovsky and William E. Watson, vol. 1, pp. 11–12.

27. *Medieval Russia's Epics, Chronicles, and Tales*, ed. Serge A. Zenkovsky (New York: Meridian, 1974), p. 48.

28. Julius Brutzkus, "The Khazar Origin of Ancient Kiev," p. 117.

29. Norman Golb and Omeljan Pritsak, *Khazarian Hebrew Documents of the Tenth Century* (Ithaca, NY: Cornell University Press, 1982), p. 55.

30. *Readings in Russian History*, eds. Alexander V. Riasanovsky and William E. Watson, vol. 1, p. 64.

31. Julius Brutzkus, "The Khazar Origin of Ancient Kiev," p. 108.

32. Omeljan Pritsak, "The Pre-Ashkenazic Jews of Eastern Europe...," in *Ukrainian-Jewish Relations in Historical Perspective*, p. 7.

33. Julius Brutzkus, "The Khazar Origin of Ancient Kiev," pp. 110, 112–114, 118.

34. Norman Golb and Omeljan Pritsak, *Khazarian Hebrew Documents of the Tenth Century*, p. 56.

35. Michael F. Hamm, *Kiev* (Princeton, NJ: Princeton University Press, 1993), p. 10.

36. Ibid., p. 3.

37. Norman Golb and Omeljan Pritsak, *Khazarian Hebrew Documents of the Tenth Century*, pp. 57–58.

38. Ibid., p. 57.

39. George Vernadsky, *A History of Russia*, vol. 1 (New Haven, CT: Yale University Press, 1948), p. 333.

40. Csanád Bálint, "Some Archaeological Addenda to P. Golden's Khazar Studies," p. 404.

41. Constantine Zuckerman, "On the Date of the Khazars' Conversion to Judaism and the Chronology of the Kings of the Rus Oleg and Igor," *Revue des Études Byzantines* 53 (1995): 269.

42. Omeljan Pritsak, "The Pre-Ashkenazic Jews of Eastern Europe...," in *Ukrainian-Jewish Relations in Historical Perspective*, p. 8.

43. Shmuel Ettinger, "Kievan Russia," in *The Dark Ages*, ed. Cecil Roth and I. H. Levine (New Brunswick, NJ: Rutgers University Press, 1966), pp. 320–321.

44. George V. Gubaroff, *Cossacks and their Land*, trans. John N. Washburn (Providence, RI: Cossack American National Alliance, 1985), p. 53.

45. Bozena Werbart, "Khazars or 'Saltovo-Majaki Culture'? Prejudices about Archaeology and Ethnicity," *Current Swedish Archaeology* 4 (1996): 209.

46. Svetlana A. Pletnyova, Khazary, p. 28.

47. Omeljan Pritsak, "The Khazar Kingdom's Conversion to Judaism," *Harvard Ukrainian Studies* 3:2 (Sept. 1978): 262.

48. René Grousset, *The Empire of the Steppes*, trans. Naomi Waldorf (New Brunswick, NJ: Rutgers University Press, 1970), p. 577. Pritsak associated Tarqu with Balanjar, rather than with Samandar (see Omeljan Pritsak, "The Khazar Kingdom's Conversion to Judaism," p. 263).

49. Vladimir F. Minorsky, "A New Book on the Khazars," *Oriens* 11 (1959): 127.

50. Vladimir F. Minorsky, *Hudud al-'Alam (The Regions of the World)*, p. 162.

51. Svetlana A. Pletnyova, *Khazar*, p. 27.

52. Douglas M. Dunlop, *The History of the Jewish Khazars*, p. 95.

53. Ibid.

54. George Vernadsky, *A History of Russia*, vol. 1, p. 216.

55. Carlile A. Macartney, *The Magyars in the Ninth Century* (Cambridge, England: Cambridge University Press, 1930), p. 74.

56. The word Sarkel consists of two elements: *sar* (a contraction of *sarigh*, meaning in this instance "white") + *kel* ("fortress," also spelled *kil*).

57. Bozena Wyszomirska, "Religion som enande politisk-social länk—exemplet: det Kazariska riket," in *Arkeologi och Religion*, p. 139.

58. Antal Bartha, *Hungarian Society in the 9th and 10th Centuries*, pp. 13–14. Other fortresses in the Khazar kingdom were also constructed from bricks that contained Turkic tamga symbols.

59. Bozena Wyszomirska, "Religion som enande politisk-social länk—exemplet: det Kazariska riket," in *Arkeologi och Religion*, p. 137.

60. Csanád Bálint, "Some Archaeological Addenda to P. Golden's Khazar Studies," p. 398.

61. Bozena Werbart, "Khazars or 'Saltovo-Majaki Culture'? . . .," p. 210.

62. István Fodor, *In Search of a New Homeland*, trans. Helen Tarnoy (Gyoma, Hungary: Corvina, 1982), p. 239.

63. Csanád Bálint, "Some Archaeological Addenda to P. Golden's Khazar Studies," p. 399.

64. Antal Bartha, *Hungarian Society in the 9th and 10th Centuries*, pp. 12–13.

65. Neal Ascherson, *Black Sea* (New York: Hill & Wang, 1995), p. 9.

66. Leonid S. Chekin, "Samarcha, City of Khazaria," *Central Asiatic Journal* 33:1–2 (1989): 28. Samkarsh is sometimes spelled as Samkarch.

67. *An Ethnohistorical Dictionary of the Russian and Soviet Empires*, ed. James S. Olson (Westport, CT: Greenwood Press, 1994), p. 308; Vsevolod L. Vikhnovich, "From the Jordan to the Dnieper," *Jewish Studies (Mada'e ha-Yahadut)* 31 (1991): 19.

68. Douglas M. Dunlop, "The Khazars," in *The Dark Ages*, ed. Cecil Roth and I. H. Levine (New Brunswick, NJ: Rutgers University Press, 1966), pp. 354, 449. The *Mandgelis Docu-*

ment was discovered by Abraham Firkovitch (1786–1874) in the Mandgelis (Medgelis) Synagogue in the Caucasus during the 1840s. The document mysteriously vanished in 1876, but was rediscovered over a century later by V. V. Lebedev.

69. Antal Bartha, *Hungarian Society in the 9th and 10th Centuries*, p. 62.

70. Ibid., p. 201.

71. George Vernadsky, *A History of Russia*, vol. 1, p. 157.

72. Vladimir Ia. Petrukhin, "The Normans and the Khazars in the South of Rus' (The Formation of the 'Russian Land' in the Middle Dnepr Area)," *Russian History/Histoire russe* 19 (1992): 396.

73. Bozena Werbart, "Khazars or 'Saltovo-Majaki Culture'? . . .," p. 213.

74. Julius Brutzkus, "The Khazar Origin of Ancient Kiev," p. 118. In ancient times, Yevpatoria was known by the Greek name Kerkinitida. The Crimean Tatars call it Gözleve.

75. Ibid.

76. Peter B. Golden, *Khazar Studies*, vol. 1, p. 75.

77. Bozena Werbart, "Khazars or 'Saltovo-Majaki Culture'? . . .," p. 209.

78. Lev N. Gumilev, "New Data on the History of the Khazars," pp. 81–83.

79. Julius Brutzkus, "The Khazar Origin of Ancient Kiev," pp. 112, 118.

80. Svetlana A. Pletnyova, *Khazary*, p. 29.

81. Douglas M. Dunlop, *The History of the Jewish Khazars*, p. 252.

82. Thomas S. Noonan, "Why Dirhams First Reached Russia: The Role of Arab-Khazar Relations in the Development of the Earliest Islamic Trade with Eastern Europe," *Archivum Eurasiae Medii Aevi* 4 (1984): 241.

83. Simon Szyszman, "Le roi Bulan et le problème de la conversion des Khazars," *Ephemerides Theologicae Lovanienses* 33 (1957): 73.

84. Alexander A. Vasiliev, *The Goths in the Crimea*, pp. 98, 103–104. Phullai was located where Planerskoye is today, on the Crimean coast midway between Sudak and Feodosia.

85. Thomas S. Noonan, "Why Dirhams First Reached Russia. . .," p. 239.

3

THE STRUCTURE OF THE
KHAZAR GOVERNMENT

In Sefer ha-'Osher, composed in the late eleventh century or early twelfth century, Jacob ben Reuben wrote that the Khazars were mighty, with their own kingship and rule, which allowed them to avoid paying tribute to the non-Jewish nations around them. Indeed, Khazaria is the only example of an independent Jewish state in eastern Europe. The Khazars had a system of dual monarchy, which consisted of a kagan and a bek. This system was supported by additional officials at lower levels, such as tarkhans, judges, and local governors.

THE KAGAN

The supreme ruler (i.e., emperor) of the Khazars was known as the kagan; for this reason, Khazaria has been called a "kaganate." The kagan was a sacred religious figure who lived in seclusion from the general public. The Khazars believed that the kagan brought good fortune (*qut*) to the empire. The Khazar kagan established traditional law (*törü*) as the law of the kaganate.[1]

A charismatic kagan founded the Khazar kaganate by the middle of the seventh century. The kaganship was hereditary, and it is believed that the kagans of Khazaria (see Table 3–1) were members of the Asena (Ashina) royal family. The kagans of the Hsiung-nu, the eastern Turkish Empire, and the western Turkish Empire had also belonged to the house of Asena.[2]

The strange ritual of kagan-killing was found among both the western Turks and the Khazars. According to the Arab historian al-Istakhri, a limit was imposed upon the length of a Khazar kagan's life after he started ruling.[3] The nobles placed a silken cord around the kagan's neck and tightened it until he began to choke, and they asked him: "For how long do you intend to rule?" The nobles intended to kill him if his reign lasted even one day beyond the specified number of years. Ibn Fadlan, on the other hand, gave a precise figure for the maximum number of years allotted to a king's reign. If a kagan had ruled for at least forty years, he wrote, his courtiers and subjects felt that his ability to reason had become impaired, on account of his old age. As a consequence, they would kill the kagan.[4] The scenario described by al-Istakhri was virtually identical to the practice of the western Turks. The western Turks inducted a new kagan by carrying him in a felt carpet and spinning him nine times. He then mounted a horse and began to ride, but the nobles choked him with a silver scarf and asked him how long he would rule. Since he was being nearly strangled, he was unable to answer coherently, so the nobles decided the duration of his reign based on their interpretation of what he had mumbled.[5] The Khazars apparently retained this ancient Turkic tradition even after their conversion to Judaism.

The kagan's wife was known as the *khatun*. However, ibn Fadlan claimed that the kagan had a harem of twenty-five wives, all of whom were daughters of kings, as well as sixty beautiful slave-girl mistresses.[6] By ibn Fadlan's time (the early 920s), however, the kagan was a follower of Judaism. Since polygamy was not generally a Jewish custom, it is possible that the harem was the chronicler's own invention. Historians have noticed that the number twenty-five is also prominent in the sections on the Khazars in the accounts of Eldad the Danite and Elchanan the Merchant (see Chapter 1). In other words, it seems that the twenty-five "wives" symbolically represented the twenty-five peoples and kingdoms under Khazar domination.

In the years following the initial conversion to Judaism, only a Jew was eligible to become the Khazar kagan.[7] According to the *Schechter Letter*, the first Jewish kagan was an Israelite sage appointed by the Khazars. The Jewishness of the kaganship, along with the presence of Jews in other high administrative posts, indicates the privileged role of Jews in the Khazar government structure. Yet, it is not a valid conclusion that only members of the Khazar ruling elite were Jewish, since Judaism was the predominant religion of the Khazar tribe (see Chapter 6).

The kagan was allegedly given an elaborate mausoleum after his death. Ibn Fadlan described the interesting procedure for burying a deceased kagan:

> The custom of the superior king is that when he dies a great hall is built for him, containing twenty chambers. In each of these a grave is dug for him, and stones are broken till they become like powder, which is then sprinkled therein, and pitch is spread over that again. Under the building is a river. The river is large and rapid. They bring the river over the grave and say that it is in order that no devil or man, no worm or creeping beast, may come to him. When he is buried the heads of those who buried him are struck off, so that it may not be known in which of the chambers is his tomb. His grave is called Paradise, and they say, "He has entered Paradise." All the chambers are spread with silk brocade interwoven with gold.[8]

Archaeological remains of the mausoleum, if indeed they ever existed, have not survived to the present day. Indeed, al-Istakhri wrote that whoever passed within the vicinity of the Khazar kagan's tomb was required to walk rather than ride on horseback until he no longer could see the tomb.[9] This contradicts ibn Fadlan's statement that no one was supposed to know where the grave was located.

As time went on, the status of the Khazar kagan diminished. According to Omeljan Pritsak, the historian al-Ya'qubi's ninth-century account suggests that the kagan was the supreme ruler as well as the military commander until the year 799; by 833, however, the kagan shared power with the other monarch, the bek.[10] Around 943, the Arab historian Ali al-Masudi (d. 956) wrote that the kagan had limited power, since he could not give orders or decide important affairs of state.[11]

THE BEK (KING) AND HIS ARMY

In the tenth century, when the kagan had been reduced to the status of a spiritual figurehead, it was the bek[12] (i.e., *melekh*, king) who handled secular state affairs in Khazaria. Ibn Fadlan wrote that the bek had the power to bind, to punish, to release, and to govern the affairs of state. Still, the bek was considered to be the second-in-command, after the titular kagan. Unlike the kagan, the bek often appeared in public. The names of many important Khazarian beks are known from the list in *King Joseph's Reply* (see Table 3–2).

One of the most important responsibilities of the bek was leadership of the army. The bek led all military expeditions. The army consisted of a well-trained force of warriors. According to *Muruj al-Dhahab* by al-Masudi, the Khazar army included professional soldiers of the Islamic faith who originally came from Khwarizm[13] following a terrible drought in central Asia. These Muslim soldiers, collectively known as the Arsiya, were ethnic Iranians, and they served as bodyguards for the Khazar king. They were also skilled horseback archers. In 943, the Arsiya numbered about seven thousand men. Slavic Rus'ians also served in the Khazar army.[14] Additionally, the chronicler Marvazi wrote that ten thousand Burtasian horsemen served the Khazar king. Ibn Rustah provided a colorful description of the Khazarian army led by the bek:

> When they go out in any direction, they do so armed in full array, with banners, spears, and strong coats of mail. He [the bek] rides forth with 10,000 horsemen, of whom some are regular paid troops and others have been levied on the rich.[15]

Scouts ventured ahead of the army during expeditions, carrying candles and flares made from wax to provide the army with light. Each member of the army was required to take a peg with him to be used with other pegs to encircle their own army encampments, in order to prevent enemy infiltration into their camps.[16] A shield was hung from each peg.

At the same time that Khazarian troops were engaging in battle, other troops were left behind to safeguard their families and property.

The Khazars continued the Turkic practice of taking hostages from enemy groups. They also seized valuabie treasures from the enemy. When the army took booty, it all would be collected in the bek's camp so that the bek could select some of the most prized items for himself, with the rest to be divided among the horsemen.[17]

Ibn Fadlan described what would happen in the event that the Khazar army was unsuccessful:

> When he [the bek] sends out a body of troops, they do not in any circumstances retreat. If they are defeated, every one who returns to him is killed . . . . Sometimes he cuts every one of them in two and crucifies them and sometimes he hangs them by the neck from trees. Sometimes, when he would treat them well, he makes them grooms.[18]

The army was certainly the most important element in the Khazar military system. The Khazars apparently did not have a navy.[19]

Saadiah ben Joseph, better known as Saadiah Gaon (882–942), the chief tenth-century rabbinical authority at the talmudic academy in Sura, Babylonia, recorded an interesting custom regarding the reporting of results to the bek:

> I encountered in our scriptures things that were difficult for me to understand, until it came to my mind that these same things still occur in our own times. One of these things is that I have maintained for a long time that it was Moses' habit that when he responded to a command of God he kept it in his mind until the time when the second revelation came. Moses was not allowed to break off the words of the revelation by responding to the first revelation, he had to wait until the revelation was completed, and only then could be respond.
>
> And the reader of the Torah sees a reply is not the response to the first statement. And if there is a reply to the second statement, then Moses gives it after the third one. For example, we have learned in: "And Moses reported the words of the people to the Lord" (Exodus 19:8) when: "And the Lord said to Moses: Lo, I come to you in a thick cloud" (Exodus 19:9) at the time when: "Then Moses told the words of the people to the Lord" (Exodus 19:9) and likewise when God said: "Go down, warn the people, lest they break through to the Lord . . . " (Exodus 19:21) his answer was: "The people cannot come up to Mount Sinai . . . " (Exodus 19:23). But this answer was in response to the preceding command "And you shall set bounds for the people round about, saying . . . " (Exodus 19:12.)
>
> And as concerns my explanation of the weekly Torah portion (parasha) Wa Yishma 'Yethro, it did not occur to me that this is a habit of kings until I realized that it is a habit of the kingdom of the Khazars. If a king (melekh) calls for a prince or a commander [to fulfill a request], then he carries it out and subsequently appears before him, but he does not say "O my lord, I have satisfied your wish." Instead, he waits until he is called for another request. And if he has completed that [second] request, he says: "I have fulfilled the first request." And when it became clear to me that this is a habit of kings, then I no longer stuck to my earlier interpretation.[20]

The bek lived in the capital city from December to April, celebrating Hanukkah and Pesach while there. However, the bek resided in the steppes during all the other months.

In certain respects, the bek was inferior in status—at least symbolically—compared to the kagan, as indicated by ibn Fadlan's account:

> He [the Kagan Bek] goes humbly in every day to the superior Kagan, displaying deference and modesty. He never enters except barefoot, with a piece of wood in his hand. When he has greeted him, he lights the wood in his presence, and when it has finished burning, he sits with the king on his throne at his right hand.[21]

The Khazar kagan had the power to order the bek to be put to death.[22] Since the status of the bek was less than that of the kagan, it may be assumed that in matters of disputed opinion the kagan would be consulted by the bek and that the kagan's word on the matter was decisively final. This was certainly the situation in the early periods of Khazaria's existence when all officials submitted to the kagan's authority. Yet, as time went on, the bek's power increased, surpassing the kagan's power by the mid-ninth century. Indeed, the major policymakers of Khazaria in the tenth century—Benjamin, Aaron, and Joseph—were beks. Still, the *Schechter Letter* (circa 948 or 949) described the kagan as the "judge." This seems to indicate that the kagan was the chief adjudicator in the realm, even as late as the mid-tenth century, when he no longer had legislative or executive powers.[23]

THE KENDER AND THE JAVISHGAR

The *kender* was the third-in-command in the Khazar government. The kender's deputy, the fourth-in-command, was known as the *javishgar*. It is not certain what administrative tasks were performed by these two officials.

THE TARKHAN

After the kagan, bek, kender, and javishgar, the next position in the hierarchy of power was the *tarkhan*. The tarkhans served as commanders of regiments of the Khazar army or auxiliary troops.[24] Some Alans became *As tarkhans* and, thus, participated in the Khazar government. A famous tarkhan led a large-scale military initiative against the south Caucasus in 762–764 (see Chapter 7). *Tarkhan* was also the title of the local governor of Atil in the eighth century.[25]

THE COURT PANEL

The Khazars also established an organized judicial system. Al-Masudi reported that the Khazars had a seven-member "supreme court" in Atil composed of two Jews, two Muslims, two Christians, and one pagan.[26] Al-Masudi noted that the two judges for the Khazar tribe consulted the Torah when deciding the outcome of cases. The pagan court member represented the Slavs of Khazaria.

The court in Atil dealt primarily with trading issues.[27] Peter Golden has suggested that the judges were representatives for the foreign traders living in Atil.[28]

The representation of all Khazarian religions on the court panel indicates that the court was a model of tolerance and peaceful coexistence. The diversity in the Khazar court is remarkable when compared to the turmoil in western Europe and Byzantium over religious issues during the same period.

Apparently, some traditional Turkic methods remained embedded in the legal decisions of the Khazars even after the conversion to Judaism.[29]

THE LOCAL GOVERNORS

The provincial governors in the Khazar Empire held the title *tudun* and were appointed by the Khazar kagan. The Turkic tuduns collected taxes and customs duties.[30] Khazarian tuduns controlled parts of the Crimea, including Cherson and Doros (see Chapter 2).

There were also appointed government officials with the title *baliqchi* who ruled the Bosporus (i.e., Kerch) and Tmutorokan. The title *baliqchi* means "fisherman" and reflects the Khazars' major interest in fishing. The baliqchis were seen as the guardians of the waterfront. The Byzantine historian Theophanes wrote about a prominent Khazar baliqchi who ruled Kerch at the start of the eighth century (see Chapter 7). In the late 930s, during the early years of King Joseph's reign, there was a Jewish Khazar military general in the Cimmerian Bosporus named Pesakh ha-M-Q-R "the Baliqchi." Baliqchi Pesakh is famous for his victory over Prince Oleg of the Rus (see Chapter 8).

Some Khazar localities possessed elected government leaders in addition to appointed leaders like the tuduns and baliqchis. For example, an elected "father of the city," called *babaghuq* in the Khazar language, led affairs in Cherson between about 705 and 840.[31] Another babaghuq presided over Tmutorokan in around the year 703.

Local Turkic kings were called *el-teber*. El-tebers ruled over communities of Khazars, as well as those of Magyars, Huns, Onoghurs, Volga Bulgars and Suvars, and Burtas.[32]

Ibn Fadlan reported that one Muslim official in particular was responsible for handling legal issues of concern to Atil's Muslim population (see Chapter 2). The chief representative of the Muslim community was the vizier (*wazir* in Arabic), a hereditary title. Omeljan Pritsak suggested that the vizier Kuya, father of Ahmad, was identical to the Kiy of the old Rus'ian chronicles.[33]

TAXATION

The products of blacksmiths were taxed by the Khazar government.[34] Food and drink was also taxed. For example, Mus-

lim merchants in Khazaran-Atil paid taxes in the form of food
to the Khazar kagan.[35] Along with customs duties on merchandise and transport (see Chapter 5), these taxes were important sources of revenue for the kagan's government. However,
Hudud al-'Alam reported that the maritime customs duties
brought in the most wealth to the Khazar king.[36]

TRIBUTARY PEOPLES

Khazaria may be considered an empire during the periods
when the Khazars controlled other ethnic groups. By the second half of the eighth century, the Khazars controlled a vast
land territory between the Black Sea and the Caspian Sea,
including parts of the Ural Mountains and Volga. This resulted
in the recognition of Khazarian overlordship by numerous
peoples, including the Caucasian Alans, the Hungarians, the
Bulgars, certain Slavic tribes, and the Crimean Greeks and
Goths.

Many eastern Slavs were paying tribute to the Khazars
around the middle of the ninth century. In the entry for the
year "859," the *Rus'ian Primary Chronicle* recorded that the
Khazars imposed tribute upon the Polianians, Severians, and
Vyatichians, consisting of "a white squirrel-skin from each
hearth."[37] The Radimichians also paid tribute to the Khazars.[38]
Meanwhile, the Krivichians, Slovenes, and Ieria in the north
paid tribute to the Varangians.

Prince Oleg of Kiev conquered the Severians in "884" and
the Radimichians in "885," according to the *Rus'ian Primary
Chronicle*. But recent scholarship has proven that Oleg actually reigned from 911 until 941.[39] Thus, Oleg probably conquered the Severians and the Radimichians in the 920s or
930s—before his war with the Khazars in the late 930s, his war
with the Byzantines in 941, and other raids in 943 and 944
(see Chapter 8). In one of the surviving versions of his *Reply*, Khazar King Joseph wrote (circa 955) that his empire
ruled over three Slavic groups: Sever, Slaviun, and Ventit.[40] Yet,

Constantine VII (circa 950) wrote that the Severians paid tribute to the Rus, not to the Khazars.[41]

Other tribes also had to pay the Khazars tribute on a regular basis. The Bulgars paid an annual tribute in the ninth and
tenth centuries. Almush, the ruler of the Volga Bulgars in the
early tenth century, was under the jurisdiction of the Khazars.[42]
The Burtas (a Finnic people), Pechenegs (a warlike Turkic
people), Magyars, and other tribes also paid tribute to the
Khazars. The shamanist North Caucasian Huns were vassals of
the Khazars during the seventh century.[43]

THE "KAGANS" OF KIEVAN RUS

The Khazars influenced the form of government of the emerg-
ing state of Kievan Rus. Even the Khazar title *kagan* was
adopted by the Rus'ian rulers, as medieval documents indicate. The *Annales Bertiani* (sub anno 839), the sermon "On
Law and Grace" by Metropolitan Ilarion (early eleventh century), and "The Lay of the Host of Igor" (*Slovo o polku
Igoreve*) (1185) all apply the title *kagan* to the highest Kievan
sovereign; Ilarion called the Rus princes Vladimir and Iaroslav
"kagan," and "The Lay of the Host of Igor," an epic about an
unsuccessful Rus'ian campaign against the Polovtsi (Cumans),
calls Prince Igor of Novgorod-Seversk "kagan."[44] Even *Hudud
al-'Alam* called the Rus ruler "*Rus-khaqan.*"[45] Charles J.
Halperin wrote: "That a steppe title was used in Kiev suggests
considerable cultural interaction, and the significance of this
trace of Khazar influence has long been recognized."[46]

Table 3–1. *The Khazar Kagans.*

Ziebil (Tong Yabghu), of the western Turkish Empire, 618–630.

Irbis(?), founder of Khazar kaganate, circa 650 or 652.

Busir (Ibousir-Glavan), circa 703 or 704

?, first kagan who converted to Islam, circa 737

Baghatur, circa 760

Xan-tuvan (Dyggvi), circa 830s

Zacharias, circa 861

?, second kagan who converted to Islam, circa 960s

Georgius Tzul, ?–1016

Table 3–2. *The Khazar Beks (Kings).*

Bulan (Sabriel), circa 861

Obadiah, grandson of Bulan, circa 860s

Hezekiah, son of Obadiah, ninth century

Menasheh I, son of Hezekiah, ninth century

Hanukkah, brother of Obadiah, ninth century

Yitzhak, son of Hanukkah, ninth century

Zebulun, ninth century

Menasheh II (Moses), son of Yitzhak, late ninth century

Nisi, son of Menasheh II, late ninth century

Aaron I, late 9th century or early 10th century

Menahem, late 9th century or early 10th century

Benjamin, circa 920

Aaron II, son of Nisi, circa early 930s

Joseph, son of Aaron II, late 930s to about 960

NOTES

1. Peter B. Golden, "Khazaria and Judaism," *Archivum Eurasiae Medii Aevi* 3 (1983): 143.

2. Douglas M. Dunlop, *The History of the Jewish Khazars* (New York: Schocken, 1967), p. 160. The Persian geographical treatise *Hudud al-'Alam* (The Regions of the World), compiled in 982 and 983 by an unknown author, noted that "Ansa" was the tarkhan kagan's tribal group at Atil.

3. Ibid., p. 97.

4. Ibid., p. 112.

5. Peter B. Golden, "Imperial Ideology and the Sources of Political Unity Amongst the Pre-Cinggisid Nomads of Western Eurasia," *Archivum Eurasiae Medii Aevi* 2 (1982): 46–47.

6. Douglas M. Dunlop, *The History of the Jewish Khazars*, pp. 109, 112.

7. Omeljan Pritsak, "The Khazar Kingdom's Conversion of Judaism," *Harvard Ukrainian Studies* 3:2 (Sept. 1978): 278–279.

8. Douglas M. Dunlop, *The History of the Jewish Khazars*, pp. 111–112.

9. Carlile A. Macartney, *The Magyars in the Ninth Century* (Cambridge, England: Cambridge University Press, 1930), p. 221.

10. Omeljan Pritsak, "The Khazar Kingdom's Conversion to Judaism," p. 278.

11. Vladimir F. Minorsky, *A History of Sharvan and Darband in the 10th–11th Centuries* (Cambridge, England: W. Heffer & Sons, 1958), p. 148.

12. The bek is sometimes called the "viceroy." Alternative Turkic titles for the bek included *yilig* and *shad* (*ishad* or *isha*). The title *shad* derives from *abshad*, which originally was *äbä-shad*.

13. Douglas M. Dunlop, *The History of the Jewish Khazars*, p. 206. Vladimir Minorsky suggested that the Arsiya guards were members of the Alan (As) tribe (see Vladimir F. Minorsky, "A New Book on the Khazars," *Oriens* 11 (1959): 129).

14. Peter B. Golden, *Khazar Studies*, vol. 1 (Budapest: Akadémiai, 1980), pp. 16, 81. A few members of other groups, including the Oghuz, also served in the Khazar army. The most notable Oghuz warrior in the army was Tokak Temir-Yaligh (Tokak "Iron-Bow"), the father of Seljuk. After Tokak's death, Seljuk was brought up in the Khazarian royal court in Atil. Around 985, Seljuk quarreled with the Khazar king, escaped east to Jand along the Syr Darya, and converted to Islam. Seljuk went on to found several important Turkish dynasties in Asia Minor, Syria, and Persia.

15. Douglas M. Dunlop, *The History of the Jewish Khazars*, p. 105.

16. A. P. Martinez, "Gardizi's Two Chapters on the Turks," *Archivum Eurasiae Medii Aevi* 2 (1982): 154–155.

17. Douglas M. Dunlop, *The History of the Jewish Khazars*, p. 105.

18. Ibid., p. 113.

19. Ibid., p. 211.

20. Translated from the original Hebrew text given in Abraham E. Harkavy, "Rab Sa'adyah Gaon al debar ha-Kuzarim," in *Semitic Studies in Memory of Rev. Dr. Alexander Kohut*, ed. G. A. Kohut (Berlin: S. Calvary & Co., 1897), p. 245.

21. Douglas M. Dunlop, *The History of the Jewish Khazars*, p. 111.

22. Peter B. Golden, "Khazaria and Judaism," p. 149.

23. Constantine Zuckerman agreed that after the bek took over state affairs the kagan remained the supreme judge, even over the bek (see Constantine Zuckerman, "On the Date of the Khazars' Conversion to Judaism and the Chronology of the Kings of the Rus Oleg and Igor," *Revue des Études Byzantines* 53 (1995): 252).

24. George Vernadsky, *A History of Russia*, vol. 1 (New Haven, CT: Yale University Press, 1948), p. 219.

25. Omeljan Pritsak, "The Khazar Kingdom's Conversion to Judaism," p. 262.

26. Vladimir F. Minorsky, *A History of Sharvan and Darband in the 10th–11th Centuries*, p. 147.

27. Antal Bartha, *Hungarian Society in the 9th and 10th Centuries*, trans. K. Balazs (Budapest: Akadémiai, 1975), p. 16.

28. Peter B. Golden, "Khazaria and Judaism," p. 143.

29. Ibid.

30. Peter B. Golden, *Khazar Studies*, vol. 1, p. 216.

31. Omeljan Pritsak, "The Khazar Kingdom's Conversion to Judaism," p. 264.

32. Ibid., pp. 263–264.

33. Norman Golb and Omeljan Pritsak, *Khazarian Hebrew Documents of the Tenth Century* (Ithaca, NY: Cornell University Press, 1982), p. 55.

34. Antal Bartha, *Hungarian Society in the 9th and 10th Centuries*, p. 12.

35. Ibid., p. 16.

36. Vladimir F. Minorsky, *Hudud al-'Alam (The Regions of the World)* (London: Luzac & Co., 1937), p. 162.

37. *Readings in Russian History*, eds. Alexander V. Riasanovsky and William E. Watson, vol. 1 (Dubuque, IA: Kendall/Hunt, 1991), p. 11.

38. Frederick I. Kaplan, "The Decline of the Khazars and the Rise of the Varangians," *American Slavic and East European Review* 13 (1954): 4.

39. Constantine Zuckerman, "On the Date of the Khazars' Conversion . . . ," p. 269.

40. Julius Brutzkus, "The Khazar Origin of Ancient Kiev," *Slavonic and East European Review* 22 (1944): 110–111. Brutzkus suggested that the Severians of the Chernigov area were connected with the Turkic Sever tribe (see idem., p. 123).

41. *Readings in Russian History*, eds. Alexander V. Riasanovsky and William E. Watson, vol. 1, p. 66.

42. Peter B. Golden, "Khazaria and Judaism," p. 130. Circa 921, ibn Fadlan wrote that the Volga Bulgars paid tribute to the Khazars.

43. Peter B. Golden, *Khazar Studies*, vol. 1, p. 90. These Huns lived in the Sulak River basin, north of Derbent.

44. Julius Brutzkus, "The Khazar Origin of Ancient Kiev," p. 123; Charles J. Halperin, *Russia and the Golden Horde* (Bloomington, IN: Indiana University Press, 1985), pp. 12–13;

Vladimir Ia. Petrukhin, "The Normans and the Khazars in the South of Rus' (The Formation of the 'Russian Land' in the Middle Dnepr Area)," *Russian History/Histoire russe* 19 (1992): 400.

45. Vladimir F. Minorsky, *Hudud al-'Alam (The Regions of the World)*, p. 159.

46. Charles J. Halperin, *Russia and the Golden Horde*, pp. 12–13.

4

THE KHAZAR WAY OF LIFE

*T*he daily life and culture of the Khazars is not
described in detail in historical documents. Thus, archaeological fieldwork is our primary source of reliable
information about this obscure subject.[1] Archaeological
evidence shows that the Khazars were a highly productive people, manufacturing goods of all sorts for both
internal use and export to other countries. It also confirms that the Khazars were expert farmers and herders.

LANGUAGES SPOKEN
BY THE KHAZARS

Several Arabic historians of the tenth century described the
original Khazar language as one bearing some resemblance to
the Bulgar language while retaining distinctive qualities. Al-
Istakhri wrote:

The Bulgar language resembles that of the Khazars, while the
Burtas speak another language. Similarly, the Russian language
is different from both the Khazars' and Burtas' languages.[2]

Ibn Fadlan wrote:

The language of the Khazars does not resemble the Persian
nor the Turkish languages, nor any other language in the
world, even if it does resemble the language of the Bulgars.[3]

Ibn Hauqal, writing several decades later, confirmed al-
Istakhri's notice: "The Bulgar language is like the one of the
Khazars."[4]

From these statements, it appears that the Khazar language
can be described as having affinities to the Oghuric linguistic
group, a unique branch of the Turkic linguistic family (see
Table 4–1). The modern Chuvash language, spoken by about
1.6 million people in the Chuvash Autonomous Region of
western Russia, is the only living language in the Oghuric
group.[5] Omeljan Pritsak believed that the Khazar language was
equivalent to the ancient Hunnic language.[6] In the same re-
spect, Chuvash and its extinct sister languages were classified
as "West Hunnic" languages by *An Ethnohistorical Dictionary
of the Russian and Soviet Empires.*[7] Unfortunately, we still
know very little about the grammar and vocabulary of
Khazarian, because few traces of the language have survived.

According to Pritsak, Oghuric ("Hunno-Bulgaric") and
common Turkic both were spoken in the Khazar Empire.
However, it is not yet possible to determine which type of
Turkic was predominant in Khazaria.

The Khazars wrote their original language in Turkic runic
letters. The discovery of Khazar runic writing has been a rare
occurrence. A single Turkic word was affixed to the *Kievan
Letter* (see Chapter 6). Turkic runes were found in a cave in
Kerch, on a wooden stick from the Taras-vale, on two flasks
from Novocherkask, and on stones at the Mayaki hill fort.
Other examples of Turkic (apparently Khazar) written language have been found inscribed on large stones in Khumar

(in present-day Karachay-Cherkessia), but are being misused by local residents instead of being preserved in museums and translated.[8] The main difficulty is in differentiating between Khazar-produced runes and other types of runes. Some of the runes may be in the Khazar language, while others may be in Bulgar or some other language. In fact, the only runes that may, at this time, be unquestionably classified as Khazarian are those on the *Kievan Letter*.

One of the major characteristics of Jewish life throughout history has been the use of Hebrew as a liturgical and—sometimes—a written and spoken language. When the Khazars adopted Judaism, they gradually adopted Jewish customs, including the Hebrew language. This explains why the text of the *Kievan Letter* was composed in Hebrew (see Chapter 6). There is also additional evidence that seems to demonstrate that the Khazars adopted Hebrew. For instance, the Arabic writer Muhammad ibn Ishaq an-Nadim of Baghdad, author of *Kitab al-Fihrist* (circa 987 or 988), wrote that the tenth-century Khazars used Hebrew letters when writing.[9] On the other hand, some Khazars probably spoke Greek in addition to Hebrew (see summary of the *Chronicle of Elchanan the Merchant* in Chapter 1).

The Khazars would have been able to learn how to read and write Hebrew from recent Jewish immigrants to Khazaria, as well as the old Jewish communities of the Crimea. Indeed, there exists evidence that the Crimean Jews of the Khazar era were fully acquainted with Hebrew and were willing to teach the language even to Christians. For instance, the evangelist Saint Cyril gained extensive knowledge of Hebrew during his stay in the city of Cherson in 860–861 (see Chapter 6). Using his newly acquired knowledge, Cyril incorporated elements of Hebrew letters into the Glagolithic character set he developed; for instance, the letter Ш (representing the sound *sh*) was derived from the Hebrew letter *shin*. The Cyrillic character set, created in the 890s, borrowed this letter, as well as the structure of what later became the letter Щ (representing the sound *shch* in Russian), from Glagolithic.

Evidence from the Persian work *Ta'rikh-i Fakhr ad-Din Mubarak Shah*, composed in 1206, indicates that the Khazars at some point switched from the Hebrew alphabet to a Cyrillic-like alphabet. The relevant passage reads:

> The Khazars have a script which is related to the script of the Russians [Rus]. A group of Greeks [Rum] who are near them write in this script and are called Greek Russians [Rum-Rus]. They write from left to right, and the letters are not joined to one another. They number twenty-one. The greater part of these Khazars who use this script are Jews.[10]

KHAZAR ARTS AND CRAFTS

The Arab historian al-Istakhri wrote that Khazaria produced no exportable goods except isinglass,[11] which is extracted from fish. As an example, he claimed that clothing was not produced in Khazaria, since the Khazars imported clothing from Turkmenistan, Persia, Azerbaijan, Armenia, and the Byzantine Empire. Scholars have tended to follow the assumption that the Khazars were consumers, but not producers. Ananiasz Zajaczkowski, for example, wrote:

> In productive work the Khazars had no direct participation, and their entire material culture was imported and of foreign origin. This role of an intermediary and not that of a producer is very typical of the Khazars, as of many other Turkic peoples.[12]

Yet, the historical record is not entirely correct in its assessment of Khazar commerce. Whereas al-Istakhri and other medieval written sources make it appear as if craft production was at a very low stage of development in the Khazar Empire, numerous archaeological surveys have demonstrated that the Khazars produced and exported many of their own goods as well. The discovery of many blacksmith and pottery shops during the course of excavation shows that much domestic manufacturing took place in Khazaria. Archaeology has revealed that, in addition to pottery and iron products (e.g., weapons, farming tools), the Khazars produced large quantities of leather clothing, silver and gold jewelry, ornaments, silverware, mirrors, horse saddles, decorated belt buckles, and other items. This evidence led Thomas Noonan to the conclusion that the Khazars were relatively self-sufficient in crafts production.[13]

The Saltovo-Mayaki culture of Khazaria, which especially prospered along the Don and Donets river valleys, may be described as a civilization in which creativity and skill flourished. The Khazars and other tribes in the kingdom often manufactured belt mounts and amulets decorated with plants, animals, and humans. A variety of interesting amulets were found at cemeteries in Verkhneye Saltovo and Dmitrievsky, including circular "sun amulets" and representations of horses.[14] According to archaeologist Bozena Werbart, the ring shape of the "sun amulets" was spiritually significant, representing Tengri, the shamanistic god of the sky. At Sarkel, archaeologists unearthed bracelets, sabers, bronze figurines, and other types of metalcrafts. The Saltovo peoples also were active in creating implements such as hammers, axes, knives, arrow tips, and bows.

Pottery was produced in large quantities in Crimean towns, Tmutorokan, and along the River Don (at Sarkel, Suvarovo, Podgaevka, Mayaki, and other sites). Pottery-producing kilns were found near Sarkel and Suvarovo.[15] Saltovo potters produced pottery of many kinds, often featuring lines, patterns, and designed rims.[16] Some of the pottery were marked with tamgas (tribe symbols). The Khazars produced most of their pottery from red and green clay, but Daghestani Khazars primarily used gray clay.[17]

The Khazars created an abundance of beautiful jewelry, including bracelets, rings, chains, and earrings produced from gold, silver, bronze, and glass. Some of the motifs on the jewelry have amazed archaeologists. For instance, specimens of Khazar jewelry depicting a woman have been found in the

Caucasus.[18] Some archaeologists call her the "Khazar Madonna," and she may represent a shamanistic deity.

Even more mysterious are clay scorpion sculptures which have been unearthed at some Khazar sites. Their meaning is unclear.

Some members of the Saltovo-Mayaki culture, particularly those near the western border of the Khazar Empire, lived in close proximity to Slavs. For instance, some lived in the land that at present is Bogatoye in the Izmail raion of the Odessa oblast (southern Ukraine). Remains of a yurt were found there. During the ninth and tenth centuries, the Saltovo peoples operated a pottery shop and an iron workshop in Bogatoye.[19] Archaeologists discovered that the Saltovo craftsmen of Bogatoye often sold their goods to their Slavic neighbors.

The material culture of early Kiev—including weapons, belts, belt buckles, and harnesses—bears a resemblance to the characteristic Saltovo style.[20] The extent to which the Khazars and other Turkic tribes influenced the arts and crafts of the Kievan region is a subject worthy of continued investigation.

The Khazars were apparently the first makers of paper in Europe. A "ritual structure" near the Khazar fortress of Sarkel included a skeleton with henna and paper. According to Werbart and Artamonov, this paper was made locally but was based upon the methods of China and Samarkand.[21] By comparison, paper was first made in Italy and Spain in the twelfth century—over two centuries later. On the other hand, Bálint and Noonan favored the view that the paper was actually made in Samarkand and imported to Khazaria.[22] The Muslims in Samarkand had learned the paper-making process from Chinese craftsmen who were held hostage by Ziyad ibn Salih in 751.[23]

KHAZAR AGRICULTURE AND FOOD-GATHERING

Agriculture, fishing, livestock-breeding, and hunting were very important activities in Khazaria.

Crop agriculture prevailed in many parts of the Khazar Empire, particularly in the northern forest zone, while nomadic pastoralism prevailed in some parts of the southern steppe zone. Archaeologists conducting excavations on the Crimean and Taman peninsulas and along the River Don have gathered evidence that the peoples of Khazaria used plows, hoes, sickles, scythes, and other agricultural tools. The hoes and plows were used for working the soil, while the sickles and scythes were used for cutting grains at harvesting time. The Saltovo farmers of the Don valley used two different types of wooden plows, one heavier than the other; the heavier plow was used for harder work and had a colter.[24] Whereas large scythes were used for harvesting grains for human consumption, short scythes were used for harvesting hay for animals.

Among the crops cultivated in the steppe lands in Khazaria were millet, wheat, barley, rye, hemp, and garden vegetables (e.g., peas).[25] The farmers of the Don valley and Daghestan operated millstones for grain-grinding. They stored their excess yield in grain pits. Several grain pits were found at Dmitrievko in the Belgorod oblast and at Tmutorokan. Melon and cucumber seeds and the remains of grapes and cherries were also found during excavations of Khazar settlements.[26] A grapevine-pruning knife was found during digs at Tsimlyan near the Don's right bank.[27] The town of Balanjar was also one of the grape- and cherry-growing centers in the kingdom. Grape-growing was certainly one of the most productive activities for the Khazar farmers. Wines were produced on the Crimean and Taman peninsulas in large quantities.

According to the *Reply of King Joseph to Hasdai ibn Shaprut*, the Khazars of Atil lived in their city during the winter, but in the month of Nisan (March–April) they would go to the fields and gardens for the cultivation of their crops. Each Khazar family had its own hereditary estate. King Joseph also reported that there were many orchards and vineyards in the Khazar Empire. However, he added that rainfall was not frequent around Atil. The fertility of the land of the lower

Volga region depended largely on rivers, streams, and springs. The Khazars tended to engage in agriculture along the edges of rivers, while pursuing nomadic pastoralism elsewhere, according to Bartha.[28] The Khazars created irrigation canals between the Terek and Sulak rivers and other parts of the northeastern Caucasus because of the lack of sufficient rainfall.[29] By contrast, in the Don valley there was already sufficient rainfall, so irrigation was not necessary in order to produce a bountiful harvest.

Crops were transported both by river and by carts, according to al-Istakhri. The Khazars used skiffs for sailing along the Volga.[30]

Al-Istakhri wrote that rice and fish were the staple foods in the diet of the residents of Khazaran-Atil.[31] The Khazars caught many kinds of fish, including sturgeon, carp, sterlet, perch, and beluga. Archaeologists have located a net ballast, fishing hooks, and spears that once belonged to Saltovo fishermen.[32]

Nomadic pastoralism and animal-keeping took place in many parts of the southern steppes of Khazaria. Livestock domestication was practiced by many of the Khazars, Alans, and Bulgars. Horses were bred for riding, pulling carts, and meat. Sheep were raised for wool. The breeding and raising of cattle, goats, birds, donkeys, pigs, and oxen was also commonplace in the kingdom. The Khazars along the Don and the Donets kept their animals in stables. Aside from farm animals, the Khazars possessed many camels.[33] Archaeological studies have concluded that beekeeping also took place in Khazaria.[34]

The peoples of Khazaria hunted wild boars, beavers, elks, foxes, birds, and rabbits. For hunting, the Khazars and other tribes used arrows, bows, spears, axes, and lassos.[35]

THE STRUCTURE OF KHAZAR HOMES

Most domiciles in Khazaran and Atil were felt tents (*yurts*), along with a smaller number of clay houses, owing to the fact that the kagan did not allow people to build houses with brick; thus, only royal and public buildings were built from brick.[36] Stone and wood were also utilized for a variety of buildings constructed in the empire, including homes.

At Balanjar, dwellings were generally small, circular, single-room yurts with an open fireplace in the center. These dwellings were typical of nomads. However, some of the residents of Balanjar lived in dwellings with two or more rooms and stone foundations.

Similarly, some of the Saltovo-Mayaki Turks of the southern Don valley lived in round, yurt-like homes with open fireplaces in the center, resembling the yurts of central Asia and southern Siberia. By contrast, a typical farmer of northern Khazaria would live in a permanent square-shaped house (e.g., a home with walls made from wood logs or from reeds, mud, and wooden stakes) and would create a stove out of stone and place it in a corner of his home, rather than in the center. As time went on, the nomadic herdsmen of southern Khazaria also transformed their living quarters into more permanent structures by sinking their tents into the ground and covering the sides of the tents with turf for warmth during the winter season.[37] At some Khazarian settlements along the Don, such as the Tsimlyanskaya hill fort, both nomadic yurts and permanent structures existed.[38] Permanent Saltovo homes often featured earthworks and ditches.

KHAZAR COSTUME AND HAIRSTYLE

Al-Istakhri wrote: "The dress of the Khazars and surrounding nations is coats and tunics."[39] The Rus'ians wore the "short coat," while the Khazars, Bulgars, and Pechenegs wore the "full coat."[40] These "full coats" were essentially kaftans—similar to the long gowns worn by some Ashkenazic Jews in the nineteenth century.

Turkic men and women wore their hair in braids. According to a seventh-century Chinese account, only the Turkic kagan could have long flowing hair (tied with a ribbon), so the nobility and warriors wore braided hair instead.[41] Proof that this Turkic custom was inherited by the Khazars comes from two archaeological relics: an eighth-century or ninth-century Khazar silver scoop, found at Kotskii Gorodok on the Ob River in western Siberia; and a drinking horn from beneath the Chernaya Mogila ("Black Barrow") mound in Chernigov, dating from the 960s. The artwork on these relics depicts the Khazar epic motif of the defeat of the kagan during a fight with his rival. It has even been suggested that these images represent the ancient Turkic tradition of the ritual burder of the kagan,[42] which was discussed in Chapter 3.

The rim of the Khazar scoop from Kotskii Gorodok features two dismounted horsemen engaged in fighting. One of the fighters has loose hair tied with a ribbon, but the other has braided hair.[43] They are surrounded by their bows and horses.

A silver mounting on the drinking horn from Chernigov shows two running archers. The Khazar archer has long braided hair, whereas the Rus (Viking) enemy chasing after him has loose hair and outstretched hands. Accompanying the image are two birds, two gryphons, and three other animals. The creatures were portrayed according to Nordic artistic traditions.[44] The archer with loose hair was probably considered by the artist to be the prince (*kagan*) of Kievan Rus.

KHAZAR GRAVES

The Chernaya Mogila site reveals its connection to Khazarian traditions in another significant way: its funeral pyre—with swords, spears, and other arms melted by the fire—is similar to eighth-century Khazar pyres from Voznesenka and Malaya Pereshchepina (both situated near the Dnieper River).[45] Yet, the site is also connected to Scandinavian rituals. The findings at the mound testify to the multiethnic blend in Kievan Rus, where elements from the Khazarian culture were combined with elements from non-Turkic cultures.[46]

Burials in the Khazar Empire took many forms, including cenotaphs, catacomb graves with underground chambers, burials in pits with horses, and the burial of men and women together.[47] The various peoples under Khazar rule seem to have had different types of graves.

Many Khazar nobles were buried in accordance with ancient Turkic tradition. The Voznesenka and Malaya Pereshchepina monuments were erected as memorials to the Khazar nobility. At the Voznesenka site, the Khazar custom of gathering weapons and harnesses in a heap was followed.[48] By contrast, typical Jewish graves are simpler and do not contain possessions of value. Jewish law also prohibits any form of cremation. These monuments therefore must predate the Khazar nobles' conversion to Judaism.

In the Greek-controlled town of Sudak on the southern Crimean coast, a Khazar nobleman was buried in a stone tomb according to both Jewish and shamanistic traditions.

Khazarian graves—including those at Verkhneye Saltovo, Bulganakskoye in the Crimea, Martan-Chu in modern-day Chechen-Ingushetia, and Nizhne-Arkhyzsk in modern-day Karachay-Cherkessia—often included glass beads, glass vessels, glass bracelets, mirrors, and other glassware products.[49] Most of these were products of the Saltovo-Mayaki culture. This seems to confirm Samuel Kurinsky's theory that glassmaking technology spread from the Middle East to Khazaria (see Chapter 9). Shamanistic Khazars also put other items in their graves, including buttons, belt buckles, earrings, rings, bronze ornaments, stone beads, pottery, saddles, iron swords, bows, arrows, axes, and lances. Khazar graves sometimes contained foreign-made objects, attesting to cultural interactions with much of the rest of the world through trade.

In the Volga delta region, a young Khazar girl was buried along with two pots placed behind her head. One of the pots was black clay stucco with a grey surface and external horizontal grooves; the other was red with stripes, a decorative garland, and a handle. Bronze earrings were also buried with her. The girl's head faced the east, yet an infant buried next to the girl had been placed toward the southwest.[50] This southwest orientation (i.e., in honor of the holy city of Jerusalem) was probably typical of Jewish burials in Khazaria.

At present, many Jewish gravesites from Khazaria (even those on the Taman and Crimean peninsulas, which have been known for many decades) remain to be fully catalogued. Further studies should be undertaken to help us better understand the way in which the Khazars honored their dead and the degree to which Jewish law affected the preparation of their ninth-century and tenth-century graves.

Table 4-1. *The Turkic Linguistic Family.*

SIBERIAN (NORTHERN)

Southern Altai, northern Altai, Chulym, Dolgan, Karagas (Tofa), Khakas (Abakan Turkic), Shor, Tuvinian, Yakut (Sakha)

KIPCHAK (CENTRAL)

Bashkir, Belarusian-Lithuanian Tatar,* Crimean Tatar, Cuman (Kipchak),* Karachay-Balkar, Karaim, Karakalpak, Kazak, Krymchak,* Kumyk, Kyrgyz, Nogay, Pecheneg,* Tatar (Volga Tatar)

CHAGATAY (EASTERN)

Aynu, Chagataysh,* Ili Turki, Salar, Uyghur, Yellow Uyghur (West Yugur), southern Uzbek, northern Uzbek

OGHURIC (WESTERN)

Chuvash, Danubian Bulgart,* Khazar,* Volga Bulgar*

OGHUZ (SOUTHWESTERN)

Southern Azeri, northern Azeri, Balkan Turkic, Gagauz Turkish, Ottoman Turkish,* Qashqai, Quchani (Khorasani Turkish), Salchuq, Turkish (Anatolian Turkish), Turkmen

---

* extinct language

NOTES

1. Russian archaeological studies continue to be published on a regular basis. The interested reader may wish to consult the following new studies for additional evidence pertaining to the Khazar way of life: Svetlana A. Pletnyova's *Sarkel i "Shiolkovyi" Put'* (Moscow: Izdatel'stvo Voronezhskogo gosudarstvennogo universiteta, 1996) explains the architecture and artifacts of Sarkel; Valerii S. Flerov's *Rannesrednevekovye yurtobraznye zhilishcha vostochnoi Evropy* (Moscow: Institut arkheologii RAN, 1996) discusses yurts in historical eastern Europe; Flerov's *Pogrebal'nye obriady na severe Khazarii: Mayatskii mogil'nik* (Volgograd: Peremina, 1993) examines burial customs along the River Don; Valentina E. Flerova's *Graffiti Khazarii* (Moscow: Editorial URSS, 1997) discusses over three thousand drawings on stones, bricks, bones, pottery, and wood from the Khazar Empire.

2. Gyula Pauler and Sandor Szilágyi, *A magyar honfoglalás kútföi* (Budapest: Nap, 1995), p. 239.

3. Ibid., p. 216.

4. Ibid., p. 239. In *Al-Athir al-Baqiyah* (Ancient History and Geography), Abu Raihan Muhammad ibn Ahmad al-Biruni (973–1048) wrote that the Suwars and Bulgars of Volga Bulgharia spoke a language that was a combination of the Khazar and Turkic languages (see Peter B. Golden, *An Introduction to the History of the Turkic Peoples* (Wiesbaden, Germany: Otto Harrassowitz, 1992), p. 235).

5. The precise origins of the Chuvash people are still a mystery. The Chuvash may be descended from Suwar or Sabir people who mixed with Finnic tribes (including the Mari, Mordvin, and Burtas) and Turkic tribes (including the Bulgars) (see Peter B. Golden, *An Introduction to the History of the Turkic Peoples*, p. 396).

6. Omeljan Pritsak, "The Pre-Ashkenazic Jews of Eastern Europe in Relation to the Khazars, the Rus' and the Lithuanians," in *Ukrainian-Jewish Relations in Historical Perspective*, ed. Howard Aster and Peter J. Potichnyj (Edmonton, Alberta, Canada: Canadian Institute of Ukrainian Studies Press, 1990), p. 4.

7. *An Ethnohistorical Dictionary of the Russian and Soviet Empires*, ed. James S. Olson (Westport, CT: Greenwood Press, 1994), p. 163.

8. Ehud Ya'ari, "Skeletons in the Closet," *The Jerusalem Report* (Sept. 7, 1995): 27.

9. Peter B. Golden, "Khazaria and Judaism," *Archivum Eurasiae Medii Aevi* 3 (1983): 142.

10. Ibid.; Douglas M. Dunlop, *The History of the Jewish Khazars* (New York: Schocken, 1967), p. 120.

11. Douglas M. Dunlop, *The History of the Jewish Khazars*, p. 96.

12. Ananiasz Zajaczkowski, "Khazarian Culture and its Inheritors," *Acta Orientalia Academiae Scientiarum Hungaricae* 12 (1961): 300.

13. Thomas S. Noonan, "The Khazar Economy," to appear in *Archivum Eurasiae Medii Aevi* 9.

14. Bozena Werbart, "Khazars or 'Saltovo-Majaki Culture'? Prejudices about Archaeology and Ethnicity," *Current Swedish Archaeology* 4 (1996): 204, 205.

15. Antal Bartha, *Hungarian Society in the 9th and 10th Centuries*, trans. K. Balazs (Budapest: Akadémiai, 1975), p. 13.

16. Bozena Werbart, "Khazars or 'Saltovo-Majaki Culture'? . . . ," p. 213.

17. Thomas S. Noonan, "The Khazar Economy."

18. Ehud Ya'ari, "Skeletons in the Closet," p. 30.

19. Thomas S. Noonan, "The Khazar Economy." Archaeologists found slag (refuse from iron-smelting) at the iron workshop.

20. Vladimir Ia. Petrukhin, "The Normans and the Khazars in the South of Rus' (The Formation of the 'Russian Land' in the Middle Dnepr Area)," *Russian History/Histoire russe* 19 (1992): 397.

21. Bozena Werbart, "Khazars or 'Saltovo-Majaki Culture'? . . . ," p. 211.

22. Csanád Bálint, "Some Archaeological Addenda to P. Golden's Khazar Studies," *Acta Orientalia Academiae Scientiarum Hungaricae* 35:2–3 (1981): 399; Thomas S. Noonan, "Russia's Eastern Trade, 1150–1350: The Archaeological Evidence," *Archivum Eurasiae Medii Aevi* 3 (1983): 254.

23. Wasilii V. Barthold, *Turkestan Down to the Mongol Invasion*, 3rd ed., trans. H. A. R. Gibb and T. Minorsky (London: Luzac & Co., 1968), pp. 236–237.

24. István Fodor, *In Search of a New Homeland*, trans. Helen Tarnoy (Gyoma, Hungary: Corvina, 1982), p. 219.

25. For instance, archaeologists excavated millet and wheat grains at the Khazar village Chopolav-tepe in Daghestan.

26. Csanád Bálint, "Some Archaeological Addenda to P. Golden's Khazar Studies," p. 407; Thomas S. Noonan, "The Khazar Economy."

27. Antal Bartha, *Hungarian Society in the 9th and 10th Centuries*, p. 52.

28. Ibid., p. 54.

29. Thomas S. Noonan, "The Khazar Economy."

30. Vladimir F. Minorsky, *A History of Sharvan and Darband in the 10th-11th Centuries* (Cambridge, England: W. Heffer and Sons, 1958), p. 148.

31. Douglas M. Dunlop, *The History of the Jewish Khazars*, p. 93.

32. Csanád Bálint, "Some Archaeological Addenda to P. Golden's Khazar Studies," p. 407; Thomas S. Noonan, "The Khazar Economy."

33. Douglas M. Dunlop, *The History of the Jewish Khazars*, p. 224.

34. Bozena Wyszomirska, "Religion som enande politisk-social länk—exemplet: det Kazariska riket," in *Arkeologi och Religion*, ed. Lars Larsson and Bozena Wyszomirska (Lund, Sweden: University of Lund, 1989), p. 138.

35. Thomas S. Noonan, "The Khazar Economy."

36. Douglas M. Dunlop, *The History of the Jewish Khazars*, p. 92.

37. István Fodor, *In Search of a New Homeland*, p. 215.

38. Bozena Werbart, "Khazars or 'Saltovo-Majaki Culture'? . . . ," p. 211.

39. Douglas M. Dunlop, *The History of the Jewish Khazars*, p. 96.

40. Ibid., p. 99.

41. Vladimir Ia. Petrukhin, "The Early History of Old Russian Art: The Rhyton from Chernigov and Khazarian Tradition," *Tor* 27:2 (1995): 482–483.

42. Ibid., p. 483.

43. Ibid., p. 481.

44. Ibid., p. 477.

45. Ibid., p. 476. Malaya Pereshchepina is a village in the Poltava oblast of modern Ukraine, thirteen kilometers from the city of Poltava. Voznesenka is located in the Melitopol raion of the Zaporizhzhye oblast of Ukraine. Interestingly, the seventh-century tomb of Bulgar khan Kubrat was also found near Malaya Pereshchepina.

46. Another steppe practice that was adopted by the residents of Kievan Rus was the manner in which men were buried next to their horses in the grave. This custom was followed in the Kiev, Chernigov, and Gnezdovo regions.

47. Bozena Werbart, "Khazars or 'Saltovo-Majaki Culture'? . . . ," p. 213.

48. Vladimir Ia. Petrukhin, "The Normans and the Khazars in the South of Rus' . . . ," p. 398.

49. Thomas S. Noonan, "The Khazar Economy."

50. Lev N. Gumilev, "New Data on the History of the Khazars," *Acta Archaeologica Academiae Scientiarum Hungaricae* 19 (1967): 78.

5

KHAZARIAN TRADE

Commercial activity flourished in southern Russia and Ukraine during the Khazar era. The major traders in Khazaria were the Radhanites and the Rus. Arabs, Chinese, Oghuz Turks, and other peoples also traded with the Khazars.

KHAZARIA AS A GREAT MEDIEVAL TRADING CENTER

Khazaria was a major center for trade, especially in the eighth and ninth centuries. The classic Persian geographical essay *Hudud al-'Alam* described Khazaria as a land of plenty: "This is a very pleasant and prosperous country with great riches. From it come cows, sheep, and innumerable slaves."[1] Thus, it naturally attracted much commercial activity. The Khazars controlled several trade routes that connected Asia and Europe. One of the most important of these was along the Volga.

Other significant Khazar trade routes were those along the River Don, Azov Sea, Black Sea, and Caspian Sea.

The Khazar kagan required traders to pay customs duties and tithes on merchandise transported by both land and water routes. For example, when the Rus brought valuables that they intended to export past the city of Atil, the Khazars taxed them according to the value of the goods. Lesser chiefs also demanded payment. Ibn al-Faqih of Hamadan, the author of *Kitab al-Buldan* (circa 902), indicated that when the Rus reached Sarkel on the Don, the local Khazar governor of Sarkel took one-tenth of their merchandise.[2]

Members of the Khazar tribe were directly involved in trading. According to Gardizi, the Khazars traded candlewax and honey.[3] Khazar Jews were also merchants of wine, exporting it to the Caucasus and Mesopotamia. Archaeological research has shown that Khazarian-made silver bowls, cups, belts, and belt ornaments were exported to the Urals (the present-day Perm province), western Siberia (the Ob River region), and Kievan Rus (the Riazan province), among other places. Yet, many of the materials the Khazars exported originally came not from the Khazar territory, but rather from other locations. The Khazars often exported central Asian silver dishes and Persian coins to the Urals.[4] Until the close of the ninth century, Arabic silver was transported through Khazaria into eastern Europe. Pottery from Armenia, Iraq, Iran, Khwarizm, and other lands in the Middle East and central Asia was imported into Sarkel.[5] Spherical cones were exported from Oren-kala in Azerbaijan to the Mayaki hill fort in Khazaria.[6]

The Khazars dealt with a diversity of trading partners throughout Eurasia. Khazars traded in Khwarizm's capital, Kath, where they found a large selection of quilts, cotton goods, felt, and cushion covers.[7] Several caravan trade routes linked Khazaria with other nations. Al-Istakhri mentioned that trading caravans led from Gurganj, an Oghuz trading center in Khwarizm, to Khazaria and Khorasan.[8] Caravans also departed from the city of Bulghar on the upper Volga. It was commonplace for Khazars to arrive in Volga Bulgharia to bar-ter with the Bulgars.[9] Additionally, the Khazars in Daghestan traded extensively with the Alans. Some of the approximately one hundred Alanic tombs from Klin Yar in the north Caucasus contain Khazarian artifacts, including bronze bells and mirrors.[10]

The Khazar Empire, as a bridge between East and West, contained overland routes that led to the famous "Silk Road." After trading in Khazaria, traders sometimes traveled to Turpan, Kashgar, and the Pamir Mountains, where they met other Turkic tribes (ancestors of the Uyghurs and Kyrgyz). It was also possible to continue eastward on the route in order to reach China. Silk, incense, perfumes, spices, coral, gold and silver coins, and gems such as pearls and emeralds were among the many items transported on the Silk Road by Jews and other traders. Among the most interesting Asian imports to Khazaria were cowrie shells from the Indian Ocean and a comb made from elephant ivory.[11]

There are indications that the Khazars traded in Sweden, and even settled there in small colonies. The archaeologist Holger Arbman (1904–1968) identified several graves in Birka (a small island in eastern Sweden, south of Uppsala) that contained objects imported from Khazaria. For instance, Birka grave no. 716 (a non-coffin grave) contained a "Khazar girdle," which resembled girdles from the Verkhneye Saltovo grave fields.[12] According to Björn Ambrosiani, former Chief Archaeologist of Sweden and director of the Birka excavations, a Khazar ceramic jar was found in a Birka grave. Asiatic articles of clothing found at Birka—such as kaftans, hussar jackets, fur-trimmed hats, bronze mounts for leather belts, an "eastern" button, and balloon trousers—may also be of Khazarian origin. Arbman believed that at least two of the Birka graves belonged to members of the Khazar tribe.

Several of the objects found at Birka that apparently originated from Khazaria are characterized as belonging to a post-Sassanidic style of art. Birka grave no. 838 (a chamber grave), for example, contained a silver strap end mounting composed under the influence of Persian style. The mounting contains a plant motif and two birds of prey enclosed by rhombuses. Arbman believed that it is possibly Khazarian, since it is somewhat distinctive from similar Hungarian and Persian mountings.[13] Silver pendant pieces portraying ornamental vine-branches and palmettos were found in Birka grave no. 965 (a chamber grave), and Arbman said that these, too, were probably manufactured by the Khazars.[14] Birka grave no. 552 (a chest grave) contained multiple silver mountings, seven of which have a deformed ornamental figure. The figure is a person, sitting on a cushion, who is wearing a tight-fitting garment with downward-hanging sleeves and a belt or girdle around the waist. The head of the figure seems to be an animal's head. Arbman believed that these peculiar mountings were possibly of Persian or Khazarian origin.[15]

As the archaeological expeditions in Sweden, Ukraine, and Russia unearth more artifacts, the extent of Khazar trading activity will become clearer.

THE JEWISH RADHANITES

The Jewish Radhanite merchants were among the traders who crossed Khazaria when venturing to and returning from China, India, and other parts of Asia. The Radhanites also traveled to Spain.

While it is often assumed that the Radhanites originated in Provence (southern France), Moshe Gil argued that they actually came from the east shore of the Tigris in Iraq, known in medieval times as the district of Radhan.[16] Multiple accounts indicated that Radhan was a region in the vicinity of Persia and Baghdad. A fertile land with many date palms and wheat fields, Radhan was inhabited by numerous Christians and Jews. There was also a village called Radhan in the vicinity of Baghdad, according to ibn al-Athir, al-Bakri, and al-Suyuti.[17]

Radhanite trading activity prospered especially from the 750s to the 830s. The Radhanites exported many items from eastern Asia, including cinnamon, musk, and camphor. In addition, they exported swords, silk, furs, and slaves from Europe. Ibn Khordadbeh, an Arab geographer and traveler, stated in his mid-ninth-century work *Kitab al-Masalik wa'l-Mamalik* (Book of Routes and Kingdoms) that the Radhanites spoke the Persian, Slavic, Spanish, French (?), Greek, and Arabic languages.[18] Their remarkable multilingual ability was a useful asset, since they encountered trading partners from many diverse cultures. They often traveled between Persia and Europe by way of the Caucasus Mountains, and went as far east as China. Evidence of Radhanite trading activity in China includes a letter from an early eighth-century Persian Jewish merchant that was found at Khotan in western China (Xinjiang province).[19]

The traveling Radhanites established social and cultural relations between central Europe and Kievan Rus and Khazaria. Beginning in the middle of the ninth century, trading became extensive between Regensburg (a major southern German city) and the Khazar capital, Atil; the cities of Vienna and Kiev served as major trading centers along the route.[20] Over the years, the Khazars came increasingly into contact with western Jews, in large part because of the Regensburg-Kiev-Atil route.

After the Rus conquered Atil in the 960s and the Khazar Empire subsequently fell apart (see Chapter 8), the northwestern shores of the Caspian no longer served as a central station for Jewish traders. Although Atil was cut off from the route by the eleventh century, Kiev remained an integral part of it. In addition to the traditional Regensburg-Kiev route, a new Jewish trading route was developed that led from Prague across Poland into Kiev. The 1031 Hebrew account of Rabbi Yehudah ben Meir ha-Kohen of Mainz, titled *Sefer ha-Dinim*, named Przemysl (a Polish city) and Kiev as major trading sites along the Radhanite route in his time. A French Jewish trader from Doreville named Yitzhak Dorbelo wrote in the twelfth century that he arrived in Poland accompanied by the Radhanites.[21]

According to the 1150 account of Eleazar ben Nathan, Jewish merchants who traversed the Kiev-Regensburg route faithfully observed their religion. The traders never drove their caravans on the Sabbath. All carriages were gathered in a circle and their merchandise was placed in the middle of the circle; then, the traders prayed and celebrated their day of rest.

Further insights into the Radhanites' lifestyle were recorded by the twelfth-century authors Raban and Yitzhak ben Asher ha-Levi of Speyer. They indicated that the Radhanites created trade unions and pooled their money into a common account from which money was withdrawn when purchases were made in Kievan Rus. When merchandise was brought back from the Rus'ian land, it was shared among Radhanite families by a lottery system.[22]

Customs documents from 1191 (issued under the rule of Ottakar I of Bohemia) and 1192 (issued under Count Leopold of Austria) stated that Jewish merchants from Regensburg traded weapons, saddles, spices, wood products, slaves, and silk, wool, and linen fabrics in Kiev.[23]

A thirteenth-century document by Rabbi Zedakiah ben Abraham ha-Rofe 'Anav of Rome discussed two German Jewish merchants from Regensburg, Abraham and Yaakov, who traveled through Hungary along the Danube when going to and from Russia during the mid-eleventh century.[24]

The Jewish Khazars of Kievan Rus probably kept in touch with western Jewish educational centers in the eleventh and twelfth centuries in large part by way of the Radhanite caravans. It is often suggested that the Khazars adopted religious customs from the Radhanites.

RUS TRADERS IN KHAZARIA

The Rus were originally Viking traders from Scandinavia. According to ibn al-Faqih's *Kitab al-Buldan*, the Rus traded in the Byzantine Empire and the city of Tmutorokan. Their ships traveled from the Severskii Donets to the Don and then along the Volga until they reached the Caspian Sea, where they traded with Iranian coastal ports.[25] The Rus also traveled on land by caravans from central Asia through Iran to Iraq.

The Rus merchants transported beaverskin furs, black foxskins, sword blades, and other items past Khazaran-Atil. They had extensive trading relations with the Khazars that included active coinage exchange. Ibn Khordadbeh wrote that the Rus traders often arrived at the Khazar city of Khamlikh, where the Khazar king collected tribute from them.[26]

ARAB TRADERS IN KHAZARIA

Some Arab merchants traversed the country of the Khazars. No doubt many of them journeyed to the predominantly Muslim city of Khazaran.

According to *Derbend-Nameh* (The History of Derbent), Arab traders from Derbent were required (during the 730s) to pay Arab authorities a ten percent tax on their goods if they decided to go north to trade in Khazaria.[27]

CHINESE TRADERS IN KHAZARIA

Trade between Khazaria and China was widespread. Items transported from China to the Khazars included Chinese silk dresses[28] and Chinese mirrors.[29] A large Chinese mirror was found in an eighth-ninth century Saltovo cemetery at Yutanovka in the Volonkonovka raion of the Belgorod oblast. Another Chinese mirror, from the T'ang dynastic era, was found in a Khazar-era cemetery in Armiev in the Shemysheika raion of the Penza oblast. A tenth-century Chinese copper coin was excavated from a kurgan in a cemetery at Tsarev, in the Leninsk raion of the Volgograd oblast.[30]

There is some evidence indicating that Chinese merchants set foot in the Khazar territory. For example, a rose-colored paper in Chinese writing, listing income and expenses, was found at Moshchevaya Balka in the north Caucasus.[31] Some fragments of Chinese manuscripts also were found.

COINAGE

Scholars have debated whether or not coins were produced in Khazaria.[32] The debate partly centers around dirhem coins from the 830s which were found in southern Russia. They contain a mysterious Arabic inscription specifying their minting location as 'Ard-al-Khair (Land of the Khair)—a place that has not been identified. Some scholars have amended this phrase to 'Ard-al-Khazar (Land of the Khazar), but this interpretation is not universally accepted. It is sometimes conjectured that these coins were engraved by Jewish Khazars, since the phrases on the coins do not adhere to the classical grammatical forms of the Arabic language.[33]

Experts have also examined eighty-six peculiar dirhem coins unearthed at the village Devitsa in the Voronezh oblast of southern Russia. These coins, dating from the 750s through the 820s, had numerous chronological errors, since the engraved ruling dates of the caliphs do not correspond to the years when those caliphs actually ruled. There were also spelling mistakes on the engravings of caliph and place names (e.g., Sarkand for Samarkand).[34] Forty-two of the eighty-six coins from Devitsa have the Turkic sign, which was the Turkic letter representing the sound sh. This sign is similar to runes found on Khazar pottery from Sarkel, as well as on other artifacts from the Saltovo-Mayaki region. According to the Russian numismatist Aleksei Andreevich Bykov, these forty-two coins provide the most convincing evidence for Khazar coinage.[35] On the other hand, Thomas Noonan argued that the Turkic marks easily could have been engraved by Pechenegs, rather than by Khazars.[36]

Through the process of trade, coins from many parts of the medieval world—especially the Byzantine Empire and the Islamic Caliphate—reached Khazaria. Byzantine coins minted during the reigns of emperors Justinian II (restoration 705–711); Leo III (717–741); Constantine V (741–775); Michael III (842–867); Basil I (867–886); Leo VI (886–912); Romanus

I Lecapenus (920–944); Constantine VII Porphyrogenitus (913–959); Romanus II (959–963); Nicephorus II Phocas (963–969); and John Tsimisces (969–976) were excavated at sites in the Khazar Empire.[37] The Khazars of Tmutorokan used coins that were produced at the Byzantine mint in Cherson on the Crimea during the ninth century. Arabic silver dirhems were found in Khazar graves in the Atil region, Verkhneye Saltovo, Zhitkov, and the Rostov oblast. Persian drachms minted during the reign of Khusrau (Chosroes) II Parviz (590–628) were found in Khazar-era cemeteries in the present-day Chechen-Ingushetia region.[38]

NOTES

1. Vladimir F. Minorsky, *Hudud al-'Alam (The Regions of the World)* (London: Luzac & Co. 1937), p. 161.

2. Omeljan Pritsak, "An Arabic Text on the Trade Route of the Corporation of Ar-Rus in the Second Half of the Ninth Century," *Folia Orientalia* 12 (1970): 257.

3. Douglas M. Dunlop, *The History of the Jewish Khazars* (New York: Schocken, 1967), p. 107. Al-Istakhri claimed that all the honey and wax in Khazaria was brought there from the lands of the Rus and Bulgars, but this must be an exaggeration.

4. Csánad Bálint, "Some Archaeological Addenda to P. Golden's Khazar Studies," *Acta Orientalia Academiae Scientiarum Hungaricae* 35:2–3 (1981): 410.

5. Thomas S. Noonan, "Russia's Eastern Trade, 1150–1350: The Archaeological Evidence," *Archivum Eurasiae Medii Aevi* 3 (1983): 254.

6. Thomas S. Noonan, "The Khazar Economy," to appear in *Archivum Eurasiae Medii Aevi* 9.

7. Vladimir F. Minorsky, *Hudud al-'Alam (The Regions of the World)*, p. 121. Kath, also known as Kazh and Shahristan, was a center for scholarship and outstanding architecture.

8. Carlile A. Macartney, *The Magyars in the Ninth Century* (Cambridge, England: Cambridge University Press, 1930), p. 222.

9. A. P. Martinez, "Gardizi's Two Chapters on the Turks," *Archivum Eurasiae Medii Aevi* 2 (1982): 157.

10. A. Belinsky and H. Härke, "Cemetery Excavation at Klin Yar, North Caucasus, 1993–94," *Newsletter of the Centre for the Archaeology of Central and Eastern Europe* No. 3 (1995): 4–5.

11. Thomas S. Noonan, "The Khazar Economy."

12. Bozena Wyszomirska, "Religion som enande politisk-social länk—exemplet: det Kazariska riket," in *Arkeologi och Religion*, ed. Lars Larsson and Bozena Wyszomirska (Lund, Sweden: University of Lund, 1989), p. 142. Several golden Khazar or Avar girdle mountings with plant ornamentations from the first half of the ninth century were also discovered in Silesia and central Poland.

13. Holger Arbman, "Einige orientalische Gegenstände in den Birka-Funden," *Acta Archaeologica* 13 (1942): 306.

14. Ibid., p. 308.

15. Ibid.

16. Moshe Gil, "The Radhanite Merchants and the Land of Radhan," *Journal of the Economic and Social History of the Orient* 17:3 (1976): 300.

17. Ibid., p. 314.

18. *Jewish Travellers*, ed. Elkan N. Adler (London: George Routledge & Sons, 1930), p. 2. In the original text, the word interpreted as "French" by Adler and others is *ifraniya*. According to Gil, *ifraniya* may actually be a designation for the language of Frankish-controlled Italy, rather than a reference to

the French spoken in France (see Moshe Gil, "The Radhanite Merchants and the Land of Radhan," p. 310).

19. Moshe Gil, "The Radhanite Merchants and the Land of Radhan," p. 313.

20. Omeljan Pritsak, "The Khazar Kingdom's Conversion to Judaism," *Harvard Ukrainian Studies* 3:2 (Sept. 1978): 265. Kalonimus ben Shabtai, a tenth-century author, made reference to Jewish trading between Regensburg and eastern Europe (see Paul Wexler, "The Reconstruction of Pre-Ashkenazic Jewish Settlements in the Slavic Lands in the Light of Linguistic Sources," *Polin* 1 (1986): 12).

21. Itzhak Schipper, "Dzieje gospodarcze Żydów Korony i Litwy w czasach przedrozbiorowych," in *Żydzi w Polsce Odrodzonej*, ed. A. Hafftka, Itzhak Schipper, and A. Tartakower (Warsaw, 1936), p. 116.

22. Ibid., p. 114.

23. Ibid.

24. Raphael Patai, *The Jews of Hungary* (Detroit: Wayne State University Press, 1996), pp. 31–32.

25. Omeljan Pritsak, "An Arabic Text on the the Trade Route of the Corporation of Ar-Rus...," p. 248.

26. *Readings in Russian History*, ed. Alexander V. Riasanovsky and William E. Watson, vol. 1 (Dubuque, IA: Kendall/Hunt, 1991), p. 64.

27. Thomas S. Noonan, "Why Dirhams First Reached Russia: The Role of Arab-Khazar Relations in the Development of the Earliest Islamic Trade with Eastern Europe," *Archivum Eurasiae Medii Aevi* 4 (1984): 265–266.

28. Csánad Bálint, "Some Archaeological Addenda to P. Golden's Khazar Studies," p. 410.

29. Thomas S. Noonan, "The Khazar Economy."

30. Ibid.

31. Thomas S. Noonan, "Why Dirhams First Reached Russia. . .," p. 257.

32. For discussion, see Thomas S. Noonan, "Did the Khazars Possess a Monetary Economy? An Analysis of the Numismatic Evidence," *Archivum Eurasiae Medii Aevi* 2 (1982): 220–223. Additional information may be found in the newly released book by Omeljan Pritsak, *The Origins of the Old Rus Weights and Monetary Systems* (Cambridge, MA: Harvard Ukranian Research Institute, Harvard University Press, 1998), pp. 22–32.

33. Bozena Wyszomirska, "Religion som enande politisk-social länk—exemplet: det Kazariska riket," in *Arkeologi och Religion*, pp. 140–141.

34. Thomas S. Noonan, "Did the Khazars Possess a Monetary Economy? . . .," p. 241.

35. Ibid., pp. 223, 242.

36. Ibid., p. 245.

37. Ibid., pp. 255–257.

38. Thomas S. Noonan, "The Khazar Economy."

6

THE KHAZARS' CONVERSION TO JUDAISM

*O*ne *of the most remarkable and unique events in Khazar history was the large-scale adoption of Judaism in the kingdom. The Khazars chose to adopt the standard rabbinical form of Judaism rather than the beliefs of the Karaite sect.*

This chapter explores the circumstances that led to the conversion of the Khazars, as well as the documents and artifacts that verify the existence of widespread Khazar Judaism. Primary sources of information concerning the conversion episode include: (1) Khazar documents, such as the Reply of King Joseph, the Schechter Letter, and the Kievan Letter; (2) reports from Arab and Persian historians, travelers, and commentators, such as ibn Fadlan, al-Istakhri, ibn Rustah, and 'Abd al-Jabbar ibn Muhammad al-Hamdani; (3) the Persian treatise Denkart; (4) the Frankish commentary Expositio in

Matthaeum Evangelistam by Druthmar of Aquitaine; (5)
Jewish books, such as Sefer ha-Qabbalah by Abraham ibn
Daud and Sefer ha-Kuzari by Yehudah HaLevi; and (6)
several Karaite texts.

The conversion episode has sparked the imagination
of countless people, both Jewish and non-Jewish,
throughout the ages. In the twentieth century, it became
a popular topic for novels, the most famous being Dictionary of the Khazars *by the Serbian writer Milorad*
Pavic (1988).

PRELUDES TO CONVERSION

Archaeological evidence indicates that Jews have lived in the
Balkans, in the Caucasus (including Georgia), along the north-
ern shores of the Black Sea, and in other areas of eastern
Europe since Roman times.

Jewish settlements and synagogues existed in Roman-gov-
erned Pannonia (modern-day Hungary) as early as the third
century C.E. Archaeological discoveries have included stone
markers upon which Jewish names and menorah (candlehold-
er) images were engraved.[1] The text of the markers was often
written in the Latin language. One of the early third-century
tablets from ancient Pannonia includes a reference to Cos-
mius, the head of the synagogue at Spondilla. In some cases,
the Jewish identity of the inscribed names is known because
the ethnic terms *judeus* and *Judaea* were appended. Engravings of the seven-branched menorah also were found on Pan-
nonia-era rings and amulets as well as a clay oil lamp.[2]

Jews also lived in Moesia and Thrace during Roman times.
A third-century tombstone from near Gigen village, Nikopol
district, in northern Bulgaria (near the Romanian border) refers to a man named Iosses by the title *archisynagogus*, which
means "synagogue chief."[3] Additional evidence for Jewish
settlement in early Bulgaria also exists.

Perhaps the most significant of ancient Jewish settlements in eastern Europe were those on the Crimean and Taman peninsulas. In the premedieval period, thousands of Jews from Egypt, Judea, Syria, and Asia Minor migrated to the Hellenic kingdom of Bosporus, settling in Crimean towns (including Pantikapeum [later called Kerch] and Theodosia [later called Feodosia]), the towns of Gorgippia (later called Anapa) and Phanagoria (later called Tmutorokan; both Gorgippia and Phanagoria were located across the Kerch Strait from Crimea, in the present-day Krasnodar region), and the town of Olbia (located northwest of Crimea, at the Bug River's estuary, along the Black Sea coast). The Jews of the Crimea were actively engaged in jewelrymaking, potterymaking, and trading in grain, fish, and slaves.[4] The Crimean Jews spoke the Greek language, as demonstrated by Greek marble plaques created by Jews in Pantikapeum, Olbia, Gorgippia, and other towns in the Crimean region from the first to the third centuries.[5] The Greek inscriptions contain Jewish names, such as Yehudah and Enokh.

Some of the inscriptions reveal that synagogues in the Greek colonies welcomed slaves to become members of Jewish communities. For example, a marble inscription in Greek found in Phanagoria, dating from 51 C.E., mentions the liberation of a slave that was "to be guaranteed by the guardianship of the Jewish community."[6] Another inscription from the kingdom of Bosporus, dating from 80 C.E., says that the slave Heraclas was freed by a woman named Chreste in a *proseuche* (Jewish house of prayer).[7] It says that Heraclas, the former slave, could travel freely on the condition that he attended the synagogue's services devoutly. The evidence that slaves came under the protection of the synagogue's members and adopted the Jewish faith shows that the ancient Crimean and Tamanian Jews derived their origins from multiple ethnic groups.

Archaeological findings at Chersonesus (later called Cherson) were particularly interesting. There, in the fifth or sixth century, the Byzantines built a Christian basilica above an earlier structure that seems to have been an ancient synagogue. A stone found in the basilica contains carvings of the lulav (palm branch), shofar (ram's horn), and menorah, and Hebrew writing was found on a plaster fragment from a wall in the basilica.[8] These artifacts date from the second, third, or fourth century. The plaster fragment is in Hebrew and Greek, and refers to a certain "Hananiah from Bosporus." It also mentions Jerusalem.

Many stones found at Pantikapeum, dating from the second to fourth centuries, are also inscribed with menorahs. The Jews flourished in Pantikapeum because it was the capital of the Bosporan kingdom and was the most prosperous of all the settlements in the Crimean region.

A variety of interesting legendary tales supplement factual records about the early history of Jews in eastern Europe (see also Chapter 1). For example, an early sixth-century Jew named Yehudah Magig supposedly wrote folktales about ancient Jewish dispersions throughout Asia and Crimea, including stories about Judeans settling in Matarkha (Tmutorokan).[9] There also exists a host of semimythical stories about Jews being forcefully deported to the Caspian region.

As we have seen, large Jewish communities existed in eastern Europe even before the Khazar Empire was established. The Romans and Byzantines later took control of the ancient Greek colonies, and the Crimean Jews began to trade frequently with the Byzantine capital, Constantinople. Several centuries later, most of Crimea was incorporated into the Khazar Empire. It is uncertain to what degree the Jewish communities of ancient Crimea survived through the centuries into the Khazar era. Many scholars believe that descendants of the early Jewish populations of the Crimea and Caucasus influenced the decision of the Khazars to convert to Judaism. According to this point of view, the Crimean Jews came into direct contact with the Khazars. This view is, perhaps, strengthened by evidence that the Crimean Jews had a missionary zeal.

Many of the early Greek residents of the Crimea were drawn to elements of Judaism and created a "cult of the Great God."[10]

KHAZARIA AS A REFUGE
FOR PERSECUTED JEWS

Khazaria became a safe haven for significant numbers of persecuted Jews from Europe and Asia.

The persecution of Jews in Sassanid-ruled Persia motivated Jews to come to eastern Europe.[11] According to the Israeli historian Michael Goldelman, the Zoroastrians in the Persia-Armenia area tried to impose their religion upon all non-Zoroastrians in the time of Persian king Yazdegard (around the 450s); thus, circa 455, Armenian and Persian Jews were persecuted, and moved to what later became the Khazar territory.

The anti-Jewish policies of the Byzantine Empire also forced many Jews to flee to less dangerous lands such as Khazaria. Several emperors initiated policies of forced baptism. In around 630–632, the Byzantine emperor Heraclius (reigned 610–641) decreed that all Jews in his empire must convert to Christianity.[12] Jews also escaped from the Byzantine Empire in around the years 722–723, during the reign of Emperor Leo III (reigned 717–741), since Leo III's policy was to force Jews to adopt Christianity.[13]

Persecutions in Byzantium remained a threat for Jews in the following century. In the 860s, Emperor Basil I (reigned 867–886) tried to convert Byzantine Jews by decree.[14] However, Basil I's conversion schemes were not successful, and persecution intensified. By the end of the ninth century, Byzantine laws decreed that Jews could not hold public office, intermarry with Christians, or own Christian slaves.[15] Jews were told to read the biblical scriptures in Greek rather than in Hebrew. Furthermore, if any Jew tried to convert a Christian, he would be killed and his property would be confiscated. Jews were not allowed to testify on behalf of Christians during legal proceedings, and could not construct new synagogues. These laws clearly were meant to codify the "inferior" status of Byzantine Jews in comparison to Orthodox Christians.

Byzantine emperor Romanus Romanus I Lecapenus (reigned 920–944) began to persecute Jews in around 932 and, like his predecessors, attempted to convert them to Christianity. Romanus I's actions led to the murder of hundreds of Jews and the destruction of numerous synagogues.[16] Jews continued to migrate to Khazaria from the Muslim and Byzantine lands circa 943, because Jews were still being forcefully converted to Christianity by Romanus I, according to al-Masudi.[17] With the continuing flight of Jews from Byzantium, Joseph, the king of the Khazars, welcomed them to his country. Obviously, the Khazar Jews despised Romanus for his persecutions, calling him "the evil one."[18] Circa 943, King Joseph reacted to Romanus' persecutions by ordering vengeful attacks upon the Taman peninsula, as well as the killing of Christians.

The tenth-century historical account known as the *Schechter Letter* said that Jews came to Khazaria to escape "the yoke of the idol-worshippers."[19] The *Letter* stated that the Jews who came through Armenia to Khazaria intermarried with the Khazars and propagated the ritual of circumcision, but it also mentioned that Sabbath observance was not universally adopted among all Khazars prior to their official conversion. The Jewish immigrants learned the customs of the Khazars and fought side-by-side with them in wars against enemy nations.

Jews from Mesopotamia (modern-day Iraq) also moved to Khazaria. Around 929, Saadiah Gaon wrote that a Jew named Yitzhak ben Abraham migrated from Mesopotamia to Khazaria.[20] The *Schechter Letter* confirmed that Jews came to Khazaria from Baghdad, as well as from the Byzantine Empire and Khorasan (eastern Persia).[21]

The Jews of Khwarizm (modern-day Uzbekistan) also fled to Khazaria, according to a controversial theory introduced by Sergei P. Tolstov and accepted by Hansgerd Göckenjan and a few other historians.[22] According to their theory, this migration of Jews came about because of the "Mazdak Rebellion," which was essentially a social revolution. They claimed that a "Judaizing" sect, led by Hurzad (a member of the Khwarizmian royal house) and the commander Hamagard, instigated revolts (circa 712–715) against Khwarizm's shah (Hurzad's brother) and the upper elite, who professed Zoroastrianism. The shah, in danger because of the revolts, requested assistance from the Arabs, who were beginning to conquer Khwarizm under their leader Kutaiba ibn Muslim. Kutaiba, the Umayyad viceroy (i.e., military governor) of Khorasan since 704 or 705, pursued an aggressive expansionist policy, attacking Tokharistan (in 705) and taking Bukhara and Samarkand (by 712) in a series of battles.[23] Kutaiba burned the idols at Samarkand and forced the residents of these conquered territories to adopt Islam. He had mosques built in Bukhara, Samarkand, and other towns.[24] After Kutaiba conquered Khwarizm, he instituted anti-Jewish policies, executed the "Judaizing" rebels, and expelled Jewish scholars, traders and artists from the region.[25] According to Giles Whittell, the expelled Jewish intellectuals and traders from Khwarizm went to southern Russia and established new trade routes along the Volga and between eastern Europe and central Asia. Simon Szyszman suggested that some of them perhaps later left Khazaria for Hungary, becoming known as the "Khalisioi" (on the Khalisioi, see Chapter 9). Tolstov's theory has undergone considerable criticism from historians, and generally is not accepted.

The multiple waves of Jewish settlers coming to the Khazarian lands appear to have played a major role in encouraging the Khazars to convert to Judaism. This is indicated by the following brief statement by the Arab historian Dimashqi (written circa 1327):

> Ibn-al-Athir [or al-Masudi?] tells how in the days of Harun the Emperor [of Byzantium] forced the Jews to emigrate. They came to the Khazar country, where they found an intelligent but untutored race and offered them their religion. The inhabitants found it better than their own and accepted it.[26]

Harun al-Rashid was the Abbasid caliph from 786 to 809. Thus, according to Dimashqi, the conversion took place at the end of the eighth century or the beginning of the ninth century.

Other historians suggest that the Khazars adopted Judaism as a conscious political decision designed to help preserve the political independence of Khazaria from the Christian and Muslim empires surrounding them.[27] Thus, Khazaria held the balance of power between the Christian Byzantine Empire and the Muslim Caliphate.

Omeljan Pritsak, on the other hand, attributed the conversion of the Khazars solely to the influence of the traveling Radhanite and Iranian Varaz merchants, who were Jewish.[28] This inference cannot be drawn from any of the surviving historical sources, but should not be entirely dismissed.

KHAZAR SHAMANISM

Before their conversion to Judaism, the Khazars were believers in shamanism and worshipped spirits and the sky. Their particular belief system is known as Tengri shamanism. The shamanistic Khazars turned to the East when they prayed.[29] The Khazarian medicine man (shaman), called *qam* or *tabib*, was highly respected. The shamans were healers and were said to be able to predict the future.[30]

The early Huns and Bulgars had a similar shamanistic tradition. The leading god of the Turkic shamanists was Tengri, the sky god, an immortal being who created the world. Umay was the mother-goddess and Yer-sub was the primary earth-water god.[31] Tengri was said to have ruled the "upper world," while the fertility goddess Umay and the earth-water deities ruled the "middle world," and Erlik-khan ruled the "lower world" ("hell").[32] The Huns of Varach'an worshipped a thunder god named Kvara. The Bulgar shamanists worshipped the sun, moon, and stars.[33]

Animals were also worshipped, and each tribe had its own totem. The horse was the primary animal sacrificed to Tengri. The old Turkic calendar, derived from the lunar calendar of the Chinese, was based on an animal cycle. The Turks generally used twelve years, and accordingly the calendar is known as the "Calendar of the Twelve Animals." The Turks along the Volga first adopted the calendar at the beginning of the seventh century. The Bulgars used a calendar containing the years of the mouse, cow, wolf or tiger, hare, snake, horse, sheep, hen, dog, and pig.[34] Many other variants of the calendar also existed. For example, some Turkic tribes borrowed the dragon from the Chinese for their calendar, while other Turks replaced it with the crocodile or the fish.[35]

As the Turks believed that divinity was present throughout nature, their belief system may also be described as a form of pantheism. Trees were considered sacred among all Turkic peoples. According to Turkic mythology, a large "cosmic tree" held up the sky and served as the gateway to a higher level of the universe.[36] Other sacred parts of the earth were mountains, rivers, and springs.

Some tribes manufactured idols from silver and bronze. Another significant element of the shamanist belief system was ancestor worship.

The opening of a shamanist Turk's tent was directed toward the East. In the *Chou-shu*, a Chinese dynastic annal completed around 629, it is said that the kagan's tent faced "towards the East because one honors the direction from which the sun rises."[37]

Every year, the Turks celebrated the beginning of spring by holding events on March 22, which they called *Ulugh-kun* (The Great Day).[38] The Great day ushered in the month of *Oshlaqay*. There were two other very important ceremonies, both of which were overseen by the kagan: Upon the arrival of summer, the Turks made offerings to Tengri; and once a year each Turk would go on a pilgrimage to his ancestral home.[39]

SAINT CYRIL'S KHAZARIAN MISSION

The increasing numbers of Jews in eastern Europe began to make their presence known to the rulers and people of

Khazaria. They created a preliminary interest among Khazars in basic elements of Judaism. The Khazars also had the opportunity to learn monotheism from Christian preachers who established themselves in Khazaria by the eighth century (see Chapter 2).

In the mid-ninth century, the Khazar people were reconsidering their religious beliefs. The *Life of Constantine* said that in around the year 860, Khazar envoys came to Constantinople to request the assistance of Christian preachers. Significantly, the Khazar envoys said:

> We have known God the Lord of everything [Tangri, the Altaic God of Heaven] from time immemorial . . . and now the Jews are urging us to accept their religion and customs, and the Arabs, on their part, draw us to their faith, promising us peace and many gifts.[40]

This statement reveals that Jews were actively seeking converts in Khazaria in 860.

In the year 860, Saints Cyril and Methodius were sent as missionaries to the Khazars by the Byzantine emperor Michael III (reigned 842–867) since the Khazars had requested that a Christian scholar come to Khazaria to debate with the Jews and Muslims. The main events of Cyril's mission were recorded in the *Life of Constantine*, which was written around the 870s, probably by Saint Methodius.

According to the *Life of Constantine*, when Cyril initially arrived in the Khazar Empire, he met a Khazar man who criticized the Byzantine manner of appointing rulers and the Christian dependence on books for religious debates. As a representative of an oral culture, the man advocated the retention of knowledge internally, saying "We . . . bring forth all wisdom from our breasts, as if we had swallowed it, not taking pride in writing, as you do."[41] However, the man was unable to answer a very specific biblical question that Cyril threw at him—how many generations lived before Moses, and for how many years did each generation last—owing to his lack of knowledge of Torah. Constantine Zuckerman suggested that this man was "one of the Khazar Jews who held to a rudimentary bookless form of Judaism before the 'return' to the proper Jewish observance."[42] On the other hand, Francis Butler proposed that the man may have been a fictional character introduced into the text to illustrate Cyril's role as a bringer of literacy and learning to pagans.[43]

Saint Cyril studied Hebrew in Cherson during the winter of 860–861. After learning Hebrew, Cyril traveled to the residence of Kagan Zacharias. Methodius accompanied him. Cyril was now prepared to engage in debate with the Jewish rabbis.

The famous religious disputation among representatives of competing faiths began in the summer of 861 at the kagan's court.[44] The kagan (at that time the highest authority in Khazaria) and the bek (second-in-command) received the Byzantine delegation, which consisted of an envoy and judges. It appears that a number of Khazars were in the audience watching the debates. During the debates, the kagan remarked to Cyril that his people believed in one God, rather than in the Christian Trinity.[45] The *Schechter Letter* recorded how the Byzantine and Arab leaders tried to discourage the Khazars from converting to Judaism. Cyril urged the Khazars to choose Christianity in order to avoid a terrible fate.

During the disputation, the Khazar leaders called themselves a "bookless crowd," but they were aware of the existence of holy books that they could consult. The reference to holy books paralleled the *Schechter Letter*'s mention of the Torah books stored in the cave of Tizul Valley. The kagan told Cyril that his words about the scriptures were proper and as sweet as honey, yet it was God's will that the Khazars be illiterate.[46] The mention of the holy books reveals that the Khazars previously had been consulting with Jews about religious matters, prior to the debate, since the Khazars themselves could not read the books.

The following day, Cyril returned to debate further with the other missionaries, and the Khazars are presented in the *Life of Constantine* as being aware of several facts described in the Torah.[47] The *Life* claimed that the Khazars were impressed by the saint's debating skills.

The rabbis in the kagan's court were unconvinced by the saint's religious arguments. Their dedication to Judaism remained as strong as ever, setting the stage for proselytism on a large-scale basis in the empire. Saint Cyril was successful in converting only two hundred Khazars to Christianity;[48] however, he did succeed in persuading a Khazar governor to stop warring against a Crimean city near Cherson, for he cared for the safety of the Christians who resided there.[49]

The *Life of Constantine* is not the only Christian account of debates between the Byzantine saints and the Khazars. A separate account said that, during his stay in Moravia, Saint Methodius held a religious debate before an audience of pagans and Jews with a Khazar named "Zambrii."[50] According to the prologue to the *Life of Methodius*, Zambrii was a "heretic" who attacked Christianity. The story boasted about how Methodius "out-argued" the Jews and "heretics" since he was "armed with the words of the prophets and apostles." Allegedly, all of Methodius' opponents were defeated, and the assembled audience fled from a raging fire.

KING BULAN'S CONVERSION

Bulan,[51] the first Jewish ruler of the Khazars, decided upon Judaism after listening to the arguments of the Arab mullah, Christian priest, and Jewish rabbi who attended the religious debate. Several sources referred to Bulan as king (i.e., *bek*, *malik*, *melekh*) rather than emperor (i.e., *Great Kagan*).[52] The *Schechter Letter* said that the first Jewish bek became the chief officer after winning victories in battles against Khazaria's enemies. Bulan and his successors to the throne all wielded considerable power as heads of the military forces of the kaganate—a role that became associated with beks and no longer applied to the kaganship. Thus, despite the suggestions of a few scholars, Bulan cannot be identified as the kagan.

The mullah, priest, and rabbi each tried to explain the benefits of his own system of belief to King Bulan. However, Bulan went a step farther by asking the Christian and Muslim representatives which of the other two religions they believed to be superior. The Christian priest preferred Judaism over Islam, and likewise the Muslim mullah preferred Judaism over Christianity. Bulan therefore saw that Judaism was the root of the other two major monotheistic religions and adopted it for himself and his people.

The date of King Bulan's conversion to Judaism traditionally has been considered to be the year 740, with the ruling aristocratic classes and many of the common people converting soon afterward, based upon Yehudah ha-Levi's statement in *Sefer ha-Kuzari* that the Khazar king converted about four hundred years before his time. Under this scenario, scholars proposed that Bulan could have been the kagan who was forced to convert to Islam in 737, although it was a short-term commitment (see also Chapter 7). Yet, as previously mentioned, Bulan was actually a bek, not a kagan. Other scholars based the date on al-Masudi's statement, written circa 943 and corroborated by Dimashqi several centuries later, that the Khazar king became a Jew between 786 and 809. These dates are not necessarily correct, since there is no evidence for Judaism among the Khazar tribe in the eighth century.

In a reassessment of the date of the conversion, which took into account the aforementioned evidence for Cyril's disputation in 861 being positively identified as the famous religious debate mentioned in *King Joseph's Reply to Hasdai ibn Shaprut*, Constantine Zuckerman explained that ha-Levi's date of circa 740 and al-Masudi's date of circa 786–809 both may be inaccurate.[53] The discrepancy in dates has often been interpreted to mean that standard rabbinical Judaism was adopted many decades after Bulan's reign and that Bulan professed a syncretic belief (such as Judaism mixed with shamanism) or a sectarian variant of Judaism (such as Karaism). Zuckerman has convincingly asserted that King Bulan ruled around 861 rather than 740, and that the conversion process in the Khazar royalty took only one stage, rather than two or three stages.[54] However, this does not rule out the strong indication that Judaism took several decades to fully spread among the populace.

The Khazars adopted the rabbinical form of Judaism rather than the Karaite variation.[55] The short version of *King Joseph's Reply* described the events that occurred after Bulan chose Judaism:

> From that time on the Almighty God helped him and strengthened him. He and his slaves circumcised themselves and he sent for and brought wise men of Israel who interpreted the Torah for him and arranged the precepts in order.

King Joseph did not reveal the identity of these "wise men of Israel."

According to *Kitab Tathbit Dala'il Nubuwwat Sayyadina Muhammad* (The Book of the Establishment of Proofs about our Master Muhammad's Status as a Prophet), written by 'Abd al-Jabbar ibn Muhammad al-Hamdani circa 1009 or 1010, one Jewish missionary in particular was primarily responsible for persuading the king and the tribes in the Khazar Empire to convert to Judaism. 'Abd al-Jabbar emphasized that the conversion took place "without [any recourse to] violence and the sword" and listed some of the Jewish rituals and laws that the Khazars adopted (among them circumcision, adherence to kosher eating practices, and abstinence from work on the Sabbath).[56] Medieval Jewish scholars, including Rabbi Moses ben Nahman (Nahmanides) in *Torat Adonai Temimah* in the thirteenth century and Rabbi Yehudah Aryeh ben Joseph Moscato in *Kol Yehudah*[57] in the sixteenth century, suggested that Yitzhak ha-Sangari (Isaac Sangari)[58] was the name of the Jewish rabbi who was involved in the religious disputation at Bulan's court and who converted the king and taught him the principles of Judaism.

The story of Bulan's conversion to Judaism was embellished by the Sephardic Jewish philosopher and poet Yehudah ben Samuel ha-Levi (c. 1080–1141), a native of Toledo, Spain, in his famous masterwork *Kitab al-Hujjah wa'l-Dahl fi Nasr al-Din al-Dhalil* (The Book of Argument & Proof in Defense of the Despised Faith), which was composed in 1120–1140 and translated from Arabic to Hebrew in the mid-twelfth century. It is popularly known by the title The Book of the Khazars (*Sefer ha-Kuzari* in Hebrew, *Kitab al-Khozari* in Arabic). The book consists of five chapters and presents the merits of Judaism.

Sefer ha-Kuzari stated that an angel spoke to Bulan one night while he was dreaming, explaining that while his "intentions are desirable to the Creator" his continued observance of Khazarian shamanistic rites and sacrifices was objectionable. Ha-Levi explained that the angel's repeated warnings that Bulan's religious activities were not correct

> prompted the king to explore other belief systems and religions. Ultimately, the king and all the subjects of his kingdom converted to Judaism. The arguments of the rabbi [Sangari] were the catalyst for this event, for, through them, the king found spiritual peace and intellectual harmony.[59]

A parallel to the *Kuzari*'s reference to an angel appearing before Bulan was contained in Rabbi Petakhiah's travelogue *Sibbuv ha-Olam*:

> To the seven kings of Meshech an angel appeared in a dream, bidding them to give up their laws and statutes, and to embrace the law of Moses, son of Amram. If not, he threatened to lay waste their country. However, they delayed until the angel commenced to lay waste their country, when the kings of the Meshech and all the inhabitants of their countries became proselytes, and they sent to the head of the academy a request that he would dispatch to them some disciples of the wise. Every disciple of the wise that is poor goes there to teach them the law and the Babylonian Talmud. From the land of Egypt the disciples go there to study.[60]

Ha-Levi proceeded to explain Bulan's increasing devotion to Judaism after an expedition to the Warsan Mountains.[61] He continued:

The king and his chief officer went to these mountains, which were in the desert by the sea. The books say how, in the middle of the night, they reached a cave where Jews used to observe the Sabbath every week, and how they revealed themselves to the Jews, and converted to Judaism—which included being circumcised in that very cave. They returned to their country with their hearts committed to Judaism, but they initially hid their faith. Using wise discretion, they slowly began to divulge their secret, little by little, to a select group of their inner circle. Their numbers grew, until finally they revealed their secret to the public and prevailed upon the rest of the masses to convert to Judaism. They brought in Jewish sages and books from different countries and learned the Torah from them.

The Khazar books detail all their successes in vanquishing their enemies, conquering various lands, discovering hidden treasures, and amassing armies numbering in the hundreds of thousands. They also detail how the Khazars loved the Torah and yearned for the Temple—to the point where they erected a facsimile of the Tabernacle that Moses built. They gave honor to their local Jews, and took pride in them.[62]

The adoption of Judaism by the Khazars was one of the most interesting events in medieval European history. It was once thought that Yehudah ha-Levi created the conversion episode as an imaginary tale, but it has become clear that the story of the conversion of the Khazars in the *Kuzari* reflected actual events. In 864, only a few years after Saint Cyril's Khazarian mission, the Khazars were described for the first time (in *Expositio in Matthaeum Evangelistam*) as observers of Judaism (see Chapter 1). Bulan's conversion was the beginning of an unparalleled period of greatness and splendor for the Jews of eastern Europe.

THE SCHECHTER LETTER

Around the summer of 948, Yitzhak bar Nathan met a knowledgeable Khazar Jew in Constantinople who was scholarly and a "favorite" of the kagan. At Yitzhak's request, this Jew, whose name is unknown, wrote an essay about Khazar history.[63] The original letter was written around 949, according to Zuckerman.[64] Zuckerman also wrote:

> There is actually every reason to believe that the Letter was produced no more than five years after the events described and was delivered to the messengers of Hasdai ibn Shaprut in Constantinople, where every detail in it could be easily verified.[65]

Today, the text is known as the *Schechter Letter* or *Cambridge Document.* In the late 1890s, Solomon Schechter discovered this and other important Genizah documents in an old synagogue in Cairo, Egypt.[66] The Cairo Genizah materials had been stored in a dark room where they were left untouched for hundreds of years. The documents were brought to Cambridge, England in 1896, and the Taylor-Schechter Collection at Cambridge University now preserves these valuable medieval works.

The *Schechter Letter* described how the Khazars and the Jews who had migrated there from Armenia intermarried and "became one people."[67] A particular Jewish warrior was a noble fighter for Khazaria's cause and won a great victory over enemies, so the Khazars appointed him as the army's chief officer (i.e., *bek*). He thus is to be regarded as the founder of the dynasty of Jewish kings, according to the author.

Next, the *Letter* presented another version of the events leading to the religious disputation and the formal adoption of Judaism by the royal house and the common people. God influenced the bek to restore his faith in Judaism. His wife Serakh and her father also encouraged him to return to Judaism. The Byzantine and Arab rulers were incensed that the king chose to adopt all elements of Judaism.[68] The king sent for Jewish, Christian, and Muslim sages to come to his court to describe their respective religions. Each debated the merits of the three faiths, but when the Jewish sage described the

Torah and the settlement of ancient Israel, the Greek and Arab sages confirmed that what he said was right. However, some issues still were not resolved, so the Khazar officials asked for the books of the Torah that were kept in a cave in the plain of Tizul. After the Jewish sages explained these books, the Khazars and the Israelites fully embraced Judaism. It is at this point that the immigration of Jews to Khazaria from Greece, Baghdad, and Khorasan is mentioned. A Jewish sage was appointed as judge (*kagan*). Meanwhile, the bek's name became Sabriel.[69]

The document continued with a description of the military affairs of tenth-century Khazaria, especially relating to Alan-Khazar and Rus-Khazar interactions (see Chapters 7 and 8).

The events recorded in the *Letter* have been proved historically accurate. The document itself is known to be authentic since it was mentioned by Rabbi Yehudah ben Barzillai of Barcelona in *Sefer ha-'Ittim* (circa 1100), a treatise on the laws of the Sabbath and the Jewish festivals.[70]

The *Schechter Letter* was addressed to Hasdai bar Yitzhak ibn Shaprut, a prominent Sephardic Jewish diplomat. Many scholars suggest that Hasdai read the *Letter* prior to writing to King Joseph and that, therefore, the document further inspired him to try to correspond directly with the Khazar ruler.

THE KHAZAR CORRESPONDENCE

Hasdai ibn Shaprut's famous "Khazar Correspondence" with tenth-century Khazar king Joseph came about because of Hasdai's interest in finding further confirmation that an independent Jewish kingdom still existed.[71]

Hasdai resided in Cordoba, Spain. He was a physician as well as the vizier to the Umayyad caliphs Abd-al-Rahman III (reigned 911–961) and Hakem (reigned 961–976). Hasdai wrote to Joseph that he initially learned about the existence of the Jewish kingdom called Khazaria from traveling merchants of Khorasan. At first he was skeptical, but then Byzantine ambassadors to the Caliph confirmed that Khazaria really existed. The ambassadors told Hasdai that the kingdom *Al-Kuzari* was ruled by King Joseph and that traders came from Khazaria to Byzantium with fish, skins, and many other goods.[72]

With increased hope, Hasdai tried to make arrangements for the transport of a letter to the Khazar king. Yitzhak, son of Nathan, met Hasdai and offered to take his letter to the Khazars, but because the route to Khazaria was dangerous— on account of intertribal warfare and turbulence in the Black Sea that prevented safe navigation—Yitzhak did not make it past Constantinople. However, as mentioned previously, he did successfully obtain the *Schechter Letter* account. Hasdai contained to look for ways to transport his letter. Around the year 953, two central European Jews, Saul and Joseph (ambassadors of the "King of the Givlim"), agreed to send the letter from the *Saqlab Givlim* (Slavic Croatians) to Jews in Hungary, where it would be transmitted to the Rus'ians and then Bulgars before finally reaching Khazaria. Saul and Joseph told Hasdai that around the year 947 they had met a blind Khazar Jewish scholar named Mar 'Amram. 'Amram was a wise Israelite who lived in the Khazar king's house and ate at the king's table.[73]

Circa 954,[74] Menahem ben Jacob ibn Saruq,[75] Hasdai's literary secretary, composed the final draft of the query letter according to Hasdai's instructions. In the letter, Hasdai asked the Khazar king many questions, such as what their land, army, government, and observance of Judaism were like, and which tribes lived under his jurisdiction. The letter was transmitted eastward to the Khazar king by Rabbi Jacob ben Eliezer, a German Jew.[76]

King Joseph's Reply reached Hasdai around the year 955. It stated that Joseph's ancestor, King Bulan, was circumcised, officially converted to Judaism, and drove out sorcerers and idolaters from the kingdom and trusted in God alone. The *Reply* indicated that after a Khazar-led attack on the town of Ardabil,[77] located south of the Caucasus Mountains, a tabernacle was established along the biblical model, with an ark, candlestick, table, sacred vessels, and altar. Bulan set up the tabernacle because the angel in his dream told him to do so. He was promised God's assistance if he observed the commandments and had a synagogue constructed.

Also noteworthy in the *Reply* is Joseph's statement that King Obadiah, Bulan's successor, invited Jewish sages from many lands to come to Khazaria in order to explain the meaning of the Torah, Talmud, Mishnah, and prayers:

> After those days, there arose from the sons of his [Bulan's] sons a king named Obadiah. He was an upright and just man. He reorganized the kingdom and established the [Jewish] religion properly and correctly. He built synagogues and schools, brought in many Israelite sages, and honored them with silver and gold, and they explained to him the twenty-four books [the Torah], Mishnah, Talmud, and the order of prayers [established by] the Khazzans. He was a man who feared God and loved the law and the commandments.

King Obadiah's religious renaissance occurred around the 860s or 870s.[78] According to many scholars, Obadiah's religious zeal led the Khazar populace to became familiar with the holy Jewish works, and, thus, many more Khazar shamanists converted to Judaism than otherwise would have been the case. The fact that the Khazars studied the Mishnah and Talmud— rabbinical documents rejected by the Karaite sect—indicates their affinity to rabbinical Judaism.

Obadiah was succeeded to the throne by his son Hezekiah and then by Hezekiah's son Menasheh. Then, because Menasheh left no living heirs, Obadiah's brother, Hanukkah, became king. All the Khazar kings who followed also had Hebrew names. According to Yehudah ben Barzillai, the names of the Jewish kings, in order of succession, were as follows: Bulan, Hezekiah, Menasheh I, Yitzhak (Isaac), Menasheh II, Benjamin, Aaron, and Joseph.[79] *King Joseph's Reply* gave a more complete enumeration: Bulan, followed by one or several other kings, then Obadiah, Hezekiah, Menasheh I, Hanukkah, Yitzhak, Zebulun, Menasheh II, Nisi, Aaron I, Menahem, Benjamin, Aaron II, and Joseph. As may be readily seen, Obadiah was not included in Yehudah ben Barzillai's enumeration, but that does not necessarily mean that he did not exist, as Zuckerman claimed. In any case, both lists confirm that the two Khazar kings who preceded Joseph were Benjamin and Aaron.

Both copies of *King Joseph's Reply* are now widely known to be based upon an authentic document, not forgeries.[80] Rabbis Yehudah ben Barzillai and Abraham ibn Daud both referred to the *Reply* in their twelfth-century books.

THE KIEVAN LETTER

The *Kievan Letter* was discovered in 1962 when Norman Golb examined a collection of previously unidentified documents from the Cairo Genizah. The letter does not contain a date, which makes precise dating difficult, but it is generally assumed to be from the tenth century. According to Omeljan Pritsak, it dates back to around the year 930, during the time when Kiev was under Khazarian rule.[81] On the other hand, Leonid Chekin argued that it may have been composed between 870 and 930, earlier than Pritsak and Golb suggested.[82] The *Kievan Letter* was written on parchment. It is the only new Khazar document to have surfaced in recent years, and it is the oldest one ever found.

The subject of the letter is the unfortunate circumstance facing Jacob ben Hanukkah. The Khazar Jews of Kiev wrote this letter of recommendation on Jacob's behalf. Jacob's brother had borrowed a sum of money (as a loan), but afterward he was attacked and killed, and his money was stolen. When the moneylenders learned about this incident, they imprisoned Jacob, who was his brother's guarantor. Jacob remained in captivity for one year, until the Khazar Jews of Kiev freed him and paid sixty gold coins to the moneylenders. The

purpose of the letter was to help raise the forty coins that
remained to be paid from among other Jewish communities.
The authors urged their fellow Jews to contribute money to
Jacob as an act of kindness:

> So now, O our masters, raise up your eyes to heaven and do
> as is your goodly custom, for you know how great is the vir-
> tue of charity. For charity saves men from death.[83]

The document was written in square Hebrew letters and
in the Hebrew language, but a Turkic runiform word was
added with a brush pen in the lower-left-hand corner of the
page. The six-letter runic word reads *[h]oqurüm*, which in the
Khazarian language means "I have read [it]."[84] The fact that
this word appears on a Hebrew document shows that the
Khazar officials who processed the letter understood both
Hebrew and the Khazarian language.

Particularly fascinating are the signatures of the eleven
Khazar Jews who wrote this letter for Jacob, since their names
are of mixed Hebrew and Khazarian origins. The following are
the names of members of Kiev's Jewish community in the early
tenth century:

Abraham ha-Parnas ("the Benefactor")	Kufin bar Joseph
Yitzhak ha-Parnas ("the Benefactor")	Reuben bar Simson
Yehudah bar Yitzhak Levi	. . . el bar Manäs
Gostata bar Kiabar Kohen	Hanukkah bar Moses
Manär bar Samuel Kohen	Yehudah called Sawarta
Sinai bar Samuel	

The large majority of these Khazars were probably descended
from proselytes, although two of the signatories were Kohens
and one was a Levite. Although the titles *Kohen* ("Aaronide
priest") and *Levi* (designating a member of the Israelite tribe
of Levi) are usually inherited, Golb suggested that Tengri
shamanist priests (*qams*) in Khazaria adopted these titles af-

ter converting to Judaism.[85] Israel Kasovich even claimed that
the Khazar kings after Bulan, all of whom claimed descent
from Japheth rather than Shem, "styled themselves
Cohanim."[86] A number of scholars disagree with Golb's hypothesis, arguing that non-Israelites are not allowed to adopt
the titles Kohen and Levi because of the rabbinical law of
descent through the male line. A possible explanation, then,
is that the Kohanim and Levites in Khazaria descended in part
from Middle Eastern Jewish men who had intermarried with
Turkic women.

The question of the origins and meanings of the names in
the *Kievan Letter* has aroused much discussion among scholars. Gostata's father's name, Kiabar, seems to indicate that he
was a Kabar.[87] Kiabar may very well have been connected with
the Kopyrev konets district of Kiev, which was populated by
Jews, according to Kievan chroniclers (see Chapter 2). Pritsak
claimed that Gostata was named after the Turkic Bulgar clan
member Gostan.[88] Other Oghuric Turkic names among the
signatories include Manär ("great man") and Manäs ("great
great").[89] Pritsak associated the name Kufin with the Kuban
River in the north Caucasus and the Kup'i Bulgar tribe that
lived in that region. He also noted that Yehudah's appellation
"Sawarta" may indicate his membership in the Turkic Sabir
tribe.[90] The Russian historian A. N. Torpusman, on the other
hand, suggested that Gostata (Gostyata?), Kufin (Kupin?), and
Sawarta (Severyata?) are actually East Slavic names.[91]

What else do we learn from the *Kievan Letter*? Many of the
phrases in the letter—such as "nor are we as warners but
rather those who remind" and "you shall eat the fruits in this
world"—are rabbinical idioms typical of those used in other
Jewish letters of recommendation during the medieval era.[92]
Thus, the obvious conclusion we must draw, according to
Golb, is that the Khazars living in Kiev practiced standard
rabbinical Judaism. Golb also explained that the letter demonstrates that many non-royal Khazars had in fact adopted
Judaism as their faith:

The new Kievan Letter may thus be said to support, and indeed to demonstrate, the authenticity of other Hebrew texts pertaining to the Khazar Jews, and together with them shows that Khazarian Judaism was not limited to the rulers but, rather, was well rooted in the territories of Khazaria, reaching even to its border city of Kiev.[93]

THE DEGREE OF JUDAIZATION AMONG THE KHAZARS

A variety of medieval documents that illuminate the Khazars' Judaism have survived to the present day. The contemporary quotes from Arabic, Karaite, and other sources indicate that the Jews exerted an enormous amount of influence over Khazarian affairs, and that a great many of the Khazar people became Jewish.

The conversion of the Khazar kings was only the first step in a transition to Judaic practices. Judaism started to spread widely in Khazaria toward the end of the ninth century, partly because of the enthusiastic pro-Judaism policies of King Obadiah and his successors.[94] There are many indications that Judaism was the predominant religion among the Khazar people themselves by the tenth century.

There is no evidence that any of the Khazar kagans or beks were Jewish in the eighth century. The *Life* of Saint Abo explicitly described the Khazar kagan as a pagan in the year 782.[95] The kagans of this period—such as Kagan Baghatur—had Turkic names, and no trace of Judaic influence can be detected. Indeed, many Jewish communities existed in Khazaria at this time—such as the immigrants from Armenia and the colonies on the Crimean and Taman peninsulas—but they had not yet persuaded even the kagans and beks to adopt their religion, much less the population at large.

In the early stages of Judaization in Khazaria, the Jewish religion was predominant only among the ruling classes of Khazaria, while the majority of the Khazars still worshipped Tengri rather than Yahweh. If Yehudah ha-Levi can be trusted, the king (presumably the bek) converted in around 740. If, on the other hand, al-Masudi's date is accurate, the king converted between 786 and 809. Ibn Khordadbeh wrote between 846 and 885 that only the Khazar lower-king (bek) was Jewish.[96] Unfortunately, the *Schechter Letter* does not provide dates for when a victorious chief warrior of mixed Khazarian-Israelite origins became the first Jewish bek, Bulan (Sabriel), or for when a Jewish sage was appointed as the first Jewish kagan. However, the sequence of these two events was established: A Jewish bek was installed on the throne before a Jew became kagan. One may assume that the first Jewish bek, not being fully knowledgeable about the rituals and laws of Judaism, was responsible for bringing about only a basic level of Judaism in Khazaria before the decisive switch in 861. It is entirely possible that Bulan ruled Khazaria during the 840s and 850s, if not earlier, without adhering to Judaism properly and sincerely or spreading the religion among his people, thus leading ibn Khordadbeh to conclude that none of the Khazar people were Jewish. The kagan, meanwhile, remained a dedicated shamanist, and the subordinate bek still remained under the kagan's religious influence, which would explain his continued worship at the pagan shrines (as described in *Sefer ha-Kuzari*), despite his nominal Jewishness.

Ibn Khordadbeh's account described the very earliest stages of Judaism in the Khazar Empire. Around the 860s, the kagan's throne was, for the first time, occupied by a Jew. This situation was discussed by the Persian historian ibn Rustah, who wrote circa 903 that the Khazar rulers (the kagan, bek, generals, and chiefs) and nobles professed Judaism, but that the rest of the Khazars still practiced shamanism.[97] Ibn Rustah's information most likely comes from an unnamed archaic report of the late ninth century.[98] Therefore, it does not reflect the situation in the tenth century.

The Jewish kagans and beks certainly remained committed to their new religion. As an example of the dedication of the kagans to Judaism, the Arab traveler ibn Fadlan mentioned that when the kagan of the Khazars learned that Muslims had destroyed a synagogue in Dar al-Babunaj, he retaliated by destroying a minaret at a mosque in Atil and killing the muezzins.[99] The commitment of the rulers to Judaism obviously influenced the populace at large.

The final stage in the Judaization of the Khazars—the propagation of Judaism among the common people—took place sometime between the reign of King Obadiah and the 930s. Ibn Fadlan wrote circa 921 or 922 that: "The Khazars and their king are all Jews."[100] Ibn al-Faqih wrote circa 902 (or 930): "All of the Khazars are Jews. But they have been Judaized recently."[101] Al-Masudi reported in 943 that the Jewish religion was professed by the kagan, his "entourage," and members of the Khazar tribe.[102] Circa 985, al-Muqaddasi compiled a work titled *Descriptio Imperii Moslemici*, in which he said: "Sheep, honey, and Jews exist in large quantities in that land [Khazaria]."[103] It is of major significance that 'Abd al-Jabbar—whom I cited earlier in this chapter—wrote that the Khazars agreed to meet all the obligations set forth in the Torah, including not working on the Sabbath day or on holidays; refraining from eating the meat of forbidden animals; circumcision; and washing rituals. Druthmar of Aquitaine wrote in *Expositio in Matthaeum Evangelistam* (864) that ". . . all of them [the Gazari] profess the Jewish faith. The Bulgars, however, who are of the same race, recently became Christians."[104] These sources demonstrate that large numbers of non-aristocratic Khazars adopted Judaism.

There also exist some other Arabic accounts—from the tenth to the thirteenth centuries—that on the surface appear to contradict these statements. For example, al-Istakhri's account (written circa 932 or 951) stated that the Jews were numerically the smallest group in Khazaria compared to the Muslims and Christians, except among government officials.[105] However, he added that Judaism was practiced by the king and his officers. Similarly, al-Bakri wrote (around 1094) that most people in the Khazar Empire were Muslims and Christians, ". . . but there are idolaters among them, and the people of a section among them, and their king, are of the Jewish faith . . ."[106] An anonymous twelfth-century source, *Risalat fi'l Aqalim*, said that the people in Khazaria were mostly Muslims, but that their king was a Jew. In a summary of earlier Arabic accounts, Yaqut wrote (around 1229) that there were more Muslims and Christians in Khazaria compared to the number of Jews.[107] I believe that these four Arab accounts should be interpreted as follows: Whereas the Khazar Empire encompassed many non-Jewish peoples (e.g., Muslim Bulgars, pagan Slavs, and pagan Huns), the ethnically Khazar people—who were outnumbered by other groups—were Jewish to a large extent, as further evidence suggests. In other words, these accounts appear to describe the extent of Judaism among all inhabitants of the Khazar Empire rather than among the Khazar tribe alone. There are at least three other possibilities as to why these four sources did not admit to a large Jewish presence in Khazaria: The Arab writers were referring to the population of Khazars along the Volga and Caspian rather than to those living in western territories (e.g., Crimea, Sarkel, Kiev), where Judaism may have been more prevalent; the writers, being Muslims, were reluctant to acknowledge Judaism's appeal in the kingdom, whereas some Jewish writers were proud to point it out; or the writers based their information on outdated sources such as ibn Rustah.

Further evidence that Judaism was the primary religion among the Khazars comes from Karaite, Persian, and Jewish sources. Around the first half of the tenth century, the Karaite historian and biblical commentator Jacob al-Kirkisani wrote in *Kitab al-Riyadh wa'l-Khada'iq* (Book of Gardens and Parks) that the Khazars adopted Judaism.[108] Other Karaite writers scorned the Khazar Jews and called them mamzerim rather than "true Jews." For example, Jacob ben Reuben of Byzantium wrote:

Now, [the prophet] Zachariah has already said (Zachariah 9:6), "And a bastard shall dwell in Ashdod," alluding to the Khazars who shall enter the Jewish fold in the Diaspora.[109]

An additional Arabic Karaite commentary, written either by Japheth ben Ali or Jeshuan ben Yehudah, also used Zachariah's verse to explain that the Khazars were "illegitimate" bastards:

And we explain that this was the condition of the nations before the rise of Nebuchadnezzar and he made them disappear from their land, and they intermixed and perhaps the unknown laws were similar to those of the Moabites and the Ammonites. [This continued] until the arrival of the man [Eliyahu the Prophet] who separated between non-Jews (al-Goyim). And they became acquainted with each other as Mishpakhot ha-Goyim and their condition returned to what it was [before]. And it was said "And a bastard shall dwell in Ashdod" (Zachariah 9:6) and that was an indication that the Israelites gave Ashdod and its surroundings to them as a place to live. And it has been suggested that they were the Khazars who adopted the religion of Israel in the time of Exile. As for those who adopted Judaism before the Exile, the Almighty God had made them already dwell between the Israelites, in accordance with the verse in Ezekiel 47:23: "And in what tribe the stranger sojourneth, there shall ye give him his inheritance."[110]

Another medieval source, the Persian *Denkart*, also criticized the Khazars' Judaism, but for a different reason:

As for religion, it is evident that when it was propagated among them, the strength, the splendor, and the *xvarrah* of the Zoroastrian religion eliminated the strife from their lives, and established joy and profit; but that [when] false doctrines descended upon them and wove their way among them, they were changed. Thus, it is clear that the false doctrine of Jesus in Rome, that of Moses among the Khazars, [and] that of Mani in [Uyghur-ruled] Turkistan removed the strength and bravery that they formerly possessed, and [as a result] these people returned to a state of weakness and decadence when among their rivals; and Manichaeism was ruined just like the philosophy in Rome.[111]

Several erudite Sephardic scholars wrote about the Khazars' conversion to Judaism. Abraham ibn Daud (circa 1110–1180), a Spanish Jewish writer, included the following in his 1161 work *Sefer ha-Qabbalah* (The Book of Tradition):

> You will find the communities of Israel spread abroad from the town of Sala at the extremity of the Maghrib, as far as Tahart at its commencement, the extremity of Africa [Ifraqiyah, Tunis], in all Africa, Egypt, the country of the Sabaeans, Arabia, Babylonia, Elam, Persia, Dedan, the country of the Girgashites which is called Jurjan, Tabaristan, as far as Daylam and the river Itil where live the Khazar peoples who became proselytes. Their king Joseph sent a letter to R. Hisdai, the Prince bar Isaac ben-Shaprut and informed him that he and all his people followed the Rabbanite faith.[112]

Also very significant are several descriptions of Jewish Khazars who were living abroad after Khazaria's downfall. It is true that ibn Miskawayh wrote that in 965 "all" of the Khazars adopted Islam,[113] except for the Khazar king, but he was referring only to those Khazars who were conquered by the Khwarizmians (see Chapter 8). This particular group of Khazars was forced to largely abandon Judaism for political reasons rather than out of voluntary choice. Meanwhile, a large number of Khazars remained Jewish. This is confirmed by such sources as the *Rus'ian Chronicle* and Rabbi Petakhiah's travelogue, as well as by several vague records of a twelfth-century Khazarian Jewish messianic movement, led by the Khazars Solomon ben Duji and his son, Menahem ben Solomon (see Chapter 9).

The majority of sources quoted in this section are consistent with the evidence for Khazar Judaism in the *Schechter Letter*, *King Joseph's Reply*, *Kol Yehudah*, *Sefer ha-Kuzari*, the *Kievan Letter*, and Dimashqi's report, all of which were discussed earlier in this chapter.

ARCHAEOLOGICAL EVIDENCE

There is considerable archaeological proof of the existence of non-royal Khazar Jews that supplements the aforementioned historical evidence.

It is certain that Khazar Jews lived in Phanagoria (Tmutorokan), since over sixty tombstones bearing Jewish symbols (such as seven-branched menorahs, shofars, and lulavs) on one side and Turkic tribe symbols (*tamgas*) on the other side were found on the Taman peninsula.[114] Many of these tombstones date from the eighth or ninth century.

Khazarian tombstones on the Crimean peninsula also depict the shofar, menorah, and staff of Aaron, as well as Turkic tribe symbols.[115] One of the Hebrew-lettered gravestones from Chufut-Kale seems to date from the year 846. Many others originate from the tenth and eleventh centuries (see Chapter 9). Khazar Jewish graves were also found in Kerch's straits.[116] In 1996, a Russian expedition found several engravings of the menorah etched into the side of a mountain in Kerch.

The artifacts from Taman and Crimea are extremely significant since their tamgas show that these Jews were ethnic Turks.

Some of the most interesting evidence comes from Sarkel. Bricks and stones found at Sarkel contain engraved depictions of living creatures as well as geometric patterns and symbols, Turkic runes, and the Jewish menorah, and some of the Khazar symbols appear to be Hebrew square-style letters similar to those recovered from ancient Crimean sites.[117] Engravings of the six-pointed Jewish star of David were found on circular Khazar relics and bronze mirrors from Sarkel and Khazarian gravefields in Verkhneye Saltovo.[118] A few archaeologists argue that the center of Sarkel housed a synagogue. In a village near Sarkel, an actual Khazarian menorah made of gold was discovered.

Scholars at a museum in Rostov-on-Don have attempted to reconstruct what seems to be a Khazarian tabernacle from parts of a folding altar that were unearthed.

It is hoped that new archaeological discoveries will follow in the future, since it is not expected that more previously unknown medieval documents will be located.

CONCLUSIONS

The accumulated evidence contradicts popular but antiquated views, such as those expressed by Vladimir Minorsky:

> The propagation of Judaism among the Khazars had but a restricted scope and concerned only the top of the social pyramid, while the majority of the people must have stuck to the old nomad practices. . . .[119]

Similarly, Dunlop commented:

> The character of the Khazars as Judaized Turks has constantly to be kept in mind. This probably means that their Judaism— limited no doubt in any case to a comparatively small group— was always superficial.[120]

These opinions can now be discarded. The discovery of new documentary and archaeological evidence has proved that Judaism was widespread among the common Khazar people.

In conclusion, it is clear that it was not just the Khazar kings and the upper class who became Jews, and the Khazar form of Judaism is to be characterized as standard rabbinical belief.

Notes

1. Alexander Scheiber, *Jewish Inscriptions in Hungary from the 3rd Century to 1686* (Budapest: Akadémiai, 1983), pp. 14, 17, 59.

2. Raphael Patai, *The Jews of Hungary* (Detroit: Wayne State University Press, 1996), pp. 23–24.

3. Vicki Tamir, *Bulgaria and Her Jews* (New York: Sepher-Hermon Press, 1979), p. 3.

4. Zev Katz, "The Jews in the Soviet Union," in *Handbook of Major Soviet Nationalities*, ed. Zev Katz, et al. (New York: The Free Press, 1975), pp. 358–359.

5. Vsevolod L. Vikhnovich, "From the Jordan to the Dnieper," *Jewish Studies (Mada'e ha-Yahadut)* 31 (1991): 17–18.

6. Robert S. MacLennan, "In Search of the Jewish Diaspora: A First-Century Synagogue in Crimea?" *Biblical Archaeology Review* 22:2 (March/April 1996): 46.

7. Ibid., pp. 46–47.

8. Ibid., pp. 49–50.

9. Vsevolod L. Vikhnovich, "From the Jordan to the Dnieper," pp. 16–17.

10. Ibid., p. 18.

11. The Sassanid dynasty ruled Persia from circa 226 to circa 641.

12. Constantine Zuckerman, "On the Date of the Khazars' Conversion to Judaism and the Chronology of the Kings of the Rus Oleg and Igor," *Revue des Études Byzantines* 53 (1995): 241.

13. Salo W. Baron, *A Social and Religious History of the Jews*, vol. 3 (New York: Columbia University Press, 1957), p. 176.

14. Constantine Zuckerman, "On the Date of the Khazars' Conversion . . . ," p. 255.

15. Stanford J. Shaw, "Christian Anti Semitism in the Ottoman Empire," *Belleten C.* 54:68 (1991): 1081.

16. Ibid., p. 1080.

17. Vladimir F. Minorsky, *A History of Sharvan and Darband in the Tenth–Eleventh Centuries* (Cambridge, England: W. Heffer and Sons, 1958), p. 146.

18. Norman Golb and Omeljan Pritsak, *Khazarian Hebrew Documents of the Tenth Century* (Ithaca, NY: Cornell University Press, 1982), p. 115.

19. Ibid., p. 107.

20. Abraham E. Harkavy, "Rab Sa'adyah Gaon al debar ha-Kuzarim," in *Semitic Studies in Memory of Rev. Dr. Alexander Kohut*, ed. G. A. Kohut (Berlin: S. Calvary & Co., 1897), p. 245.

21. Norman Golb and Omeljan Pritsak, *Khazarian Hebrew Documents of the Tenth Century*, p. 111.

22. For discussion, see V. Altman, "Ancient Khorezmian Civilisation in the Light of the Latest Archaeological Discoveries (1937–1945)," *Journal of the American Oriental Society* 67:2 (1947); Itzhak Ben-Zvi, *The Exiled and the Redeemed*, trans. Isaac A. Abbady (Philadelphia: The Jewish Publication Society of America, 1961), p. 212; Hansgerd Göckenjan, *Hilfsvölker und Grenzwächter im mittelalterlichen Ungarn* (Wiesbaden, West Germany: Franz Steiner, 1972), p. 45; Simon Szyszman, "Le roi Bulan et le problème de la conversion des Khazars," *Ephemerides Theologicae Lovanienses* 33 (1957): 74; Giles Whittell, *Cadogan Guides—Central Asia* (London: Cadogan Books, 1996), p. 183.

23. Luc Kwanten, *Imperial Nomads* (Philadelphia: University of Pennsylvania Press, 1979), p. 47.

24. Wasilii V. Barthold, *Turkestan Down to the Mongol Invasion*, 3rd ed., trans. H. A. R. Gibb and T. Minorsky (London: Luzac & Co., 1968), p. 185.

25. The chronicler al-Biruni wrote about the expulsion of Khwarezmian scholars, which took place in 712. Kutaiba ibn Muslim was killed in 715 after losing the support of his army.

26. Douglas M. Dunlop, *The History of the Jewish Khazars* (New York: Schocken, 1967), pp. 89–90.

27. Proponents of this view have included, among others, Antal Bartha, Douglas M. Dunlop, Arthur Koestler, Paul Wexler, and Ananiasz Zajaczkowski.

28. Omeljan Pritsak, "The Khazar Kingdom's Conversion to Judaism," *Harvard Ukrainian Studies* 3:2 (Sept. 1978): 280–281; Omeljan Pritsak, "The Pre-Ashkenazic Jews of Eastern Europe in Relation to the Khazars, the Rus' and the Lithuanians," in *Ukrainian-Jewish Relations in Historical Perspective*, ed. Howard Aster and Peter J. Potichnyj (Edmonton, Alberta, Canada: Canadian Institute of Ukrainian Studies Press, 1990), p. 5.

29. Constantine Zuckerman, "On the Date of the Khazars' Conversion . . . ," p. 243.

30. *Asian Mythologies*, ed. Yves Bonnefoy, trans. Gerald Honigsblum, et al. (Chicago: University of Chicago Press, 1993), p. 329. Oghuz shamans entered trances to attempt to exorcise exil spirits below the earth and to win the protection of benevolent spirits.

31. Peter B. Golden, "Imperial Ideology and the Sources of Political Unity Amongst the Pre-Činggisid Nomads of Western Eurasia," *Archivum Eurasiae Medii Aevi* 2 (1982): 44.

32. Sev'yan I. Vainshtein, "The Turkic Peoples, Sixth to Twelfth Centuries," in *Nomads of Eurasia*, ed. Vladimir N. Basilov, trans. Mary F. Zirin (Seattle: University of Washington Press, 1989), p. 59.

33. David Marshall Lang, *The Bulgarians* (Boulder, CO: Westview Press, 1976), p. 33.

34. Peter B. Golden, *An Introduction to the History of the Turkic Peoples* (Wiesbaden, Germany: Otto Harrassowitz, 1992), p. 250.

35. *Asian Mythologies*, ed. Yves Bonnefoy, p. 324.

36. Ibid., p. 328.

37. Peter B. Golden, *An Introduction to the History of the Turkic Peoples*, pp. 149–150.

38. The word *Ulugh-kun* was recorded in the monumental comparative dictionary *Divan-i Lughat-it-Turk* by Mahmud al-Kashgari in the 1070s.

39. Luc Kwanten, *Imperial Nomads*, p. 45.

40. George Vernadsky, *A History of Russia*, vol. 1 (New Haven, CT: Yale University Press, 1948), p. 346.

41. Francis Butler, "The Representation of Oral Culture in the *Vita Constantini*," *Slavic and East European Journal* 39:3 (1995): 367.

42. Constantine Zuckerman, "On the Date of the Khazars' Conversion . . . ," p. 244.

43. Francis Butler, "The Representation of Oral Culture in the *Vita Constantini*," pp. 368, 377.

44. Constantine Zuckerman, "On the Date of the Khazars' Conversion . . . ," p. 245.

45. Francis Butler, "The Representation of Oral Culture in the *Vita Constantini*," p. 371.

46. Ibid., p. 372.

47. Ibid. Butler said (idem., p. 377) that the alleged knowledge of aspects of the Torah by the Khazars may be an addition by the author of the *Life* based on the author's incorrect assumption that even pagan people are aware of basic elements of the Old Testament. As evidence, Butler cites another source, the *Life of Stephen of Perm*, where Saint Stephen is said to have met pagan Finns in Perm who were familiar with facts in the Torah, although such an occurrence is questionable.

48. Constantine Zuckerman, "On the Date of the Khazars' Conversion . . . ," p. 243.

49. Alexander A. Vasiliev, *The Goths in the Crimea* (Cambridge, MA: The Mediaeval Academy of America, 1936), p. 113.

50. Roman Jakobson, "Minor Native Sources for the Early History of the Slavic Church," *Harvard Slavic Studies* 2 (1954): 65.

51. The name *Bulan* meant "an elk" in Turkic. The word *bulan* is attested in the Chuvash, Tatar, and Kipchak languages in addition to Khazarian. Bulan's Hebrew name was Sabriel.

52. Omeljan Pritsak, "The Khazar Kingdom's Conversion to Judaism," pp. 278, 279.

53. Constantine Zuckerman, "On the Date of the Khazars' Conversion . . . ," p. 246.

54. Ibid., p. 250. If the conversion took place after the eighth century, as indicated by the *Life of Constantine*, the dynasty of Jewish kings lasted only from 861 to around 965, rather than 740 to 965.

55. Peter B. Golden, *Khazar Studies*, vol. 1 (Budapest: Akadémiai, 1980), p. 23; Peter B. Golden, "Khazaria and Judaism," *Archivum Eurasiae Medii Aevi* 3 (1983): 138; Norman Golb and Omeljan Pritsak, *Khazarian Hebrew Documents of the Tenth Century*, pp. 13–15, 30. See Chapter 11 for a refutation of the claim that Karaism existed in Khazaria.

56. Shlomo Pines, "A Moslem Text Concerning the Conversion of the Khazars to Judaism," *Journal of Jewish Studies* 13 (1962): 47.

57. *Kol Yehudah* is a renowned commentary on *Sefer ha-Kuzari*. On the name Yitzhak ha-Sangari, Rabbi Moscato cited material from *Sefer ha-Emunot* ("The Book of Beliefs") by Shem Tov ibn Shem Tov (c. 1380–1441).

58. Rabbi Yitzhak ha-Sangari perhaps came from the Byzantine town of Sangarus or somewhere else along the Sangarios River (known today as Sakarya River) in northwestern Turkey.

59. Yehuda HaLevi, *The Kuzari*, trans. N. Daniel Korobkin (Northvale, NJ: Jason Aronson, 1998), p. 1.

60. *Jewish Travellers*, ed. Elkan N. Adler (London: George Routledge & Sons, 1930), p. 83.

61. The Warsan Mountains, near the Caspian seashore, are identified with Varach'an, the capital of the north Caucasian Huns (see Peter B. Golden, "Khazaria and Judaism," p. 139). *Varach'an* is the Armenian form of the Arabic rendition *Balanjar*. The Huns of Varach'an resided in the Sulak river basin, which is north of Derbent. Pritsak claimed that Varach'an is probably equivalent to modern-day Tarqu, near Makhachkala (see Omeljan Pritsak, "The Khazar Kingdom's Conversion to Judaism," p. 263).

62. Yehuda HaLevi, *The Kuzari*, p. 55–56.

63. The essay's author claimed to be part of the Khazar king's entourage (see Paul E. Kahle, *The Cairo Geniza* (London: Oxford University Press, 1947), p. 17). Ashtor speculated that the essay was originally written in the Greek language and then translated into Hebrew by a Jew who was familiar with Italian (see Eliyahu Ashtor, *The Jews of Moslem Spain*, vol. 1, trans. Aaron Klein and Jenny M. Klein (Philadelphia: The Jewish Publication Society, 1992), pp. 200, 207), but this view is generally not accepted. Pritsak suggested that the original essay was written in the Arabic script but in the Hebrew language (see Norman Golb and Omeljan Pritsak, *Khazarian Hebrew Documents of the Tenth Century*, p. 129).

64. Constantine Zuckerman, "On the Date of the Khazars' Conversion . . . ," p. 241. The extant copy of the *Schechter Letter* dates back to the eleventh or twelfth century.

65. Ibid., p. 259.

66. See Paul E. Kahle, *The Cairo Geniza*, pp. 7–8, 17.

67. Norman Golb and Omeljan Pritsak, *Khazarian Hebrew Documents of the Tenth Century*, p. 107.

68. Ibid., p. 109.

69. Ibid., p. 113.

70. Ibid., p. 75. Yehudah ben Barzillai indicated that he had personally seen a copy of the *Schechter Letter*, noting that the original was written in Constantinople and that it described the military activities of Kings Aaron and Joseph as well as the story of the conversion.

71. *Jewish Travellers*, ed. Elkan N. Adler, p. 32. The letters exchanged between Hasdai and Joseph have recently been republished in a most excellent new English translation. For Hasdai's letter, see Yehuda HaLevi, *The Kuzari*, pp. 342–349. For Joseph's letter, see idem., pp. 350–357.

72. Ibid., p. 27.

73. Ibid., p. 30.

74. Some scholars believe that *The Query of Hasdai ibn Shaprut* may have been composed as late as 961.

75. Menahem ibn Saruq is famous for his Hebrew dictionary *Mahberet*, which served as a guide to the study of the Torah but was attacked by the philologist and poet Dunash ben Labrat.

76. *Jewish Travellers*, ed. Elkan N. Adler, p. 32.

77. Allegedly, the Khazar attack on Ardabil took place around the year 730 (see Omeljan Pritsak, "The Khazar Kingdom's Conversion to Judaism," p. 274).

78. Douglas M. Dunlop claimed that Obadiah's renaissance took place around the year 800 (see Douglas M. Dunlop, *The History of the Jewish Khazars*, p. 170). But Zuckerman's analysis makes it more likely that it occurred about six or seven decades later.

79. Constantine Zuckerman, "On the Date of the Khazars' Conversion . . .," pp. 249–250. The king lists may have been derived from another Khazar document chronicling Khazaria's history—perhaps from the so-called "Books of the Khazars" alluded to by Yehudah ha-Levi in the *Kuzari*. These chronicles may have been brought to Spain by Khazar royalty and scholars (see Chapter 9) and probably included details of the Khazar occupation of Bulgar land, plus descriptions of the deeds of Joseph's predecessors to the throne.

80. Ibid., p. 248; *Jewish Travellers*, ed. Elkan N. Adler, p. 23. Pavel Kokovtsov, a translator of the texts into Russian (in his 1932 book *Evreysko-Khazarskaya perepiska v X veke*), believed in the genuine nature of the letters. The long version of the *Reply* may date from the thirteenth century, and the short version was included in the sixteenth-century manuscript *Kol Mebasser* by Yitzhak Aqrish (see Norman Golb and Omeljan Pritsak, *Khazarian Hebrew Documents of the Tenth Century*, p. 76).

81. Norman Golb and Omeljan Pritsak, *Khazarian Hebrew Documents of the Tenth Century*, p. 71.

82. Leonid S. Chekin, "The Role of Jews in Early Russian Civilization in the Light of a New Discovery and New Controversies," *Russian History/Histoire russe* 17:4 (Winter 1990): 384.

83. Norman Golb and Omeljan Pritsak, *Khazarian Hebrew Documents of the Tenth Century*, p. 15.

84. Ibid., pp. 41–42. These runic letters were written from right to left.

85. Ibid., p. 27.

86. Israel I. Kasovich, *The Eternal People* (New York: The Jordan Publishing Co., 1929), p. 305.

87. Norman Golb and Omeljan Pritsak, *Khazarian Hebrew Documents of the Tenth Century*, p. 55.

88. Omeljan Pritsak, *The Origin of Rus'*, vol. 1 (Cambridge, MA: Harvard University Press, 1981), p. 69.

89. Norman Golb and Omeljan Pritsak, *Khazarian Hebrew Documents of the Tenth Century*, p. 40.

90. Ibid., p. 38.

91. Vsevolod L. Vikhnovich, "From the Jordan to the Dnieper," p. 22.

92. Norman Golb and Omeljan Pritsak, *Khazarian Hebrew Documents of the Tenth Century*, p. 31.

93. Ibid., p. 32.

94. One theory holds that intensive Judaization may have been associated with the revolts of the Kabars. Emperor Constantine VII Porphyrogenitus (reigned 913–959) wrote in *De administrando imperio* that the Kabars were involved in a civil war against the Khazar government (see also Chapter 9). The Kabar revolts were allegedly associated, according to Antal Bartha, with the Kabars' objection to "judicial and adminis-

trative changes that followed the spread of the Jewish faith in the Khazar empire" (see Antal Bartha, *Hungarian Society in the 9th and 10th Centuries*, trans. K. Balazs (Budapest: Akadémiai, 1975), p. 63). According to Omeljan Pritsak, a major Kabar rebellion took place in the 830s because the Khazar bek supported Judaism while the Khazar kagan, named Xan-tuvan (Dyggvi), was opposed to Judaism (see Omeljan Pritsak, *The Origin of Rus'*, vol. 1, pp. 28, 171, 182). The supporters of this kagan would have been those who were hostile to the spread of Judaism in the empire. After a series of conflicts, many of the rebels were killed and the kagan was defeated. The kagan became a fugitive, fleeing from the Jewish bek along with his supporters. Pritsak argued that the kagan and surviving rebels resettled in Rostov and became acquainted with the Scandinavians, who founded the first Rus'ian kaganate by 839. He speculated that the kagan may have married one of the Scandinavian girls. It is known that the Kabar rebels later migrated to Hungary and Transylvania (see Chapter 9). In the absence of further documentation, these theories must be regarded as speculative and unproved, because none of the surviving documents describe objections (by either the kagan or the populace) to King Obadiah's religious policies, nor do they link Obadiah with the Kabar revolts.

95. George Vernadsky, *A History of Russia*, vol. 1, p. 292.

96. Omeljan Pritsak, "The Khazar Kingdom's Conversion to Judaism," p. 279.

97. Douglas M. Dunlop, *The History of the Jewish Khazars*, p. 104.

98. Constantine Zuckerman, "On the Date of the Khazars' Conversion . . .," p. 253. Another illustration of the antiquated nature of ibn Rustah's account is the fact that he called the bek the *isha*, which was the bek's former title. By the 830s, the bek was already known by his new title. Thus, some of ibn Rustah's sources may even go back to before the 830s (see Douglas M. Dunlop, *The History of the Jewish Khazars*, p. 108).

99. Peter B. Golden, "Khazaria and Judaism," p. 153.

100. Ibid., p. 140.

101. Ibid.

102. Vladimir F. Minorsky, *A History of Sharvan and Darband in the 10th–11th Centuries*, p. 146.

103. Salo W. Baron, *A Social and Religious History of the Jews*, vol. 3, p. 197.

104. Omeljan Pritsak, "The Khazar Kingdom's Conversion to Judaism," p. 271.

105. Douglas M. Dunlop, *The History of the Jewish Khazars*, pp. 91–92.

106. Frederick I. Kaplan, "The Decline of the Khazars and the Rise of the Varangians," *American Slavic and East European Review* 13 (1954): 8.

107. Peter B. Golden, "Khazaria and Judaism," p. 142.

108. Zvi Ankori, *Karaites in Byzantium* (New York: Ams Press, 1968), p. 67.

109. Ibid., p. 71.

110. Translated from the original Hebrew text given in Abraham E. Harkavy, "Rab Sa'adyah Gaon al debar ha-Kuzarim," in *Semitic Studies in Memory of Rev. Dr. Alexander Kohut*, pp. 246–247.

111. Translated from the French edition: *La légende de Zoroastre selon les textes pehlevis*, ed. Marijan Molé (Paris: C. Klincksieck, 1967), p. 237.

112. Douglas M. Dunlop, *The History of the Jewish Khazars*, p. 127.

113. Ibid., p. 244.

114. Vsevolod L. Vikhnovich, "From the Jordan to the Dnieper," p. 19; J. G. Lipman, "Taman," in *The Jewish Encyclopedia*, vol. 12 (New York: Ktav, 1901–1906), p. 40.

115. Norman Golb and Omeljan Pritsak, *Khazarian Hebrew Documents of the Tenth Century*, p. 27.

116. Ehud Ya'ari, "Skeletons in the Closet," *The Jerusalem Report* (Sept. 7, 1995): 27.

117. Bozena Wyszomirska, "Religion som enande politisk-social länk—exemplet: det Kazariska riket," in *Arkeologi och Religion*, ed. Lars Larsson and Bozena Wyszomirska (Lund, Sweden: University of Lund, 1989), pp. 137–138.

118. Ibid., pp. 138, 143, 144. It is, of course, possible that these stars from Khazaria were actually created by pagan Slavs or shamanist Turks. For a detailed history of the symbolism associated with the hexagram (six-pointed star), see Gerbern S. Oegema, *The History of the Shield of David: The Birth of a Symbol* (Frankfurt am Main: Peter Lang, 1996). According to Oegema, the hexagram originated in Asia among non-Jews and used to be called the "Seal of Solomon." By the thirteenth century, it began to be called the "Shield of David" and to be used for Jewish magic and heraldic seals. Flags from medieval Morocco and Turkey displayed the hexagram, and Oegema thought that this particular use of the star spread from Muslim countries to Spain and then to central Europe (see idem., p. 74). In the 1350s, the hexagram was added to the flag of the Jews of Prague. The six-pointed star came into use among Christian Germans and West Slavs also (see Paul Wexler, *The Ashkenazic Jews* (Columbus, OH: Slavica, 1993), p. 123). The symbol spread thereafter from central Europe to the Jews of Poland and Russia (see Oegema, pp. 129–130). Unfortunately, Oegema did not discuss the Khazarian hexagrams nor the theory that the hexagram is called the "Shield of David" because of the legendary Khazar David al-Roy (the assumed name of Menahem ben Solomon).

119. Vladimir F. Minorsky, "A New Book on the Khazars," *Oriens* 11 (1959): 122.

120. Douglas M. Dunlop, *The History of the Jewish Khazars*, p. 195.

7

RELATIONS BETWEEN THE KHAZARS AND OTHER PEOPLES

*A*s *a powerful kingdom on the periphery of the Byzantine and Persian Empires, the Khazar Empire engaged in many of the important military and political affairs of the early medieval era. The Khazars did not always maintain consistent relations with their neighbors. As we shall see, the Khazars sometimes befriended the Byzantines, Alans, and Oghuz, while at other times they were their fiercest enemies.*

THE ARAB-KHAZAR WARS AND RELATIONS WITH LEADERS OF THE SOUTH CAUCASUS

Khazaria occupied a strategic position as a link between Europe, Asia, and the Middle East. The Khazars aggressively supported the expansion of their territory. In particular, the kagans challenged the caliphs and amirs for control of the border fortress of Derbent and territories in the south

Caucasus (Azerbaijan, Georgia, and Armenia) and the northern Middle East. It was therefore inevitable that the Khazars
would meet organized resistance from the Arabs. The Arabs
and the Khazars warred against each other in the seventh and
eighth centuries. These conflicts are known collectively as the
Arab-Khazar Wars.

Over a century before the beginning of the Arab-Khazar
Wars, the Khazars were already ambitiously expanding their
domains and involved in affairs immediately to the north of
Persia and Mesopotamia. According to the ninth-century Arab
historian Ya'qubi, a representative (khalifa) of the Khazar-
Turkic kagan ruled over Georgia (Jurzan) and ancient Albania (Arran) in the south Caucasus sometime between the years
488 and 531.[1] The Sassanids later took control of these lands.
The famous fortress of Derbent, whose Arab name Bab al-
Abwab meant "Gate Barrier," was built under the direction of
the Sassanid Persian emperor Khusrau (Chosroes) I
Anushirvan (reigned 531–578) and served as a gateway separating the Hunno-Turkic north from the Arabo-Persian south.
Derbent, highly prized for its strategic location, was to become
the site of numerous struggles during the Arab-Khazar Wars.
However, in this early period, the Islamic religion had not yet
been developed, and therefore the relentless Muslim expansionist programs were not yet a factor for the Turkic tribes to
contend with.

Early in the seventh century, Muhammad, a member of the
Quraysh tribe of Arabia, began to preach that only one god
(Allah) exists and that the idol worship among the Arabs of
his native city of Mecca was sinful. His beliefs, or "revelations,"
were codified in the Koran, the Islamic holy book. The
Meccans initially rejected this new monotheistic faith.
Muhammad arrived in the oasis city of Medina in September
622 and encountered resistance from its Jewish and Christian
residents. At that time, the two tribes in Medina were engaged
in intense disputes. Muhammad managed to mediate in the
tribal conflicts and became the leader of Medina. Over the

next few years, he gained support for Islam among an increasing number of Arabs. In 630, Muhammad coerced the Meccan populace to adopt Islam. In 633, Muslim Arab troops began to penetrate Persia; by 641, the old Sassanid dynasty had fallen, and the Muslims had seized full control. During the remainder of the seventh century, the Muslims conquered North Africa, Spain, and all of the Middle East and established strong ruling dynasties. It was not long before the Muslims turned their attention to the pagans of the steppes.

The First Arab-Khazar War lasted from 642 to 652. It began in 642 when the Arab general 'Abd ar-Rahman attacked Khazaria. From 651 to 652, Arab troops attempted to invade Khazaria, and they succeeded in passing north of Derbent but were then defeated by the Khazars at Balanjar, the original Khazarian capital city, which they had attempted to capture. As a result of the fighting in 652, four thousand Arabs lost their lives, including a prominent commander named Salman ibn Rabiyya. Yet, hostilities between the two sides did not cease completely even after the first series of conflicts. An army of Khazars from Samandar, supported by a number of Abkhazians and Alans, was assembled in around 655 to go against an Arab army that was led by Habib ibn Maslama.[2] This confrontation was further provoked by the fact that Habib had been ordered to take revenge against the Khazars for Commander Salman's death three years earlier. In 661–662, the Khazars raided Albania in the south Caucasus, but the prince of Caucasian Albania defeated them and prevented further Khazar looting in his territory.

Between 683 and 685, the Khazar army invaded Caucasian Albania, Armenia, and Georgia, destroying many areas and taking booty and prisoners. The Arab troops in Armenia suffered heavy losses. The rulers of both Armenia and Georgia fell in battle against the Khazar invaders.

In 713 or 714, Maslama ibn 'Abd-al-Malik, an experienced military general, captured Derbent and unsuccessfully tried to capture the lands of the north Caucasian Huns.[3] Around the same time, a Khazar army of eighty thousand men temporarily captured Caucasian Albania. When the Khazars followed up with another southward expedition to Azerbaijan in 717, Caliph 'Umar ibn 'Abd-al-'Aziz (reigned 717–720) sent troops to confront the Khazars and force them to leave the area. The caliph's commander, Hatin ibn al-Nu'man, took fifty Khazars as prisoners.

The Second Arab-Khazar War lasted from 722 to 737 and had a profound impact upon the future of the Caucasus. Thirty thousand Khazar soldiers invaded Armenia in 722 or 723 and soundly defeated the Arab army (led by Thubayt al-Nahrani) at Marj al-Hijara in Armenia.[4] The Arabs fled to Syria. In retaliation, a Muslim army led by Jarrah ibn Abdullah al-Hakami proceeded north, penetrating the Khazar lands around 723 or 724. Jarrah's troops took Balanjar from the Khazars (circa 723), killed many Khazars in battle, and enslaved numerous Khazars. Some of Balanjar's people were drowned.[5] The Khazar governor of Balanjar escaped to Samandar. Balanjar's remaining residents left the city and resettled farther north.[6] The Arab army reached as far as Samandar but then retreated south. Maslama ibn 'Abd-al-Malik was pronounced Jarrah's successor as the Umayyad Caliphate's new governor of Armenia and Azerbaijan. Apparently, Maslama's deputy attacked Khazaria in 725 or 726 and captured some villages there. The son of the Khazar kagan, named Barjik, then led an expedition southward into Azerbaijan circa 726 or 727, but the Khazars were defeated by the Arabs at the Araxes River.

Maslama led another invasion of Khazaria in 727 and 728. In 728, Maslama fought the kagan's army for almost a month, but then heavy rain made the kagan flee. Khazars who raided Azerbaijan in 729 or 730 were defeated, and the Arabs reached Al-Bayda, the Khazar capital on the lower Volga. However, in a major victory at the Battle of Ardabil in Persia in 730, the Khazars led by Barjik (having again invaded Armenia and Azerbaijan) defeated almost an entire Arab army after three days of war.[7] One of the major Arab casualties of this battle was General Jarrah.[8] Commander Barjik, however, survived. The Khazars successfully captured the town of Ardabil and killed its men. Azerbaijan, Tabriz, and Armenia all were despoiled. The Khazars raided as far south as Al-Mawsil (Mosul) in northern Iraq. However, Arab troops stopped their advance and killed much of the army. The remainder of the Khazars fled north, back to their homeland.

Thomas Noonan commented on the significance of the first half of the Second Arab-Khazar War:

> Though the Khazars had been defeated eventually, one conclusion emerged very clearly from these events. The Khazars were a most formidable foe who could undertake large expeditions into the South Caucasus, destroy Arab armies led by seasoned commanders such as Jarrah, penetrate to the very borders of Iran and Iraq, and threaten the very fabric of Arab rule in Arminiyah and Adharbayjan.[9]

The forces led by Maslama ibn 'Abd-al-Malik surged past Derbent and again invaded Khazaria toward the end of 730, but they retreated because of the cold wintry weather. The Khazars retook Derbent from the Arabs in 731 and installed a large garrison there. Maslama reacted by invading the interior of the Khazar kingdom (in 731) and again reaching Balanjar and Samandar. Maslama killed Barjik, the Khazar kagan's son,[10] and the kagan was injured. Although the Arabs could claim victory in the latest battle, they were forced to retreat southward when some Khazars pursued them from the north. The Khazar garrison at Derbent dispersed after the Arabs poisoned the water supply. Thus, Derbent again came into solid Arab control in 732.[11]

The Arabs, under the leadership of General Marwan ibn Muhammad, the Caliphate's governor of Armenia, defeated the Khazar soldiers in a major battle in 737. Marwan and his troops passed through the Darial Pass (Alan Gate), located in the center of the Caucasus mountain range, and marched into

Balanjar, Samandar, and Al-Bayda.[12] The Khazars were unprepared for Marwan's forces since they were deceived into thinking that the Arabs wanted to sign a peace treaty with them. When Marwan invaded Daghestan, the Khazars fled and were forced to transfer their capital from Samandar to Atil. While Marwan's army advanced along the right bank of the Volga and attacked the Burtas, the Khazar army remained on the Volga's left bank. When the Arabs crossed the Volga and assaulted the Khazars, the Khazar tarkhan was killed, and Marwan captured the Khazar kagan. Marwan forced the kagan to pledge support for the Muslim Caliphate and to adopt Islam, although it is suspected that he rejected the faith soon afterward.[13] Marwan's army then returned south of the Caucasus.

The Khazars' attempt to control the south Caucasus had failed. The Caucasus Mountains and the fortress city of Derbent became the southern boundary of the Khazar Empire, and the Arabs preserved control over the lands south of Derbent's Gate. Yet, despite being forced in 737 to pledge their allegiance to the Caliphate, and although for a while they paid annual tribute to the Caliphate in the form of corn and slave children, the Khazars maintained their kingdom's independence. Military power was essential to the preservation of Khazaria as an independent state. With a large supply of horses and a professional army, the Khazars were able to maintain control of their heartland. On the other hand, it must be mentioned that the second round of Arab-Khazar battles took a drastic toll upon the Khazar settlements in the Terek and Sulak river valleys, many of which were abandoned or destroyed.[14]

The most important outcome of the Arab-Khazar Wars was that the Khazars were able to prevent the Arabs from advancing into eastern Europe. As a consequence, the Arabs did not have the opportunity to spread the Islamic religion among large numbers of the peoples north of the Caucasus Mountains.[15]

The second round of conflict in the 720s and 730s did not end the tensions between the Khazars and other tribes.

Soon after 754, the Arab Governor Yazid ibn Usaid al-Sulami of Armenia sought to create a relationship with the Khazar royal family in order to establish long-lasting peace with the kagan and the Khazar soldiers and thus help Armenia survive in the face of Khazaria's strength.[16] Yazid wanted to establish an alliance with the kagan. Circa 758, the Abbasid Caliph, Mansur, ordered Yazid to marry one of the kagan's daughters. Yet, while starting out ideally, this situation ultimately led to more fighting between the Khazars and the Muslims.

The Khazar kagan around this time was named Baghatur, according to the account of ibn A'tham. He gladly accepted Yazid's offer to marry his daughter. The Armenian historian Levond called Baghatur the *Xak'an* (i.e., kagan) and "the king of the North," and described his daughter by the title *Xat'un* (i.e., khatun), meaning "princess." The marriage between Yazid and Baghatur's daughter took place in 759 or 760. Baghatur paid 100,000 dirhems as dowry.

There was an elaborate procession following the marriage. The bride was escorted south to the Muslim town of Bardha'a by ten thousand elite Khazars, who took with them thousands of horses, camels, mules, and sheep, not to mention servants.[17] They also brought along covered wagons with silver- and gold-plated doors, as well as a variety of utensils and vessels made from precious metals.

The khatun told her new husband of her desire to learn the Islamic faith and how to read the Koran, so he hired some Muslims to assist her. For a while, things went well, and peace between the Khazars and Arabs finally became a reality. Yet, after only two years and four months of marriage, the khatun died in Bardha'a, and her two young children also died. Yazid was devastated by the loss of his wife and children. The Khazars interpreted her death as the result of a deliberate plot of the Muslims, since the khatun's courtiers suggested to the kagan that she was poisoned.

With the assumption of foul play, the Khazars took revenge. Tabari wrote that, in 762, the Khazars and other Turks passed

Derbent and headed south, killing Muslims in Armenia.[18] As (Ras) Tarkhan, a Khwarizmian mercenary, was the commander of the Khazar army.[19] Thousands of Georgians were captured around this time. During 763 and 764, the Khazars tried to capture Yazid, but he fled; even so, many Muslims were killed. In 764, Khazar soldiers occupied Albanian territories in Azerbaijan, and then took principalities in eastern Georgia (Grusia) and the city of Tbilisi (Tiflis). The Khazars also destroyed parts of Armenia in that year. In the end, As Tarkhan's horde retired northward with numerous captives and a substantial booty.[20]

Another story seems to resemble the account of Baghatur's daughter's marriage to Yazid. According to Georgian chroniclers, circa 796 or 797 a Khazar kagan learned that one of the four daughters of Georgian king Archil, the princess Shushan, was immensely beautiful, and he asked to marry her, promising to free Georgia (K'artl'i) from the K'aghrt' people.[21] Shushan's mother and brothers opposed such a marriage arrangement, but the kagan continued to insist on it. Three years later, the kagan sent the Khazar general Buljan (Bulch'an) with a large army to capture Shushan. Buljan's troops entered Kaxet' and encircled the fortress where Princess Shushan and her brother, Prince Juansher, lived. Soon afterward, his troops occupied Tbilisi and all of Georgia. Meanwhile, Shushan happened to be wearing a ring that had poison beneath its gemstone. She removed the gem and deliberately consumed the poison, preferring death to marrying the kagan; Prince Juansher buried her. The Khazar kagan was angry at Buljan for Shushan's death and for the fact that her corpse was not brought to his court, so he ordered his subordinates to tie a rope around Buljan's neck and sever his head. Juansher was allowed to return to Georgia after the kagan set him free seven years later.[22] Because of the similarities between this story and the aforementioned Yazid story, some scholars have suggested that the engagement of Shushan to the kagan may be a fictional epic tale.[23]

There is a third story based on the same theme. The governor of the south Caucasus territories, Fadhl ibn Yakhya al-Barmaki, attacked a Khazar fortress near Derbent in the 790s. Originally, he planned to marry a daughter of the Khazar kagan circa 798 or 799, but she died on the journey to Bardha'a.[24] Khazar nobles told the kagan that she died as a result of foul play. This infuriated the kagan greatly, and the kagan sent a large army into the south Caucasus with the purpose of generating destruction. This story closely resembles the stories of Yazid and Shushan, and it is not clear whether the episodes are completely historical or merely a recurrent motif. Thomas Noonan maintained that these related episodes were historical in nature and that they were, in fact, separate events,[25] despite their similarities.

The Georgian *eristavi* (prince) Nerses and Abo of Tbilisi, who later became a Christian saint, both visited Khazaria around 780. The *Life* of Saint Abo noted that the Khazar kagan warmly received Nerses and provided him and his companions with generous nourishment. Nerses told the kagan that his kingdom was engaged in combat with the Arabs, but the kagan refused to pledge the support of his army for Nerses' cause. Sometime after his visit to the Khazarian royal court, Saint Abo was baptized in Khazaria by a Christian priest, and died in January 786.

Abkhazia (Ap'xazet'i), a Byzantine dependency in western Georgia, was ruled by the Christian eristavi Leon II, a grandson of the then-reigning Khazar kagan, around the 780s.[26] Leon II proclaimed the independence of Abkhazia from the Byzantines, and in 786 the Khazar kagan lent his support to the quest for Abkhazia's freedom. As a result of these circumstances, Abkhazia became a dependency of Khazaria toward the end of the eighth century, as ibn Rustah recorded.[27]

Several further conflicts destroyed the fragile Arab-Khazar peace. Sa'id ibn Salm, the governor of Armenia around the year 796, executed Najm ibn Hashim, the Arab commander of Al-Bab (Derbent). As a result, Najm's son obtained the support of a large Khazar army, which ravaged the south Caucasus. In 799, the Khazar kagan and his army traveled with the rebel Hayyun (son of Najm ibn Hashim) toward the south Caucasus, where they harmed many Muslims and inflicted much damage.[28] This Khazar army continued its invasion as far as the Araxes River in Azerbaijan. This was the last major Khazar raid against Arabs in Transcaucasia.

The Khazars gained many new affiliates just north of the Caucasus range in the beginning of the tenth century. Shandan, a nation northwest of Derbent, allied with Khazaria in 912.[29] When, in 909 or 912, the Muslim rulers of Shirvan (a region in Azerbaijan) and al-Bab attacked Shandan, the Khazars and the Sarir sent them away.[30] The king of Shirvan circa 912 or 913, 'Ali ibn Haytham, died in battle against the Khazars.

Around 916 or 917, a Khazar army assisted the *salifan* (prince) of Qaytaq (Khaydaq) in the rescue of the amir of al-Bab, 'Abd-al-Malik ibn Hashim, after 'Abd-al-Malik solicited help from the Khazars.[31] 'Abd-al-Malik had taken power on January 4, 916, but his nephew Abul-Najm vigorously opposed his rule. The combined Khazar-Qaytaq forces succeeded in capturing Abul-Najm and his associates,[32] and 'Abd-al-Malik retained his rightful position as amir.

These events make it clear that the Khazars were involved in the affairs of the Caucasus on an ongoing basis, at times playing a historically significant role.

RELATIONS WITH THE BYZANTINE EMPIRE

The Byzantines and the Khazars had a long period of relations, starting in the seventh century.

The Byzantine emperor Heraclius formed a military alliance with the Khazars in 626 as a bloc against the Persians. The alliance came about as the result of a meeting in 626 at Tbilisi between Heraclius and Ziebil, the kagan of the western Turkish Empire (including Khazaria), following a Khazar-Turkic expedition to Azerbaijan. When he was offered marriage to Heraclius' daughter, named Epiphania[33] or Eudocia,[34] Ziebil offered forty thousand men to serve in the Byzantine army as an auxiliary force. Although Ziebil was engaged to Eudocia, he died circa 630 in an internal dispute.[35]

Under the terms of the alliance, the Byzantines and the Khazars jointly fought against the forces of Persian emperor Khusrau (Chosroes) II Parviz. The Byzantine and Khazar troops were able to destroy the Sassanid Persian state after winning the Battle of Nineveh (627). Khusrau II was killed by the spring of 628, and the Persians were forced to sign a peace treaty with Byzantium.

Activities then shifted from Persia to the south Caucasus. Kagan Ziebil's forty thousand horsemen invaded and plundered Tbilisi in 628 or 629 and were immensely successful. The Khazars took many prisoners and treasures in their conquest of Tbilisi, as Bartha explained:

> The great variety of precious vessels seized by the Khazars is remarkable: there were dishes, platters, cups, goblets, drinking-horns and big drinking-vessels called "tsorom."[36]

Viroy, a Christian church leader (*catholicos*), met the Khazar warriors at their victory camp and observed them holding a celebratory feast, consisting of wine, camel's milk, and cold meat dipped in salty water.

The Khazars also occupied the Qabala region (east of Shakki, in ancient Albania and present-day northern Azerbaijan) in the late 620s.[37] The Khazars gave the Caucasian Albanians an ultimatum: Either surrender and become vassals to the Khazar state, or males over fifteen years of age would be slaughtered and women and children would become enslaved.[38] The Caucasian Albanians were able to prevent their demise by handing over a large fortune to the Khazars' army commander. All of the Caucasian Albanian prisoners were subsequently released by the Khazars. Still, territories in Caucasian Albania, as well as Derbent and Lp'ink', became incor-

porated into the Khazar realm. People living along the Kur
and Araxes Rivers were taxed by the Khazars around 629–
630.[39] Similarly, in 629 the Khazar kagan imposed taxes on the
people of Tbilisi and directed Khazarian government officials
to control artwork, metal production, fishing, and commercial activities.[40] A Khazar army invaded Armenia and successfully fought back against Persian counterattacks. Thus, the
Khazars ruled Georgia, Caucasian Albania, and part of Armenia during this time, but the Byzantines held onto most of Armenia.

Around 630, the western Turkish kagan was overthrown
after internal disputes (see Chapter 1). As a consequence, the
Khazars' dominance over the southern Caucasus ended. The
Persians regained contol over Armenia and Azerbaijan by 632.
Furthermore, upon Ziebil's death, Emperor Heraclius lost his
alliance with Khazaria. Thus, this initial Byzantine-Khazar alliance lasted only about four years. Two other Byzantine-Khazar
royal marital engagements would follow in successive years, as
noted below.

In 695, after a revolt, the Byzantine emperor Justinian II
was deposed and exiled to the Crimean city of Cherson. Sometime between 700 and 704, Justinian II left Cherson and fled
to Doros. It was around this time that he entered into relations with a royal Khazar woman. He asked the Khazar kagan
Busir[41] for asylum. The kagan fulfilled this request and allowed
him to marry his (the kagan's) sister, Theodora. The marriage
between Justinian II and Theodora took place in around the
year 703 or 704. After her marriage to the emperor, Theodora
became a Christian.[42] Theodora and Justinian II settled in
Tmutorokan and had a son named Tiberius, who was born
in Khazaria while Justinian II was abroad. Tiberius, their only
son, was killed at the age of six.

Soon after the marriage, friendly ties ceased to exist between Justinian II and the Khazars. For example, the chronicler Theophanes wrote that the Khazar kagan instructed
Papatzi (the Khazar representative in Tmutorokan) and

Balghitzi (the baliqchi of Bosporus) to kill Justinian II. The kagan gave this instruction because he was tempted by the new Byzantine emperor Apsimar-Tiberius, who, in the words of Vasiliev, "promised him rich presents if he would deliver up Justinian, living or dead."[43] After a slave of the kagan told Theodora about her husband's "death sentence," she proceeded to warn him. The kagan tried to prevent Justinian II from escaping from Tmutorokan by placing him under a guard's watch, but he escaped (circa 704).

In 705, Justinian II was again restored to his former position as Byzantine emperor. He sought war as a mechanism of revenge against the Khazars, who had seized control of Cherson. The Khazar tudun who presided over Cherson at this time was named Zoilus. Justinian II sent forces to Cherson to reclaim it for his empire; as a result, a great many of the people of Cherson (including Crimean nobles) were tortured and executed, and Tudun Zoilus and other officials and nobles were imprisoned and sent to Constantinople.[44] Justinian II was forced to return the Khazar tudun to Cherson after the city's newly installed rulers sought the kagan's assistance. The tudun died while being returned, so Khazar soldiers killed numerous Byzantine troops. The people of Cherson rejected the authority of Justinian II and pledged their support to Philippicus (Bardanes), an Armenian. Justinian II sent another expedition to Cherson to fight with Khazar troops. Philippicus fled the scene and sought sanctuary with the kagan. A curious thing happened next: The members of the Byzantine army, who were being directed by Justinian II, eventually supported Philippicus instead.

The Khazars allied with Cherson's rebels in 711 and thus directly helped to overthrow Justinian II. Consequently, Philippicus became the new Byzantine emperor in 711, when Justinian II was assassinated. After Justinian II's final deposition in 711, the Khazars restored friendly relations with the Byzantine rulers; yet, a military conspiracy in 713 dethroned Philippicus.

The third engagement between the royal houses of the Khazars and the Byzantines was between Emperor Constantine V, the son of Emperor Leo III, and the Khazar princess Chichek (Chichak).[45] In 730, Leo III sent envoys to the kagan to request that his son be married to her. The marriage took place in either 732 or 733. Chichek was known as Tzitzakion by the Byzantines, and her name means "flower" in Turkic.[46] Chichek adopted the Christian name Irene after her marriage to Constantine V. The son of Chichek and Constantine V was Leo IV (b. January 25, 749), known as "the Khazar," who reigned as Byzantine emperor from 775 to 780. Chichek died in 752.[47] The genealogy of Leo IV's family is given in Table 7-1.

Some Byzantines other than royalty also claimed Khazar roots. Photius (b. about 820, d. about 891), a Byzantine philosopher and Patriarch of Constantinople (from 858–867 and again from 877–886), was partly Khazarian in origin.[48]

Some Khazar warriors served the Byzantine Empire in the late ninth century. Khazars served as imperial bodyguards for the Byzantine emperor Leo VI "the Wise" (reigned 886–912). When Leo VI's soldiers attacked the forces of Bulgarian emperor Simeon I, during the Bulgar-Byzantine War of 894–897, the Bulgars struck back, soundly defeating the Byzantine army and capturing the Khazar bodyguards. Ibn Rustah wrote circa 903 about Khazar guards at the gates of the palace in Constantinople.[49] Khazar guards were also stationed at the gates of the palace circa 950, during the reign of Constantine VII Porphyrogenitus (913–959), and they were often in attendance at Byzantine feasts and ceremonies.[50]

Byzantine-Khazar relations deteriorated by the mid-tenth century (see Chapter 6 on King Joseph's retaliation against Romanus I, and see Chapter 8 on the Byzantine-assisted destruction of Georgius Tzul's kaganate in 1016). The last mutually cooperative venture between the two empires was the construction of Sarkel's fortress in the 830s (see Chapter 2). One explanation for the hostility Byzantium directed toward

Khazaria in the tenth century is Khazaria's conversion to Judaism in 861. The Jewish kingdom was seen as a threat to Orthodox Christianity. The persecution of Jews by Byzantine emperors (see Chapter 6) was matched by an equal animosity toward the Jewish king of Khazaria.

RELATIONS WITH THE ALANS

The Alans, a people of the Caucasus who spoke an Iranian language, did not have a consistent diplomatic relationship with Khazaria. They were allied with the Khazars on certain occasions, yet fought them bitterly at other times.

As mentioned earlier in this chapter, the Khazars cooperated militarily with the Alans in around the year 655. This association did not last into the eighth century. For instance, it is known from the chronicles of Tabari and Ya'qubi that the Khazars attacked the Alans in 721–722. The *Schechter Letter* reported that King Sabriel—who probably can be identified as Bulan—made peace with the Alan king,[51] whose name is not given. The *Letter* did not describe the earlier Alan-Khazar relations, but it can be assumed that they were less than cordial. This peace treaty gave the Khazars a new valuable and mighty ally. The other nations developed a fear of the Khazars, but the possibility that another war might stir up between Khazaria and other nations always existed. During the war of the Burtas, Oghuz, Byzantines, Pechenegs, and Black Bulgars against the Khazars, the Alans maintained their allegiance to Khazaria, since some of them observed Jewish religious laws.[52] The Alan king successfully fought back against the enemies of Khazaria.

Benjamin was the king of the Khazars around the year 920.[53] The Burtas (steppe Alans or As) were among Benjamin's multiple enemies.

Benjamin's successor was King Aaron, who ruled in the early 930s.[54] According to the *Letter*, the Byzantine emperor persuaded the Alan king to fight against the Khazars, and thus

the Alan king became one of Aaron's most formidable enemies. King Aaron quickly took measures to counteract this
dangerous situation. After requesting help from the Oghuz
king, Aaron hired Oghuz troops to go to battle against the
Alan king, who was captured and sent to Aaron.[55] However,
in an amazing turn of events, the Alan and Khazar kings soon
became allies. This new alliance had two important consequences. First of all, Aaron's son Joseph married the Alan
king's daughter. Second, the Alans rejected Christianity[56] and
more of them fully embraced the Judaism of the Khazars (see
Chapter 10).

Unfortunately, Khazaria's latest alliance with Alania was a
short-lived one. The Alan-Khazar friendship, which had been
forged on both political and religious dimensions, reverted to
hostility after Aaron's reign ended and Joseph took power,
even though at first Joseph and the Alan ruler had cordial ties.
Thus, in the middle of the tenth century, Emperor Constantine VII Porphyrogenitus recorded in *De administrando imperio* (circa 950) that the Byzantines supported the Alans
against the Khazars.[57] Constantine VII wrote that the Alans
would bring much hardship and cause great damage to the
Khazar land if a war were to break out between the Alans and
the Khazars.

RELATIONS WITH OTHER
TURKIC TRIBES

The Turkic Oghuz people (also known as Torks, Uz, and
Ghuzz) allied with the Khazars in wars against the Pechenegs
at the end of the ninth century.[58] In 913, the Khazars and
Oghuz forced the Pechenegs to vacate the area between the
Volga and Ural Rivers and move westward.[59]

The Khazar-Oghuz alliance lasted until the ascendancy of
Benjamin to the Khazar throne. In addition to the Burtas,
King Benjamin counted among his enemies the Byzantines,
the Oghuz, and the Pechenegs, as reported by the *Schechter*

Letter. Gardizi wrote about the Khazar wars with the Pechenegs, Oghuz, and Burtas, and Gardizi and ibn Rustah both mentioned that the Khazars raided the Pechenegs on an annual basis.[60] In his famous travelogue, ibn Fadlan recorded that the Khazar king held Oghuz hostages in 922.[61] Yet, while the Khazars warred against the Oghuz in around 921, the *Schechter Letter* reported that King Aaron allied with them in a war that took place in 932.[62] Several years later, during the reign of King Joseph, the Khazars entered into an alliance with the Oghuz, Circassians, Burtas, Bab al-Abwab, and the "Northmen."

The Bulgars and the Khazars, while blood relatives, started to go their separate ways by the tenth century. Politically and religiously, the Bulgars became quite distinct from Khazaria and its Judaism. In 922, the Volga Bulgars adopted Islam as their state religion and built mosques and schools. The Bulgars also adopted the Arabic script in place of the Turkic runic script. Almush, son of Prince Shilki, was the Volga Bulgar el-teber (ruler) in 921 or 922. Ibn Fadlan visited Volga Bulgharia in 922 and reported that the Khazar king wanted to marry one of Khan Almush's daughters, but was unsuccessful since one died and the other already was married to another ruler.[63] The Bulgars of the Ural Mountains established Volga Bulgharia as a fully independent state after the conquest of Khazaria by the Rus. In 1236, the Mongols conquered Volga Bulgharia and destroyed its autonomous existence.

The Khazars maintained close contact with the Huns of the north Caucasus. Alp, the el-teber of the North Caucasian Huns around the late seventh century, was a Khazar vassal who often lent assistance to the Khazar kagan's forces during battle.[64] After Alp invaded Caucasian Albania and took much booty, he married the kagan's daughter. Chat-Khazr ("Chat the Khazr") served as an ambassador and chamberlain of the Hunnic prince Awch'i T'arkhan in the Huns' capital city, Varach'an, according to the late-tenth-century Armenian historian Moses Kalankatvats'i.[65]

RELATIONS WITH THE HUNGARIANS

The Magyars (Hungarians) came into contact with the Khazars during the course of their multiple westward migrations. Most of the Magyars left their old homeland and resettled in Lebedia (Levedia) in the first half of the eighth century, continuing to live there until the middle of the following century. Lebedia was located within the borders of the Khazar Empire, and included the lands between the River Don, the Donets River, and the Sea of Azov.

The early Magyars were connected with Turkic culture. This explains why early Slavic and Byzantine sources called the Magyars *Ungroi* (Onogurs), *Ungry, Unnoi,* and *Turkoi.*[66] Constantine VII Porphyrogenitus wrote (circa 950) that the Magyars in Lebedia were allied with the Khazars.[67] The Magyars and the Khazars fought many wars against common enemies.

Most Magyar tribal names were Turkic in origin.[68] In addition, hundreds of words of Turkic origin exist in the modern Hungarian language. The following are some examples of Turkic words in Hungarian (C = Chuvashic; K = Khazar; OH = Old Hungarian; T = Turkic):[69]

Magyar	*Khazar/Turkic*
alma ("apple")	T: alma ("apple")
atya ("father, patriarch")	T: ata ("father)
búza ("wheat")	T: bughdai ("wheat")
csicsóka ("Jerusalem artichoke, a weed plant with large yellow flowers")	K, T: chichek ("flower")
etel ("river," in OH)	K: atil ("large river"), C: as-til ("great waters")
érdem ("merit, worth")	T: erdäm ("merit, worth")
jobagy (ruler title, in OH)	K: yabghu, T: jabghu (ruler title)

kende, künde ("sacral, theocratic king")	K, T: kender ("sub-king")
köldök ("navel")	T: kindik, C: kentek ("navel")
sárga ("yellow")	T: sarigh ("yellow")
sátor ("tent")	K: chater, T: chadir ("canvas, tent")
tábor ("camp")	K: tovar, T: tabur ("camp")
talyiga ("wagon, cart, wheelbarrow")	K: talyga ("wagon, chariot")
teve ("camel")	T: deve ("camel")
túzok ("bustard")	T: toghdaq ("bustard")

Other Magyar words of Turkic origin include betú ("letter"), disznó "(hog"), gyapjú ("wool"), ír ("writes"), szó ("word"), and tyúk ("hen"). Historians have not reached a consensus on whether the Turkic words in Hungarian were derived from the Khazar language or from the Bulgar or some other language. According to István Fodor, many of the words encompassing agriculture, horticulture, animals, and dairy products came into the Hungarian language from the Bulgar tongue.[70] Even if it is true that the Magyars borrowed these words from the Bulgars, the Bulgar words were probably similar to the Khazar equivalents, since the Bulgar language was closely related to the Khazar language (see Chapter 4).

Around the year 833, the Magyars were still living between the Don and the Dnieper. Then, around 840–850, the Magyars were forced to migrate from Lebedia to the region known as Etelköz (Etelküzü).[71] They were driven westward from Khazaria by the Pechenegs of the Pontic steppes.[72] Etelköz included territories between the Dnieper and the Dniester (including the plain between the Pruth and the Dniester), as well as some lands to the west and east of these two rivers. The Magyars remained residents of Etelköz until 894–896.

After the Pechenegs forced the Magyars to leave Lebedia for Etelköz, the Khazar kagan advised the seven Magyar tribes to unite under one prince. According to Constantine VII Porphyrogenitus, a Khazar kagan gave a noble Khazar woman in marriage to the Magyars' top chief (*voievoda*)—one of several chiefs presiding over the seven Magyar tribes—whose name was Levéd (variants: Lebedias or Elöd), in return for his military assistance and bravery.[73] The kagan offered Levéd kingship over all Magyars under Khazar suzerainty. Levéd refused to become king of all the Magyars since he was childless, and suggested that the kingship instead be given to Álmos or Álmos' son, Árpád. Thus, the forefather of the Árpád dynasty, Álmos (son of Úgyek), was elected as Magyar prince in Etelköz. Under Álmos, the Magyars took control of Kiev by 840.[74] The presence of Magyars in the Kiev region in the late ninth century is evidenced by the Ugorskoye site near Kiev.[75] Álmos's successor, Árpád, was installed (circa 890) as the next Magyar chief by the Khazars' customary procedure. It became customary for Magyar kings to be chosen from the descendants of Árpád, and the Árpád dynasty lasted until 1301, when King Andrew III died childless.

Ibn Rustah described Etelköz as a fertile land abounding in trees and water and capable of sustaining agriculture. During their domination of Etelköz, the Magyars imprisoned Slavs and sold them as slaves to the Byzantines at Kerch.[76] Yet, the East Slavs of Kiev and the Magyars generally had good relations.[77]

During the period of the Magyars' residency at Etelköz, the Khazars had not yet integrated themselves with the Magyars. In 881, for instance, the Kabars were fighting near Vienna separately from the warriors of the seven Magyar tribes.[78] However, in 894, Levente, Árpád's oldest son, led a Kabar army against Bulgaria,[79] indicating the emergence of closer ties.

Most Hungarian scholars agree that the Khazars influenced the governmental structure of the early Hungarians. The

Magyars adopted the Khazars' dual-kingship system, for they had a *kende* (chief "sacral king," first-in-command) and a *gyula* (second-in-command and the actual manager of state affairs, including the army). Árpád was the second gyula. The Magyars also had a third-in-command, called the *harka*. Eventually, the gyula became more important than the kende, just as in the Khazar Empire, where the bek's power came to overshadow that of the kagan.

In 893, a new series of westward migrations was triggered by Ismail ibn Ahmed, the amir of the Iranian Samanid dynasty, who attacked the Oghuz and drove away their herds.[80] The Pechenegs, who formerly dwelled between the Ural and the Volga, in turn were forced by the Oghuz to go across the Volga, and they also crossed the Don. The Pechenegs allied with the Danube Bulgars and attacked the Magyars of Etelköz. This attack forced the Magyars to flee westward into the Carpathian Basin (in 895–896). This migration is commemorated by the Hungarians to this day.

Even after 896, when the Hungarians settled in central Europe, the Khazars lived among them and mixed with them (see Chapter 9).

RELATIONS WITH THE RUS

The relations of the Khazar Empire with the Rus can be characterized as turbulent and aggressive. The Khazar Empire was almost constantly at war with the Rus, as King Joseph related in his *Reply to Hasdai ibn Shaprut*. Extensive coverage of the Rus-Khazar conflicts and their devastating consequences for the Khazars may be found in Chapter 8.

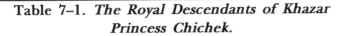

Table 7–1. *The Royal Descendants of Khazar Princess Chichek.*

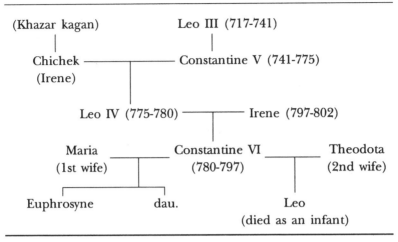

NOTES

1. Douglas M. Dunlop, "The Khazars," in *The Dark Ages*, ed. Cecil Roth and I. H. Levine (New Brunswick, NJ: Rutgers University Press, 1966), p. 326.

2. Thomas S. Noonan, "Why Dirhams First Reached Russia: The Role of Arab-Khazar Relations in the Development of the Earliest Islamic Trade with Eastern Europe," *Archivum Eurasiae Medii Aevi* 4 (1984): 179.

3. Ibid., p. 183. One of General Maslama's most powerful enemies was a Khazar chief named Samsam (al-Simsam), who became the administrator of the village of Mukrak (Mikrakh), located on the Samur River in the Lakz area (on the left bank of the Usugh-chay), during the Khazars' domination of Shirvan (see Vladimir F. Minorsky, *A History of Sharvan and Darband in the Tenth through Eleventh Centuries* (Cambridge, England: W. Heffer & Sons, 1958), p. 81).

4. Douglas M. Dunlop, "The Khazars," in *The Dark Ages*, p. 329; Thomas S. Noonan, "Why Dirhams First Reached Russia. . .," pp. 183–184.

5. Svetlana A. Pletnyova, *Khazary* (Moscow: Nauka, 1986), p. 26.

6. Thomas S. Noonan, "Why Dirhams First Reached Russia. . .," p. 184. Some residents of Balanjar went as far north as Volga Bulgharia. Thousands of "Baranjars" who had adopted Islam were encountered there by ibn Fadlan in 922.

7. Ibid., p. 187. Only about a hundred Arab soldiers escaped alive.

8. Douglas M. Dunlop, "The Khazars," in *The Dark Ages*, p. 329.

9. Thomas S. Noonan, "Why Dirhams First Reached Russia. . .," p. 188.

10. Károly Czeglédy, "Khazar Raids in Transcaucasia in 762–764 A.D.," *Acta Orientalia Academiae Scientiarum Hungaricae* 11 (1960): 75.

11. George Vernadsky, *A History of Russia*, vol. 1 (New Haven, CT: Yale University Press, 1948), p. 222.

12. Vladimir F. Minorsky, *Hudud al-'Alam (The Regions of the World)* (London: Luzac & Co., 1937), p. 452.

13. Peter B. Golden, *Khazar Studies*, vol. 1 (Budapest: Akadémiai, 1980), p. 65. The kagan had a conversation with two Muslim faqihs—Nukh ibn al-Sa'ib al-Asadi and 'Abd-al-Rahman al-Khawlani—who were sent to him by Marwan. When the faqihs told the kagan about Islam's prohibition of consuming wine and certain meats, he asked them whether he could be exempted from the prohibition. They instructed him that no deviation from the law of Islam would be permitted. He finally gave in to their pressure and adopted their faith. If the kagan had continued to resist Islam, he would have been slain.

14. Thomas S. Noonan, "Why Dirhams First Reached Russia. . .," pp. 198–199.

15. Douglas M. Dunlop, *The History of the Jewish Khazars* (New York: Schocken, 1967), p. 87.

16. Károly Czeglédy, "Khazar Raids in Transcaucasia in 762–764 A.D.," p. 79.

17. Ibid., p. 80.

18. Ibid., p. 81.

19. Vladimir F. Minorsky, *Hudud al-'Alam (The Regions of the World)*, p. 451.

20. Paul Peeters, "Les Khazars dans la Passion de S. Abo de Tiflis," *Analecta Bollandiana* 52 (1934): 33.

21. *K'art'lis C'xovreba (The Georgian Chronicle)*, ed. Robert Bedrosian (New York: Sources of the Armenian Tradition, 1991), p. 97.

22. Xosroydis, the ostikan (governor) of Armenia, rebuilt Tbilisi to recover it from the devastation the Khazars had wreaked on it.

23. Paul Peeters, "Les Khazars dans la Passion de S. Abo de Tiflis," p. 51.

24. Thomas S. Noonan, "Why Dirhams First Reached Russia. . .," p. 246.

25. Ibid., p. 247.

26. Peter B. Golden, *Khazar Studies*, vol. 1, pp. 65–66. Leon II's mother was the daughter of the Khazar kagan. Abkhazia had been a part of the Byzantine Empire since 523.

27. Vladimir F. Minorsky, "A New Book on the Khazars," *Oriens* 11 (1959): 129. The Kingdom of Abkhazia lasted until 978.

28. Vladimir F. Minorsky, *A History of Sharvan and Darband in the 10th–11th Centuries*, p. 69.

29. Ibid., p. 102.

30. Ibid., p. 106.

31. Ibid., pp. 70, 93. The region of Qaytaq was located near the Darbakh River, northwest of Derbent.

32. Ibid., p. 43.

33. John J. Norwich, *Byzantium: The Early Centuries* (New York: Alfred A. Knopf, 1989), p. 294.

34. Paul Peeters, "Les Khazars dans la Passion de S. Abo de Tiflis," p. 50.

35. Thomas S. Noonan, "Why Dirhams First Reached Russia...," p. 176.

36. Antal Bartha, *Hungarian Society in the 9th and 10th Centuries*, trans. K. Balazs (Budapest: Akadémiai, 1975), p. 140.

37. Vladimir F. Minorsky, *A History of Sharvan and Darband in the 10th–11th Centuries*, p. 17.

38. Thomas S. Noonan, "Why Dirhams First Reached Russia...," pp. 174–175.

39. Ibid., p. 175.

40. Antal Bartha, *Hungarian Society in the 9th and 10th Centuries*, p. 104.

41. Busir was also known as Ibousir-Glavan and Glavianos.

42. George Ostrogorsky, *History of the Byzantine State* (New Brunswick, NJ: Rutgers University Press, 1969), p. 142.

43. Alexander A. Vasiliev, *The Goths in the Crimea* (Cambridge, MA: The Mediaeval Academy of America, 1936), p. 81.

44. Ibid., p. 82; Thomas S. Noonan, "Byzantium and the Khazars: a special relationship?" in *Byzantine Diplomacy*, ed. Jonathan Shepard and Simon Franklin (Aldershot, England: Variorum, 1992), p. 112.

45. Peter B. Golden, *Khazar Studies*, vol. 1, p. 65.

46. The Byzantines named a certain type of ceremonial robe *tzitzakion* in honor of Chichek (see Arthur Koestler, *The Thirteenth Tribe* (New York: Random House, 1976), p. 48).

47. Károly Czeglédy, "Khazar Raids in Transcaucasia in 762–764 A.D.," p. 78.

48. Omeljan Pritsak, "The Khazar Kingdom's Conversion to Judaism," *Harvard Ukrainian Studies* 3:2 (Sept. 1978): 267.

49. Douglas M. Dunlop, *The History of the Jewish Khazars*, p. 219.

50. Ibid. Many of these events were Christian, such as Easter and the Feast of the Nativity.

51. Norman Golb and Omeljan Pritsak, *Khazarian Hebrew Documents of the Tenth Century* (Ithaca, NY: Cornell University Press, 1982), p. 113.

52. Ibid., pp. 113, 115.

53. Constantine Zuckerman, "On the Date of the Khazars' Conversion to Judaism and the Chronology of the Kings of the Rus Oleg and Igor," *Revue des Études Byzantines* 53 (1995): 254.

54. Ibid., p. 255.

55. Norman Golb and Omeljan Pritsak, *Khazarian Hebrew Documents of the Tenth Century*, p. 115.

56. Constantine Zuckerman, "On the Date of the Khazars' Conversion to Judaism. . .," p. 255.

57. Alexander A. Vasiliev, *The Goths in the Crimea*, p. 117.

58. Antal Bartha, *Hungarian Society in the 9th and 10th Centuries*, p. 60.

59. René Grousset, *The Empire of the Steppes*, trans. Naomi Waldorf (New Brunswick, NJ: Rutgers University Press, 1970), p. 182.

60. Constantine Zuckerman, "On the Date of the Khazars' Conversion to Judaism. . .," p. 254.

61. Arthur Koestler, *The Thirteenth Tribe*, p. 42.

62. Constantine Zuckerman, "On the Date of the Khazars' Conversion to Judaism. . .," p. 254.

63. Arthur Koestler, *The Thirteenth Tribe*, p. 43.

64. Thomas S. Noonan, "Why Dirhams First Reached Russia...," p. 180.

65. Vladimir F. Minorsky, *Hudud al-'Alam (The Regions of the World)*, p. 411; Peter B. Golden, *An Introduction to the History of the Turkic Peoples* (Wiesbaden, Germany: Otto Harrassowitz, 1992), p. 234.

66. Z. J. Kosztolnyik, *Five Eleventh Century Hungarian Kings* (New York: Columbia University Press, 1981), p. xi.

67. István Fodor, *In Search of a New Homeland*, trans. Helen Tarnoy (Gyoma, Hungary: Corvina, 1982), p. 213.

68. Antal Bartha, *Hungarian Society in the 9th and 10th Centuries*, p. 57.

69. Some of these examples come from the following sources: ibid., pp. 50–52; István Fodor, *In Search of a New Homeland*, p. 233; Lajos M. Ligeti, "The Khazarian Letter from Kiev and Its Attestation in Runiform Script," *Acta Linguistica Academiae Scientiarum Hungaricae* 31 (1981): 15. I wish to thank the linguists Alfred Hámori and Paolo Agostini for their additional suggestions.

70. István Fodor, *In Search of a New Homeland*, pp. 224–225. According to Fodor (idem., pp. 226–227), Hungarian also has some words of Alan origin, which were added to the Magyar vocabulary during the residence of the Magyars among the Iranian Alans and Turkic Bulgars of the Saltovo region. Alan words in Hungarian include *üveg* ("glass," from the Alan word *avg*), *hid* ("bridge"), *vért* ("armor, breastplate"), *zold* ("green"), *gazdag* ("rich"), and *vendeg* ("guest"). Fodor theorized that most of the Alans of the River Don region eventually adopted the Bulgar language in its entirety, and the stones of the Mayaki Castle, located in the Alan territory of Saltovo, were inscribed with Turkic runic letters (see idem., p. 226). Clearly, then, Saltovo was a multiethnic region in which words of both Turkic and Iranian origin could be transmitted to the wandering Magyars.

71. Ibid., pp. 239–240.

72. Antal Bartha, *Hungarian Society in the 9th and 10th Centuries*, p. 64; Peter B. Golden, *Khazar Studies*, vol. 1, p. 76; René Grousset, *The Empire of the Steppes*, p. 181.

73. Carlile A. Macartney, *The Magyars in the Ninth Century* (Cambridge, England: Cambridge University Press, 1930), pp. 229–230.

74. George Vernadsky, *A History of Russia*, vol. 1, p. 332.

75. Vladimir Ia. Petrukhin, "The Normans and the Khazars in the South of Rus' (The Formation of the 'Russian Land' in the Middle Dnepr Area," *Russian History/Histoire russe* 19 (1992): pp. 396–397.

76. István Fodor, *In Search of a New Homeland*, pp. 251–252.

77. Ibid., pp. 258–259.

78. György Györffy, *King Saint Stephen of Hungary*, trans. Peter Doherty (New York: Columbia University Press, 1994), p. 27. This information derives from *Annales Iuvavenses maximi*, which referred to the battle of the "Cowari" at Culmite.

79. Ibid., p. 42.

80. Ibid., p. 16.

8

THE DECLINE AND FALL OF THE KHAZAR EMPIRE

Ultimately, the Khazars lost their kingdom on account of the military actions of the Rus, Byzantines, and Mongols. This chapter explores the events that led to Khazaria's defeat.

THE BEGINNING OF THE END

The first Rus kaganate was founded on the middle Volga during the 830s.[1] By 885, the East Slavic tribes were united and began to grow in strength, eclipsing Khazar power in the tenth century.[2] At the same time, wandering merchants and pirates from Scandinavia, called "Varang" by the Khazars and "Al-Pharange" by al-Masudi, began to integrate themselves into Kievan Rus. The Varangian chiefs were called *köl-beki* ("kings of the sea")[3] because, unlike the Khazar chiefs, they led a large number of ships.

The Khazars became entangled in various disputes with the Rus and the Daghestanis in the tenth century. For example,

189

in August 901, Khazar troops led by their "king," Tun-Kisa ibn Buljan al-Khazari, attacked the city of Derbent.[4] However, they were defeated by Muhammad ibn Hashim and the *ghazis* (Muslim warriors and freebooters) of the al-Bab region.

The Arab historian al-Masudi recorded a dramatic sequence of events in which the Khazars inflicted a serious blow on the ambitious Rus'ians.[5] Around 913, the Khazar king allowed five hundred Rus ships to voyage down the Volga, as long as they agreed to present the king with half of all booty they acquired. The Rus sailed past Atil and then traveled down the Caspian en route to Tabaristan and other coastal territories. However, the Rus began to engage in acts of pillage and violence. They killed many men, captured women and children, stole property, and burned villages. Afterward, the Rus returned northward and arrived at islands near Baku, where they slaughtered thousands of Muslims.

Several months after their stay in Baku, the Rus continued north and arrived at Atil. The Muslim Arsiya soldiers in Atil had heard that the Rus killed a multitude of their coreligionists in the Caucasus, and they notified the Khazar king of their intention to retaliate against them. The Arsiya who served the Khazar king were strong and possessed much equipment, so they felt prepared for battle. A large war broke out between the Rus and the Arsiya. Some of the Christians of Atil joined the fifteen thousand Arsiya Muslims. After a three-day battle, the Khazars emerged victorious over the Rus. Rus casualties totaled approximately thirty thousand men. Most of the Rus'ians were killed in the battle; only five thousand survived, and many of those who managed to escape up the Volga were killed by the Burtas and the Bulgars.

In 1822, Alexander Pushkin (1799–1837), a master of Russian poetry and prose, wrote a famous poem titled *The Lay of the Wise Oleg*. It declared that the Rus'ian Prince Oleg declared war on the Khazars because "The Khazars have awakened his ire; /For rapine and raid, hamlet, city, and plain/ He gives over to falchion and fire."[6] Despite the poem's assertion that Oleg's plundering led him to destroy Khazar villages and farms, and thus to attain fame and glory, the historical record shows that victory was not Oleg's ultimate destiny. The *Rus'ian Chronicle* also gave a romanticized view of Oleg's reign and declared that he died when a serpent bit him in the foot and poisoned him.[7]

A more accurate account, the *Schechter Letter*, described Oleg's activities in detail. The letter related that the Byzantine emperor Romanus I Lecapenus made overtures to the Rus king, Oleg, encouraging him to attack the Khazar city of Tmutorokan. Romanus I was reacting to King Joseph's actions against Christians in Khazaria (see Chapter 6). Oleg captured Tmutorokan one night while the military commander of Tmutorokan, the *rab hashmonai* ("Head of the Hasmoneans"), was away. Pesakh, a prominent Khazar *baliqchi*, learned of Oleg's actions and marched against several Crimean cities that belonged to the Byzantines. Pesakh conquered three cities and killed many men and women. Pesakh then came to Cherson, where he enslaved his enemies, killed all the Rus'ians he could find, and saved the Khazars who had been captured by the Rus. Pesakh also found the booty that Oleg had stolen from Tmutorokan. Oleg fought against the Khazar troops, but was forced to surrender to Pesakh.[8] The Khazars had again won a decisive victory over the Rus. This event occurred around the late 930s, according to Zuckerman.[9]

Oleg confessed to Pesakh that Romanus had enticed him to attack the Khazars. Pesakh then forced Oleg to make war against Romanus, so as to avoid another confrontation between the Khazars and the Rus. The Rus fought against Constantinople for four months at sea, from June to September in 941,[10] but they were defeated by the Byzantine navy. A large number of Oleg's troops died. Oleg and the remnants of his servicemen fled to "FRS"[11] and died there.

Prince Oleg died in the Persian Empire in 944 or 945.[12] His Rus'ian troops perished after raiding the south Caucasus, including the city of Bardha'a. Ibn Miskawayh wrote that the

Rus leader and seven hundred Rus'ian soldiers under his command were slain by troops led by Marzuban ibn Muhammad, ruler of Azerbaijan. Meanwhile, in the summer of 944, Igor, the new prince of Kievan Rus, signed a treaty with the Byzantines,[13] which guaranteed free trade and mutual assistance in times of war between the Byzantine Empire and Kievan Rus.

Hasdai ibn Shaprut's letter to King Joseph was sent from Spain to Hungarian Jews, to Rus, to Bulgars, and then to Khazars instead of directly from Kievan Rus to Khazaria, owing to hostilities between the Rus and the Khazars that continued throughout the mid-tenth century. In the mid-950s, King Joseph addressed the following remarks about Rus'ian raids in Khazaria to Hasdai:

> I live at the mouth of the river [Volga] and with the help of the Almighty I guard its entrance and prevent the Rus'ians who arrive in vessels from passing into the Caspian Sea for the purpose of making their way to the Ishmaelites [Arabs]. In the same manner, I keep these enemies on land from approaching the gates of Bab-al-Abwab [Derbent]. Because of this, I am at war with them, and were I to let them pass but once, they would destroy the whole land of the Ishmaelites as far as Baghdad.

This passage stressed the continuing turbulence between the Khazars and the Rus.

In 962, the Khazars, led by horsemen and aggressive foot soldiers, destroyed many villages and cities in Crimea to try to reassert their control over the region.[14] The Crimean Goths turned to the Rus for help in defending themselves against the Khazars. Svyatoslav answered their call for help, and set forth against the Khazar "barbarians" in the 960s.

THE RUS'IAN CONQUEST OF THE KHAZARS

An interesting prophetic legend that appears in the *Poviest' vremennykh lyet* (Story of the Times), the first section of the

Rus'ian Primary Chronicle, "predicted" the dominance of Kievan Rus over the Khazars by comparing the types of swords manufactured by each side. According to the legend, Khazar warriors approached the forested hills along the eastern shore of the Dnieper and demanded tribute payments from the Polianian Slavs who made this land their home. As a result, the Polianians gave the warriors one sword from every hut. Triumphant in their success, the warriors returned to the Khazar kagan and presented the Slavic swords to him. But the Khazar chieftains in the court warned that this tribute was a bad omen, for the Kievan swords were sharpened on both edges and were clearly superior to the Khazar swords, which were sharpened on only one edge.[15] The Khazar chieftains said: "Surely it will be that they will one day come to take tribute of us and of others."[16] Based on the inferior weaponry of the Khazars, the story foreshadowed the ascendancy of the Rus, who seized control of the south Russian and east Ukrainian lands and ended the Khazar era of political and military dominance.

A crushing blow was dealt to the Khazar Empire by Svyatoslav, Grand Duke of Kiev (ruled 962–972), the son of Prince Igor and Igor's wife Olga. His life was one of war and conquest. The *Rus'ian Primary Chronicle* recorded that, as part of his childhood upbringing, Svyatoslav was tutored by Asmund and instructed in military tactics by the *voievoda* (military commander) Svynel'd. Medieval accounts described him as a "valiant" and "strong" leader who "undertook many campaigns."

According to the *Rus'ian Primary Chronicle*, Svyatoslav conquered and seized the Khazar city of Sarkel, including its prized fortress, in 965.[17] A messenger warned the Khazars of the impending invasion in advance, so the Khazar warriors assembled on the battlefield and prepared to fight. The Khazar kagan joined his warriors during their losing battle against Svyatoslav. The details of what transpired on that fateful day remain sketchy. The number of casualties and hostages went

unrecorded. V. N. Tatishchev suggested that Svyatoslav resettled the Khazars he had captured at Sarkel on land near
the Ros' River.[18] Svyatoslav also subjugated the Alans and the
Circassians.

In 966, Svyatoslav asserted control over the Vyatichians (a
group of East Slavs) and began receiving tribute from them.
Two years earlier, Svyatoslav had asked them to whom they
paid tribute. At that time, the Vyatichians responded that they
paid one silver piece per plowshare to the Khazars.[19]

Ibn Hauqal wrote (around 975–977) that the Rus sailed
down the Volga after defeating the Bulgars and occupied the
city of Atil.[20] The seizure took place circa 967.[21] After the
conquest of Atil, the Khazars escaped. According to ibn
Hauqal, around 969 some Khazars from Atil sought refuge by
crossing the Caspian Sea until they reached an island called
Siyah-Kuh (Siacouye),[22] which was inhabited by Oghuz Turks.
Siyah-Kuh is equivalent to modern-day Manghishlaq, on the
northeastern coast of the Caspian. Another group of Khazars
went further south to another Caspian island, off the estuary
of the Terek River. A number of other Khazars fled to Baku.

Some of the Khazar refugees were attacked by Ma'mun ibn
Muhammad, the amir of Gurganj, who forced them to adopt
Islam.[23] However, Muhammad ibn Ahmad al-Azdi, the Muslim
shah of Shirvan, assisted some of the Khazars in returning to
Atil and Khazaran, although they became subject to the au-
thority of Shirvan.

The kagan of Khazaria converted to Islam in around 965–
967 in exchange for the support of Khwarizm. Al-Muqaddasi
wrote in 985 or 986 that he had heard of Arabs from
"Gurjania" attacking the Khazars and forcing the Khazar king
to accept Islam.[24] He also wrote that the Rus "conquered the
Khazars and seized their land."[25] Grand Prince Vladimir of
Kievan Rus (ruled 980–1015), son of Svyatoslav, gained con-
trol over part of the former Khazar territory, including
Tmutorokan, and the famous vineyards and gardens of
Samandar were burned. While most of the Khazars under

Khwarizmian control became Muslims, some Khazars resisted conversion. Khwarizmian troops occupied the cities of those Khazars who refused to convert to Islam.[26]

With the stunning defeat of the primary Khazar cities, Sarkel and Atil, the Rus effectively transferred control over the prestigious Volga and Don trade routes to the East Slavs. In the period following Svyatoslav's conquests, the Rus extensively colonized the Don and Donets valleys. Land was not all that the Slavs inherited from the Khazars. According to Julius Brutzkus, ancient Rus was indebted to the Khazar way of life for its customs, legal procedures, system of government, and military organization.[27] He also explained that Khazar words for clothing, utensils, trade, and transportation made their way into the early East Slavic language of Kievan Rus. Other words of Turkic origin, such as *bogatyr* (meaning "knight," from Khazarian *baghatur* or *bogatur* ["brave warrior"]), *telega* (meaning "wagon," from Khazarian *talyga* ["wagon, chariot"]), and *verv* (meaning "house community," from Khazarian *ver-evi* ["tribe town or house"]), were also added to the Rus'ian vocabulary.

THE PASSING OF THE KHAZAR EMPIRE

The Khazars maintained a degree of political independence until at least 1016. The last Khazar kagan was named Georgius Tzul, and he was apparently a Christian. Not much data are available on this kagan. Scholars are not certain whether Georgius Tzul ruled over the Crimea or the Taman peninsula, but it seems possible that he ruled over both regions. It has also been suggested that he ruled over a small territory between the Don, the Volga, and the Caucasus.

In 1016, Byzantine emperor Basil II and the Rus'ian army sent a combined force against the Khazars.[28] This collaborative force was led by Sfengus (brother of Grand Prince Vladimir) and Mongus. Georgius Tzul was imprisoned by the Rus, and the Khazars lost control of both the Crimean and

Taman peninsulas. It has been suggested that some members of the royal family of Khazaria—including the king—emigrated to Spain after their empire was destroyed.[29]

Some historians have maintained that Khazaria actually lasted for two additional centuries. Dunlop suggested that the Khazars may have revived their old town Sarighshin as Saqsin, a market town along the lower Volga, by the twelfth century.[30] Abraham N. Poliak, a professor at Tel Aviv University, claimed that the Jewish Khazar kingdom continued to exist until 1224, during the time of the Mongol invasions, although it was considerably reduced in size and strength.[31] However, it is difficult to verify these claims, because of sparse and insufficient documentation from the eleventh through the thirteenth centuries.

Some Italian documents used *Gazaria* as the term for the Crimea until the sixteenth century. Marco Polo (circa 1254–1324), for instance, wrote that the Mongols took "Gazaria" from the Cumans. Sanudo Marino also referred to the Mongol destruction of Gothia, Sugdiana, Alania, Kievan Rus, and "Gasaria" in the early 1240s. The Gothic prince Ioann (John), who emigrated to Trebizond (Trabzon) on the southern Black Sea coast with his Byzantine-Bulgarian wife Maria in the 1440s, was called "Lord of Khazaria."

The memory of the Khazars as a major power in steppeland affairs lingers in several languages, which call the Caspian Sea the "Khazar Sea": *Hazar Denizi* in Turkish, *Xêzêr Dênizi* in Azeri, *Bahr-ul-Khazar* in Arabic, and *Daryaye Khazar* in Persian.

REASONS FOR KHAZARIA'S DESTRUCTION

Douglas M. Dunlop believed that three major factors contributed to the downfall of Khazaria: the lack of natural frontiers for defense; the alleged lack of self-sufficiency for most resources; and the lack of homogeneity in the Khazarian population.[32] In addition, Dunlop thought that the Rus must have been displeased when the Khazars began to prohibit the Rus from traveling at the lower end of the Volga. Another important contributing factor was the fact that the Khazars did not possess a navy (see Chapter 4), while the Rus did. This disadvantage prevented the Khazars from remaining the masters of the seas in the same way that they were the masters of the land.

As the tenth century proceeded and Khazaria decreased in power, the Pechenegs expanded their control over parts of Crimea.[33] Peter Golden attributed the decline of Khazaria in part to the expansion of the Pechenegs.[34] As mentioned in Chapter 7, the Pechenegs forced the Magyars to migrate westward. In 968, the Pechenegs attacked Kiev. They had become a major force to contend with in eastern Europe.

The end of the Khazar Empire signified the beginning of a new era. No longer did the Jews of eastern Europe have a nation of their own. An independent Jewish state would not rise again until the establishment of Israel in 1948. Oghuric Turkic peoples no longer maintained dominance over eastern Europe's affairs after Khazaria ceased to exist.

Golden Horde Mongols controlled a large area of the former Khazar Empire around the Caspian Sea during the late Middle Ages, with their capital at Sarai in the Astrakhan area near the Volga.

As will be seen in Chapter 9, the Khazars largely survived the traumatic events described above, and continued to prosper in new environments and new nations.

NOTES

1. Omeljan Pritsak, "The Pre-Ashkenazic Jews of Eastern Europe in Relation to the Khazars, the Rus' and the Lithuanians," in *Ukrainian-Jewish Relations in Historical Perspective*, ed. Howard Aster and Peter J. Potichnyj (Edmonton: Canadian Institute of Ukrainian Studies Press, 1990), p. 4.

2. Peter B. Golden, *Khazar Studies*, vol. 1 (Budapest: Akadémiai, 1980), pp. 79–80.

3. Julius Brutzkus, "The Khazar Origin of Ancient Kiev," *Slavonic and East European Review* 22 (1944): 120.

4. Vladimir F. Minorsky, *A History of Sharvan and Darband in the 10th–11th Centuries* (Cambridge, England: W. Heffer & Sons, 1958), p. 42.

5. Ibid., pp. 151–153.

6. *The Poems, Prose, and Plays of Alexander Pushkin*, ed. Avrahm Yarmolinsky (New York: The Modern Library, 1964), p. 55.

7. *Medieval Russia's Epics, Chronicles, and Tales*, ed. Serge A. Zenkovsky (New York: Meridian, 1974), pp. 53–54. Pushkin's poem also included a reference to a snake wrapping itself around Oleg's legs and stinging him (see *The Poems, Prose, and Plays of Alexander Pushkin*, pp. 57–58).

8. This episode of the *Schechter Letter* is translated in Norman Golb and Omeljan Pritsak, *Khazarian Hebrew Documents of the Tenth Century* (Ithaca, NY: Cornell University Press, 1982), pp. 115, 117, 119.

9. Constantine Zuckerman, "On the Date of the Khazars' Conversion to Judaism and the Chronology of the Kings of the Rus Oleg and Igor," *Revue des Études Byzantines* 53 (1995): 256.

10. Ibid., p. 257.

11. Pritsak argued that "FRS" refers to the area along the south shore of the Caspian Sea (see Norman Golb and Omeljan Pritsak, *Khazarian Hebrew Documents of the Tenth Century*, p. 138).

12. Constantine Zuckerman, "On the Date of the Khazars' Conversion . . . ," p. 268.

13. Ibid., p. 266.

14. Alexander A. Vasiliev, *The Goths in the Crimea* (Cambridge, MA: The Mediaeval Academy of America, 1936), p. 129.

15. Archaeological evidence has confirmed that the east Slavs produced double-edged swords (see Antal Bartha, *Hungarian Society in the 9th and 10th Centuries*, trans. K. Balazs (Budapest: Akadémiai, 1975), p. 12; István Fodor, *In Search of a New Homeland*, trans. Helen Tarnoy (Gyoma, Hungary: Corvina, 1982), p. 255). It has also been determined that the Alans in Khazaria used sabers that were sharpened on only one edge.

16. Vasilii O. Kluchevsky, *A History of Russia*, trans. C. J. Hogarth, vol. 1 (New York: Russell & Russell, 1960), p. 51.

The legend concluded with the statement, ". . . so it has also come to pass that the Rus'ian princes rule over the Khazars even to this day."

17. *Medieval Russia's Epics, Chronicles, and Tales*, ed. Serge A. Zenkovsky, pp. 58–59. A variation on the episode concerning the capture of Sarkel's fortress was allegedly preserved by Circassian storytellers. In the tale "Sarkel Battle" by the Circassian bard Yakhutl' Shaban it is said that Hapach, son of Prince Weché (a ruler over the Bzhedukh territory), assembled a large number of horsemen to attack Sarkel (see John Colarusso, "Two Circassian Tales of Huns and Khazars," *The Annual of the Society for the Study of Caucasia* 4–5 (1992–1993): 68). The Khazarian defensive forces approached the invading horsemen, and a battle ensued. At the conclusion of the battle, the "Great Prince of Sarkel" and other Khazars were imprisoned with their legs in shackles. The remainder of the tale praises the heroic deeds of Prince Shawel, who struck fear into the Khazars with his powerful bow and curved sword. John Colarusso suggested that the tale indicates that an alliance had been formed between Circassians and Svyatoslav's Rus'ian forces, since Circassians sometimes allied with the Rus on other occasions. I would like to thank Brian Boeck for his caution against accepting this tale as a historical source, since he says it may merely reflect nineteenth century literary traditions.

18. Jurij Luciw, *Sviatoslav the Conqueror* (State College, PA: Slavia Library, 1986), p. 96.

19. *Medieval Russia's Epics, Chronicles, and Tales,* ed. Serge A. Zenkovsky, pp. 58–59.

20. Svetlana A. Pletnyova, *Khazary* (Moscow: Nauka, 1986), p. 71.

21. Peter B. Golden, *Khazar Studies*, vol. 1, p. 82.

22. Vladimir F Minorsky, *A History of Sharvan and Darband in the 10th–11th Centuries*, p. 113.

23. Douglas M. Dunlop, "The Khazars," in *The Dark Ages*, ed. Cecil Roth and I. H. Levine (New Brunswick, NJ: Rutgers University Press, 1966), p. 353.

24. The conversion of the Khazar king to Islam was also reported by Ibn al-Athir in the early thirteenth century.

25. George Vernadsky, *A History of Russia*, vol. 1 (New Haven, CT: Yale University Press, 1948), p. 289.

26. Svetlana A. Pletnyova, *Khazary*, p. 72.

27. Julius Brutzkus, "The Khazar Origin of Ancient Kiev," p. 111. Prince Svyatoslav even wore his hair in the Turkic warrior style; his head was shaven, except for a lock of hair (see Vladimir Ia. Petrukhin, "The Early History of Old Russian Art: The Rhyton from Chernigov and Khazarian Tradition," *Tor* 27:2 (1995): 484).

28. René Grousset, *The Empire of the Steppes*, trans. Naomi Waldorf (New Brunswick, NJ: Rutgers University Press, 1970), p. 182.

29. Israel Kasovich, *The Eternal People* (New York: The Jordan Publishing Co., 1929), p. 307; Herman Rosenthal, "Chazars," in *The Jewish Encyclopedia*, vol. 4 (New York: Ktav, 1901–1906), p. 6; Heinrich H. Graetz, *History of the Jews*, vol. 3 (Philadelphia: The Jewish Publication Society of America, 1896), p. 254.

30. Douglas M. Dunlop, "The Khazars," in *The Dark Ages*, p. 353. According to Svetlana Pletnyova, the population of Saqsin consisted of Khazars, Jews, Oghuz, Khwarizmians, and Cumans at the beginning of the thirteenth century (see Svetlana Pletnyova, "The Polovtsy," in *Peoples that Vanished*, ed. P. Puchkov, trans. Ye. Voronov (Moscow: Nauka, 1989), p. 31). A Rus'ian chronicle recorded that the residents of Saqsin were forced to flee from Mongol invaders in 1229, and that they arrived in Volga Bulgharia.

31. This view was also adopted by such scholars as Julius Brutzkus, Itzhak Ben-Zvi, and S. Dagoni. On May 31, 1223,

just one year prior to the final conquest of Khazaria, Chinggis Khan's Mongol warriors defeated the Rus and the Cumans at the River Kalka. Brutzkus claimed that the Jewish Khazar tribe Endzher ruled over Daghestan separately from the other Khazars, and that only this Endzher-ruled kingdom, rather than Khazaria as a whole, survived until the thirteenth century. Ben-Zvi claimed that after the Mongols conquered Khazaria, the Jews from Khazaria fled to Crimea, Daghestan, and the city of Derbent (see Itzhak Ben-Zvi, *The Exiled and the Redeemed*, trans. Isaac A. Abbady (Philadelphia: The Jewish Publication Society of America, 1961), p. 58).

32. Douglas M. Dunlop, *The History of the Jewish Khazars* (New York: Schocken, 1967), p. 234.

33. Alexander A. Vasiliev, *The Goths in the Crimea*, pp. 115–116.

34. Peter B. Golden, "Khazaria and Judaism," *Archivum Eurasiae Medii Aevi* 3 (1983): 146.

9

THE DIASPORA
OF THE KHAZARS

There are many indications of a continued presence of Khazars in eastern Europe and other parts of the world. The Khazars settled in Hungary, Romania, Ukraine, Belarus, Lithuania, Poland, Turkey, Spain, southern Russia, the northern Caucasus, Azerbaijan, the Middle East (including Egypt), and possibly also in Bulgaria and other places. Some intermarried with other Jewish communities, while others merged with Muslim and Christian populations.

KHAZARS IN HUNGARY

Hungary was settled by Jews as early as Roman times, when it was known as Pannonia. The ancient Jews of Pannonia spoke and wrote in Greek and Latin.[1] It is not certain whether these Pannonian Jews have any connection with the Hungarian Jews of later times. Raphael Patai (1910–1996) wrote that it was from the mixture of the early Pannonian Jews with the Kabars and Khazar Jews that the medieval Hungarian Jewish population derived its origins.[2]

During their westward migrations, the Hungarians came into extensive contact with Khazars, and some of the Khazars settled permanently in Hungary. Khazar Jews were among the soldiers who protected Hungary's frontier in the tenth century. The existence of Khazar settlements in Hungary has been confirmed by topographic, documentary, and archaeological evidence.

In 896, the Magyars conquered the land of Hungary under the leadership of Árpád. The land that they acquired previously had been inhabited and ruled by Avars, Bulgars, Slovenians, Moravians, and Croatians. A new confederation, called On-Ogur (Ten Arrows), was formed from the ten tribes that now resided in Hungary: seven Magyar tribes and three Khazar tribes.[3] According to Constantine VII Porphyrogenitus, the seven Magyar tribes were called Jenő, Kér, Keszi, Tarján, Kürtgyarmat, Megyer, and Nyék,[4] although Kürtgyarmat was previously divided into two separate tribes called Kürt and Gyarmat.

The Kabars, a dissident branch of the Khazars, formed the major part of the Khazar population in Hungary. The word "Kabar" probably means either "rebel" or "ethnic mixup." The Kabar horde migrated westward into Hungary around the year 895 as a consequence of revolts and rebellions that had occurred around the years 862 and 881. Some scholars suggest that the Kabars' uprising against the Khazars was motivated by the pro-Judaism policies of King Obadiah, but there is no conclusive evidence to support this claim, and the actual reason for the uprising remains a mystery.

Several Hungarian scholars have attempted to determine the names of the three Kabar-Khazar tribes in Hungary. István Herényi speculated that their names were Varsány (a name of Alan origin), Kaliz, and Székely (or Eskil). Sándor Tóth suggested that the possible names of the Kabar tribes were Varsány, Eszlar or Oszlár, Tárkány, Berény, Örs, Ladány, and Sag.[5]

These Kabar tribes can be differentiated according to their ethnic backgrounds. The Khazars were one component of the Kabars' ethnic mix. "Kaliz" is the Hungarian name for the Khwarizmians, a people of Iranian origin, who were called Khalisioi by the Greeks. "Tárkány" may have been one of the names of a Bulgaric Kabar tribe.[6] The "Oszlár" were an Alanic people, also known as the Varsány,[7] who served in the Hungarian army in the tenth century. The Berény, Örs, and Ladány were Székely tribal groups, according to György Györffy.[8] Other non-Magyar ethnic groups in early Hungary included the Barszils (Bercels) and the Bulgaric Suvars.

It has been suggested that one of the Kabar clans that settled between the Danube and the Tisza rivers professed Judaism.[9]

Many of the Kabars settled between the Tisza and Szamos rivers in eastern Hungary.[10] The chronicler Anonymus, the notary for Hungarian King Bela III (reigned 1172–1196), wrote circa 1200 about the people called "Cozar" who lived in Hungary:

> The men of chief Marót might have formerly occupied the land towards Erdély, between the river Tisza and the forest of Igfon [in Bihar county], from the river Mures up to the river Szamos. The grandson of Marót was named by the Hungarians Menmarót, and he was friendly with many people called Cozar.[11]

Morut (spelled Marót in Magyar) (b. circa 874) served as the leader of the Kabars of Bihar and conquered the Tisza and Szamos valleys. Morut was himself a member of the Khazar-Kabar tribe, and his grandson Menumorut (spelled Menmarót in Magyar) likewise served as a Khazar–Kabar ruler in eastern Hungary.[12] As the duke (*el-teber*) of Bihar, Menumorut ruled over the Khazars who inhabited the area from the Transylvanian Alps to Meszes Kapu ("Limestone Gate") along the Szamos River. After a period of resistance, Menumorut submitted to the authority of the Magyars and married his daughters to

Magyar princes. For example, one of Menumorut's daughters married Árpád's son Zoltán.[13]

The Kabars were active participants in the cultural, military, and economic life of Hungary. A significant fact attesting to continued Magyar-Kabar relations is the statement of Constantine VII Porphyrogenitus that the Magyars and Khazars learned each others' languages, such that the Khazar language was spoken in Hungary until at least the middle of the tenth century.[14]

The Magyars invaded Germany from the east in 954. In 955, Lél, a Magyar prince who ruled over the Kabars of Nyitra, fought in this western campaign.[15] Lél allied with the Magyar chiefs Bulcsú and Súr. All three chiefs were defeated by the Germans near Augsburg (in what is today southern Germany) at the Lechfeld in the Battle of Augsburg, which took place on August 10, 955. Some of the Magyar warriors drowned in the Lech River. The victors over the Magyars in this battle were the German king Otto I (reigned 936–973) and his ally Duke Conrad. The Germans relentlessly pursued the Magyars after their defeat. The Bavarian prince Henry I captured and hanged Lél and the other two chiefs at Regensburg.

The Khazarian population in Hungary further increased in size when the Hungarian Duke Taksony (reigned 955–970) invited Khazar Jews to settle in his realm.[16] As the son of Zoltán and Zoltán's Khazar wife (Menumorut's daughter), Taksony was partly a Khazar-Kabar himself. According to Anonymus, Taksony also invited many Muslims from Volga Bulgharia to settle in Hungary.

Several other early Magyar rulers had some Khazarian ancestry. For instance, the kende Kurszán (d. 904) was descended in part from the royal house of Khazaria, since his ancestor Levéd had married a Khazar princess[17] (see Chapter 7).

A silver ring found in a cemetery in Ellend, near Pécs in southwestern Hungary and not far from the villages of Nagykozár and Kiskozár, is believed to be of Khazar-Kabar origin.[18] The ring, which dates from the second half of the eleventh century, was found next to a woman's skeleton, and has thirteen Hebrew letters engraved on it as ornamentation. The ring seems to confirm the immigration of Kabars into Hungary and the Jewish beliefs of those immigrants. Since Kozár was the name of a village in Baranya County in the Danube valley of southwestern Hungary—as noted in a religious document of the fourteenth century—and since Nagykozár and Kiskozár are within close proximity to Ellend's cemetery, Attila Kiss postulated that Khazar women from Khazarian villages may have moved into Ellend.[19]

As noted above, the Kalizes seem to have been members of the Kabars who moved to Hungary, or perhaps descendants of the Khazars invited to settle in Hungary by Duke Taksony. Although many of them were Muslims, some of the Kalizes came under the influence of the Khazars' Judaism. Arab and Byzantine authors mentioned the Kaliz people's close connections to the Khazars. The twelfth-century Byzantine writer Johannes Cinnamus, in a reference to events that transpired around the year 1154, wrote that some of the "Khalisioi" (Khwalis or Kaliz) believed in "the Mosaic laws, but not in their pure form . . . . "[20] Cinnamus also stated that the Kalizes fought with Dalmatian (Croatian) troops against Byzantine Emperor Manuel Comnenus in the mid-twelfth century.[21] The Kaliz people probably used to live around the Caspian coastline, since "Khvaliskoye" was an old Russian term for the Caspian. It has been determined that the Kalizes originally came from central Asia and were Turkic and predominantly Muslim. Thus, their origins should be sought in the Khwarizm-Khiva region of central Asia. Chinese sources called the land of Khwarizm "Kua-li."[22] Following their sojourn in Khwarizm, the Kalizes migrated to the trading center of Khazaria. Close connections between the Kaliz and the Khazars are evident from the fact that the Rus called the merchant town of Khazaran "Khvalisy" (see Chapter 2), and from some early Slavic sources that called the Khazars "Khwalisses."[23]

There are other traces of the Khazars' residence in Hungary. Hungarian scholars have systematically analyzed a variety of place names in Hungary that seem to derive from "Khazar." It is believed that places named Kazár, Kozár, Kozárd, Kozárvár, etc. were named after the Khazars.[24] It is significant that these places were in the vicinity of known Kabar settlements. Hungary had four towns named Kozár, one of which was located near a tributary of the Zagyva River. The town of Kozárd was located northeast of Szirák and west of Pásztó, in County Nógrád in northern Hungary. There was another Kozár or Kozárd in County Szatmár, south of Nagyká (in the northeastern corner of Hungary), in the same area where Anonymus said that Kabars lived. A "possessio Kozar" was given to the tribe Kaplony in 1335. A "Khazar castle" (Kozárvár) was located in County Szolnok-Doboka in east-central Hungary. The village named Kazár, which still exists today, is located in County Nógrád about fifty-three miles northeast of Budapest. Khazar settlements also existed in southern parts of Hungary (County Baranya and County Tolna), including Rác-Kozár (also known as Egyházas-Kozár), Nagy-Kozár, and Kis-Kozár.

Among documents indicating the presence of Khazar people in Hungary is one dated 1337 that contained the Latin phrase "populi Kaza[r]." There is also a document from 1279 that makes reference to a place called Chazarental ("Valley of the Khazars").[25]

There was a Hungarian family named Kozárvári that flourished from the tenth to the fourteenth centuries, and it is possible that they were Khazar in origin.[26] They may have been a noble Khazar family who named themselves after the toponym Kozárvár.

A rich Jewish Khazar merchant named Teka became the financial custodian and vice-prince of the kingdom of Hungary in 1211.[27] He was forced to flee to Austria in 1233, but later returned and restored himself to his office, serving until his death in 1245.

The ultimate fate of the Khazars in Hungary has been much disputed among scholars. Sándor Tóth asserted that the Kabars in Hungary eventually abandoned Judaism and adopted Christianity, and, furthermore, that they adopted the Magyar language in place of Khazar.[28] The theory that the Khazar Jews in Hungary were absorbed by the Christian population surrounding them was shared by Péter Ujvári and Nathan Ausubel.[29] Thus, according to this view, the Kabars and the Magyars eventually assimilated and became one people, while modern Hungarian Jews trace their origins to immigrants from central Europe who came to Hungary in the late Middle Ages and had Hebrew and German names. There are Christians living in the Sopron district of northwest Hungary (bordering on Austria) who believe that they descend from Jewish Khazars, even though they no longer observe Judaism.[30] Certain family names in Hungary—Örsúr, Aba, and Bors—may be Kabar in origin.[31]

The alternative view is that the Khazars retained their Jewish faith into the twentieth century. For example, it is believed that the long-standing tradition of dueling among Hungarian Jews derives from their Khazar heritage. It appears that Jews who retained their Khazar identity still lived in Hungary as late as the fourteenth century. According to Douglas Dunlop:

> Even as late as 1309 a Council of the Hungarian clergy at Pressburg forbade Catholics to intermarry with those people described as Khazars, and their decision received papal confirmation in 1346.[32]

KHAZARS IN ROMANIA

The history of Transylvania is intertwined with that of Hungary. Towns named Kozárvár ("Khazar Castle") and Kozárd were located between the rivers Mures (Maros) and Szamos in western Romania, and Hungarian historians believe that these were founded by Khazars.[33]

An old legend states that Jewish warriors from southern Russia invaded and settled in Wallachia and Moldova. According to Alfred Posselt, these warriors were the "Red Jews" and came to Romania around the year 1100.[34]

The Jews of the Transylvanian town of Sfîntu Gheorghe (which was part of the Kingdom of Hungary and was known as Sepsiszentgyörgy until World War I) have a tradition that they descend from Turkic Jews from the East whose nation was conquered by the Rus.[35] According to this tradition, families of Jewish Turkic merchants and soldiers settled in Sfîntu Gheorghe and began to engage in agriculture. In 1360, King Lajos I of Hungary ordered the expulsion of Jews from his territories, yet the Jews in this town were listed as "Hungarians" for the census and were spared. These Turkic Jews intermarried with a few Hungarians and Romanians, but remained a cohesive community for centuries.

Some scholars have advanced the claim that the Székely people descend from the Khazars and formed a portion of the Kabar nexus. Many of the Székely live in the city of Cluj and small farming villages in the upper valleys of the Mures and Olt Rivers in eastern Transylvania. They follow Unitarian Christianity and speak a Hungarian dialect.

Centuries ago, the Hungarian dialect of the Székely people was written using a Turkic runic alphabet of thirty-two characters, along with a few additional variant characters.[36] The Székely script was written from right to left. The runes remained in use until the eighteenth century. The alleged similarity between the Khazar and Székely runes[37] led L. Ligeti and J. Németh to conclude that the alphabet originated in the Khazar territory.[38] It further led some scholars to assume that the Székely themselves came from the Khazar Empire. Edward Rockstein, an expert on the Székely runes, dismissed legends about the Székelys' descent from Huns and Avars and believed that they may indeed be of Khazar origin. According to László Makkai, "Byzantine sources, as well as local tradition, identify the Székelys as the 'kabars' who had revolted against the

Khazars."[39] It is said that the Székely functioned as border guards on the eastern Hungarian frontier in Transylvania.

It is important to realize that the Székely did not originate entirely from Khazar stock, because there were Székely people living in Transylvania prior to the Khazar and Magyar migrations, but there is little doubt that they mixed with Khazar immigrants. If the Székely are not Khazarian, they may be descended from another "Magyarized" Turkic people. The most likely answer is that the original Székelys were Huns, which explains the Székelys' self-proclaimed identification with the Huns.

KHAZARS IN LITHUANIA AND BELARUS

According to Martin Gilbert, Jews migrated from Khazaria to Lithuania in 1016.[40] Indeed, a few Jewish families from Vilnius have claimed Khazar ancestry. It seems that many rabbinical Jews from Lithuania and Poland had ancestors from the Crimea. One wonders whether some of them had escaped the Rus'ian and Byzantine armies that crushed Georgius Tzul in 1016 (see Chapter 8).

Significant evidence exists that attests to permanent Khazar settlements in the territory that is now western Belarus. Documents contained in the Russian Judaica collection of Baron Günzburg (1857–1910) and Baron Polyakov (Polakoff) indicated that the Khazars founded a glass factory in Hrodna (Grodno) in the late ninth century or the early tenth century.[41] Glassmaking also took place in Navahradak (Novogrudok), east of Hrodna, where glassware of multiple colors was unearthed during the course of archaeological expeditions.[42]

KHAZARS IN POLAND

Whether or not the Khazars settled in Poland is a controversial question. The opinion expressed by historian Norman Davies is shared by many other scholars:

There is little reason to doubt that Jews had lived in Poland
from the earliest times, and that Judaism, as preserved by the
descendants of the ancient Chazar kingdom in the south-east,
had actually antedated Christianity.[43]

According to Davies, Judaism was introduced into Poland by
the Khazars in the ninth century. Adam Vetulani suggested that
Khazar Jews arrived in Poland before 963.[44] The Polish historians Kazimiez and Maria Piechotka also believed that the
Khazars traveled to Poland:

> In the same period there began an influx of Chazar Jews from
> the East. At first this was essentially a trade immigration, but
> towards the end of the 10th century, after the fall of the
> Chazar state, it assumed larger proportions. The immigrants
> of this period turned mainly to agriculture and handicrafts.
> These colonies or settlements occurred in the southern and
> eastern parts of the future Polish state.[45]

Unfortunately, written records attesting to the Khazar presence
in Poland have not survived to the present day. Polish chronicles from before the mid-thirteenth century disappeared during the Mongol invasion period.[46] This suggests that documents
related to Khazar settlement in Poland probably existed, but
were lost. By contrast, there is ample evidence for Jewish Khazar settlement in Ukraine and elsewhere in eastern Europe.

Earlier in this century, Itzhak Schipper (1884–1943), a
Polish Jewish scholar, proposed that town names such as
Kozari and Kozarzów in Poland were named after the Khazars,
and therefore that they demarcated the settlements of the
Khazars. Others of this nature in Poland, Ukraine, and Rus-
sia included Kozarzewek, Kozarze (in the Kraków region),
Kozara (in the Lviv region), Kozaroviche (located near Kiev),
and Kozarka and Kozari (both found in Novgorod province).
The town of Koganovo supposedly derived from kagan, the
title of the supreme Khazar king. Place names such as
Żydowska Wola, Żydowo, and Żydaticze were said to derive
from Żid, meaning "Jew." Critics, notably Bernard Weinryb,

have questioned the accuracy of Schipper's etymologies, and wonder whether toponyms with the root Żid actually may have referred to settlements of German Jews. It is difficult to confirm whether these places actually have Khazar origins.

Another interesting theory suggests that the Polish villages and graveyards called Kawyory and Kawyary are of Khazar origin.[47] The word "Kawyory" means "Jewish cemetery" and appears to derive from a pre-Yiddish word in medieval Poland, such as the Hebrew word *kevarim* ("cemetery").[48] Wexler wondered whether the Aramaic word *qabra'* ("grave"), rather than *kevarim*, was its origin.

According to Schipper, the Khazar Jews in Poland were primarily farmers and craftsmen. It is certainly conceivable that the Khazars were attracted to the fertile plains of the Polish landscape.

With the immigration of Khazar Jews into multiple regions of Poland, the glassmaking industry was developed and expanded, according to a new theory proposed by Samuel Kurinsky. Glassmaking factories were established in Wolin by the early tenth century, and in Opole and Wroclaw (both along the Odra River) by the mid-thirteenth century. Factories also were built in the Poznan, Kraków, and Gdánsk regions. The glass that was exported from the Khazar factories of Silesia included Jewish motifs, and was blown and designed according to the technique and composition commonly used by the Jews of Persia and Babylonia.[49] In fact, the color, form, and motifs of Polish Jewish glassware also were similar to that of glass produced along the Danube and in Russia and central Asia, and all of them derive from an ultimately Judean style.

Some scholars claimed that twelfth-century Polish silver coins with Hebrew characters were minted by Jews of Khazar origin. This intriguing theory is difficult to verify. Alfred Posselt claimed that a rich Jewish banker of the Lublin district named Abraham ben Joseph ha-Nasi ("prince"), who lived circa 1300 and whose name was inscribed on some Polish coins, was a Khazar.[50]

Although no documents exist that explicitly state that the Khazars settled in Poland, a mysterious document authored by Rabbi Nissim in 1096 refers to a messianic movement originating from "Al-Kazariyah" around the time of the First Crusades.[51] The relevant passage pertaining to the Khazars has been translated as follows:

> And the congregations were agitated and returned to the Lord with fastings and alms. And so from the region of Khazaria there went, as they said, 17 congregations to the "wilderness of the nations," and we know not if they met with the tribes or not.[52]

Unfortunately, Rabbi Nissim did not specify the exact location of the "wilderness of the nations," but it is possible that some members of these seventeen communities of Khazar Jews settled in Poland, as Schipper suggested.

There appear to be some examples of cultural and linguistic remnants from the Khazars among the Ashkenazic Jews of Poland. For instance, Polish Jews retained Turkic styles of dress long after their Christian neighbors had abandoned them. The Yiddish word *kaftan* (*kaftn*), meaning "long male overgarment," derives from the Turkic language.[53] The "full coat" worn by the Khazars (see Chapter 4) was probably a kaftan. Polish nobles of Sarmatian origin, who possessed traits of the steppe, also wore long kaftans.[54] Even the kings of the Burtas (considered to be Turks by al-Masudi) wore kaftans.[55]

Another important Yiddish word, *yarmulka*, meaning "skullcap," also derives from Turkic or Turkish. Wexler suggested that it derives from the Turkish work *yağmurluk*, meaning "raincoat," through an intermediary Slavic language such as Polish, Ukrainian, or Russian, which contain words similar to *yarmulka*.[56]

Herbert Zeiden suggested that the Yiddish word *davenen*, meaning "to pray," comes from Turkic.[57] Zeiden noted that the verbal root *tabun-* means "pray" in the Kipchak form of the Turkic language. In Kipchak, the initial letter "t" often was transformed into "d," which in this case theoretically yielded *dabun-dum* ("I prayed"). The word *davenen* therefore may have come into usage among the Ashkenazim by way of the Khazars and the Kipchaks.

The Yiddish word *loksh* ("noodle") derives from the Turkic word *laqsha*, possibly through a Slavic intermediary.

There are also possible remnants of the Khazar or Kipchak heritage in some Ashkenazic surnames. The surname Bairak/ Beirak may derive from the Turkic word *beyraq*, meaning "flag."[58] Balaban means "falcon" in some Turkic languages.[59] Kaplan means "tiger" in Turkish; in the eighteenth century there were two Crimean Tatar khans named Qaplan Girai.[60] It is sometimes suggested that the surname Kagan/Kaghan derives from the Turkic term for "supreme king," kagan/khaqan, although others claim that it is a variant of "Kohen."

The Ashkenazic surname Alpert, which is a shortened version of Alperowitz or Alperovitch, appears to mean "Hero-man." Genealogists traditionally have viewed Alpert as a derivative of Heilbronn, a German town. However, Alp ("Hero") and Alparslan ("Hero-lion")[61] are widely used as personal names in modern Turkey, and the Turkish surname Alperoğlu ("son of Alper") resembles the Ashkenazic Alperowitz (which also means "son of Alper"). The suffix *-owitz* is almost always used as a patronymic—as may also be seen in Abramowitz, Leibowitz, and Aronowitz—rather than as an indicator of one's ancestral town. The Heilbronn theory seems to apply only to the surname Halperin/Halpern/Galpern, not to Alpert/ Alperowitz.

Old Turkic writings speak of a man named Tonga Alp Er ("Tiger Hero Man") (also known as Alp Er Tonga). In *Kutadgu Bilig*, completed in 1069, Yusuf Khass Hajib praised him highly:

> If you observe well you will notice that the Turkish princes are the finest in the world. And among these Turkish princes the one of outstanding fame and glory was Tonga Alp Er. He was the choicest of men, distinguished by great wisdom and

virtues manifold. What a choice and manly man he was, a clever man indeed—he devoured this world entire! The Iranians call him Afrasiyab, the same who seized and pillaged their realm.[62]

Furthermore, men named Olober (Alp-Ör) and Shelbir (Es Alp-Ör) were chiefs in the army of Iaroslav, the father of Igor (the twelfth-century prince honored by the famous epic *The Lay of the Host of Igor*).[63] This information is sufficient to establish Turkic as the probable origin of the surnames Alperowitz and Alpert. Noteworthy Turkic Jews probably also were known as heroic men, thus acquiring the name Alp-er. The meaning of the name was lost over the years.

According to linguist Paul Wexler, the use of Pesach as a male first name among Ashkenazic Jews may also be a reflection of Turkic Khazar usage.[64] We have already seen that the great Khazar baliqchi Pesakh had this name (see Chapter 8), as did some Polish Jews in the nineteenth century. The name Pesach was generally used only by Jews in eastern Germany (east of the Elbe River) and eastern Europe, as well as by Karaites and Iranian Jews, but was not used by Sephardic Jews.[65] The surname Pesachov is attested among the Bukharan Jews of Uzbekistan, who descend from Persian Jews and Tajiks. Some Ashkenazic Jews have the surname Pesachowitz.

Wexler claimed that the name Pesach is only one example of the once-widespread Turkic custom of naming children after the holiday, month, or day in which they were born. This ancient practice may also be seen in the Belarusian Tatar surname Ramazan (from the Muslim holy month of Ramadan) and the Mountain Jewish surname Xanukiev/Xanukaiev (from Hanukkah). Obviously, the Khazars named Hanukkah also were born during that festival. However, this naming practice is not limited to Turkic peoples or regions. The Greek Jews of Salonika named their children Mordekhai if they were born on Purim, Nisim if they were born during the month of Nisan, and Matityahu if they were born during the Hanukkah festival[66] (in remembrance of the Judean High Priest Mattathias, father of Judah Maccabee). Boys born on Hanukkah were also named Hanukkah in Izmir, and Hanukkah was a surname in Salonika. Furthermore, Pesakha was a surname and girl's name in Istanbul.

Some researchers have proposed that the wooden synagogues of early medieval Poland were designed according to a Turkic model from Khazaria. Nathan Ausubel commented:

> There are many theories about the origins and the architectural influences that entered into their building . . . . A third and more plausible conjecture is that the Middle Eastern refugees from the Jewish kingdom of Khazaria introduced them during the Middle Ages when they settled en masse in Poland. The Asiatic characteristics are obvious in the wooden synagogues. Byzantine elements are artfully mingled with Mongolian. The roofs, pagoda style, arranged one upon another and surmounted by vaulted ceilings and cupolas, sometimes create the illusion that one is in central Asia rather than Poland.[67]

Wexler, however, noticed similarities between the early synagogues and pagan Slavic temple architecture from Bulgaria and other parts of eastern Europe.

KHAZARS IN UKRAINE

The Khazars have lived in Ukraine ever since the westward expansion of the Khazar kaganate into the Dnieper valley. By the early tenth century, a substantial community of Jewish Khazars lived in the city of Kiev, as indicated by the *Kievan Letter* (see Chapter 6). The Khazars continued to live in Kiev after it was taken over by the Rus'ians. It seems that Svyatopolk invited additional Jews from Khazaria to settle in Kiev.[68]

During the tenth and eleventh centuries, workshops in the Kiev area were producing glass beads, bracelets, and other jewelry; Kurinsky was of the opinion that Khazar Jews were probably the operators of these workshops.[69] This opinion appears to be verified by the fact that the Kievan glass beads

were like those produced by the Saltovo-Mayaki culture of
Khazaria.[70]

According to the *Rus'ian Primary Chronicle*, a Khazar Jew-
ish delegation was invited to the court of Prince Vladimir in
Kiev to discuss the tenets of Judaism, since Vladimir was deciding on a new religion to replace his former paganism. The
Chronicle reported that in 986, after the prince had rejected
the Islam of the Bulgars and the Christianity of the Germans,
he met a group of Jewish Khazars (*zhidove kozarsti*).[71] The
Khazars said that they were aware of the attempts of the
Bulgars and Germans to proselytize him. They explained to
Vladimir that they "believe in the one God of Abraham, Isaac,
and Jacob" and that they adhered to Judaism, which required
circumcision, observance of the Sabbath, and abstinence from
pork and hare meat. The Khazar Jews explained that their
native land was Jerusalem and that they were part of the dis-
persion of the Judeans. Vladimir rejected Judaism because it
was the faith of a stateless and exiled people. After further
investigation, during which Judaism was no longer considered
as an option, Vladimir chose to be baptized (circa 988) into
Greek Orthodox Christianity, ushering in an era of Byzantine-
inspired culture in Kievan Rus.

Prince Vladimir died in 1015, and after his death power
struggles erupted between Prince Svyatopolk and other rivals.
The Polish king Boleslav I "the Brave" occupied Kiev in support of Svyatopolk. These events were associated with a mis-
fortune for Kievan Jewry: In 1018, Rus'ian soldiers attacked
and robbed Jewish homes in Kiev, according to the fifteenth-
century Polish chronicle *Annales seu cronice inclyti Regni
Poloniae* by Jan Długosz.[72] During this period, according to
Benjamin Pinkus, the Khazars lived in the "Khazaria" quarter
of Kiev, whereas other Jews (perhaps Byzantine and western
Jews) lived in the "Zhidovia" quarter.[73] Kazimierz Piechotka
and Maria Piechotka claimed that in 1018 the Zhidovia district was inhabited by Jewish Radhanite traders.[74] Eventually,
integration of the two Jewish communities must have taken

place, because there was no intersectarian hostility (both groups were rabbinical Jews; neither was Karaitic). The Zhidovia quarter suffered a terrible fire in 1124, as recorded by the *Suzdal Chronicle*, but Kievan Jewry rebuilt its community and again flourished years later.

Khazar communities also continued to exist in other sections of what later became Ukraine. Nine Hebrew tombstone inscriptions, dating from 956 to 1048, in a cemetery in Chufut-Kale (central Crimea) are evidence that Khazar Jews continued to live in the Crimea many years after the Rus had reduced the once-mighty Khazar Empire to a small kaganate.[75] The Khazar Jews of Chufut-Kale possessed Hebrew names such as Isaac and Abraham, but four of the twenty names on the tombstones were non-Semitic in origin. Therefore, the Jews of Chufut-Kale were largely converts, just like the Khazar Jews of Kiev. Isaac, Abraham, and eight of the other names were Pentateuchal, i.e., from the first five books of the Torah, rather than Prophetic or Extrabiblical. Isaac and Abraham were also common names among the Khazar signatories on the *Kievan Letter*, and Pentateuchal names were the most common names among the Jewish population of other parts of Khazaria (including Kiev and Atil). Thus, in terms of their naming standards, the Khazars of the Crimea followed the typical pattern exhibited by other Khazar communities.

Vsevolod Vikhnovich asserted that the Khazar Jews became Slavicized.[76] This conclusion is bolstered by evidence that some of the Jews in Kievan Rus spoke an East Slavic language during the eleventh, twelfth, and thirteenth centuries. Abraham Harkavy was one of the first scholars to demonstrate the existence of Slavic-speaking Jews. A letter discovered in Cairo that dates from the eleventh century spoke of a Jew from Kievan Rus who visited Salonika and was fluent not in Hebrew, Greek, or Arabic, but only in the "Knaanic" language of his homeland (the Jews called Slavic the "Knaanic," or "Canaanite," language because it came from the land of enslaved Slavic children, or "Canaanites").[77] The presence of Rus'ian Jews in the twelfth and thirteenth centuries who spoke Rus'ian and read Rus'ian Bibles is also confirmed by the mention of them in the responsas of German rabbis.[78]

Other groups of European Jews also spoke Slavic in the medieval period. For example, an early ninth-century Latin document indicated that a Jewish physician who resided in Salzburg (western Austria) spoke Slavic.[79] However, Yiddish linguist Max Weinreich categorized Knaanic as an East Slavic language, rather than a form of Bohemian-Moravian Slavic or some other variant.[80] This leads us to the conclusion that the Knaanic Jews were indigenous to Kiev, rather than immigrants from farther west. In other words, the Slavic-speaking Jews of Kievan Rus were Slavic and Khazarian in origin, with an added Byzantine Jewish element. In fact, the tenth-century Catalonian Jewish traveler Ibrahim ibn Yaqub wrote that the Khazars spoke the language of the "Saqalibah" (Slavs).[81] This may explain the fact that the Khazar Jews were writing in a Cyrillic-like script by around 1206 (see Chapter 4).

The *Rus'ian Chronicle* stated that in around the year 1106, during the reign of Grand Prince Svyatopolk II in Kievan Rus, a Khazar army commander from the Kievan realm named Ivan ("Ivanko Zakharich, Kozarina"), with the assistance of two other Rus'ian generals and other men, raided against the Cumans. It seems that Ivan's name is further evidence that some of the Khazars had become Slavicized.

Around the year 1117, people presumed to be Khazars fled the Cumans and sought refuge in Kievan Rus from Vladimir Monomakh. These "Khazars" settled near Chernihiv (Chernigov), northeast of Kiev, in a new town they built called Byelaya Vyezha ("White Fortress").[82] It is likely that these "Khazars" used to live in Sarkel, along the Don, which was also known by the East Slavic name Byelaya Vyezha.

Itzhak Schipper proposed that Persian Jews from the Khazar kaganate settled in Halych (Halicz), a Rusyn (Ruthenian) town on the Dniester, based on his interpretation of the sixteenth-century chronicle *Emek ha-Bakha* by Joseph ben Joshua ha-Kohen. Most historians have not accepted this suggestion.

Julius Brutzkus believed that the Crimean Jews (Krymchaks) and the Crimean Tatars were descendants of the Khazars. However, the Crimean Tatars are actually largely the descendants of the Golden Horde Mongols.

The descendants of Khazars continued to live in Ukraine until modern times. "Jewish Cossacks" who served in the Czarist army insisted that they had Khazar origins,[83] as did some Jewish families from Odessa (a major southern port city) and Ladyzhin (a village along the Bug River). These oral traditions, originating no later than the nineteenth century, undoubtedly contain a substantial amount of truth. Many modern Ukrainian Jews physically resemble peoples of the Caucasus and central Asia, including Turkic and Tatar peoples, because of their Khazar heritage:

> It is clear, however, that the influence of the Jews, who had become the most active agents of the commerce of the Caliphate, was substantial in the Khazar kingdom, and it is probable that the commonly observed mongoloid type among East European Jews, particularly in the Ukraine, Poland and Roumania, derives from the conversions and intermarriages which were no doubt frequent in the swarming trading camps of the Khaqans.[84]

Raphael and Jennifer Patai, on the other hand, emphasized that many of the Khazars did not belong to a Mongolian type, but actually resembled Europeans:

> ... one should remember that the Khazars were described by several contemporary authors as having a pale complexion, blue eyes, and reddish hair. Red, as distinguished from blond, hair is found in a certain percentage of East European Jews, and this, as well as the more generalized light coloring, could be a heritage of the medieval Khazar infusion.[85]

Some Ukrainian Jews resemble Slavic, Germanic, or Iranian peoples, rather than Turkic peoples. Clearly, the Turkic Khazars were only one of many contributions to the Ashkenazic gene pool over centuries of intermarriage.

KHAZARS IN TURKEY

In the tenth century, some Khazars visited and inhabited the land that today is part of the Republic of Turkey. The anonymous Khazarian author of the *Schechter Letter* wrote his masterwork while staying in the city of Constantinople (see Chapter 6), which today is known as Istanbul. A number of Khazars served as palace guards in Constantinople (see Chapter 7) and were subjects of the Byzantine Empire.

The last known reference to "Khazars" in Constantinople comes from Benjamin ben Jonah, a Jewish traveler from Tudela in the Navarre region of the Basque country. Benjamin of Tudela journeyed to parts of North Africa, Asia, and Europe between 1160 and 1173, and recorded his experiences in *Sefer Massa'oth*. Benjamin had the following to say about Constantinople's trading relations:

> All sorts of merchants come here from the land of Babylon, from the land of Shinar, from Persia, Media, and all the sovereignty of the land of Egypt, from the land of Canaan, and the empire of Russia, from Hungaria, Patzinakia, Khazaria, and the land of Lombardy and Sepharad.[86]

It is unclear whether the traders from "Khazaria" were ethnic Khazars or merely residents of the Crimea (Gazaria).

KHAZARS IN SPAIN

It is said that many royal Khazars emigrated to Spain in the eleventh century (see Chapter 8). It is also possible that Khazar merchants arrived in Spanish port cities, since the Moorish rulers were tolerant of Jews.

In *Sefer ha-Qabbalah*, composed in 1161, Abraham ibn Daud stated that descendants of the Khazars were in Toledo (part of Andalusia) during his lifetime.[87] Ibn Daud added that these Khazars were rabbinical Jewish students. Perhaps these scholars came to Spain from Kievan Rus, since it is known that Rus'ian Jewish scholars from Kiev and Chernigov studied in

Toledo (see Chapter 11). Another possibility is that the students were descended from King Joseph of Khazaria.

Dunlop speculated that the Khazars in Spain may have provided information to the Sephardic Jews that was later incorporated into Yehudah ha-Levi's famous book *Sefer ha-Kuzari*. In other words, "Books of the Khazars" containing historical details about the Khazars may actually have been brought to Toledo. Whether or not such books existed will probably remain a tantalizing mystery.

KHAZARS IN AZERBAIJAN

The Khazars were among the Turkic settlers of Azerbaijan during the early medieval period.

After the Arab general Marwan ibn Muhammad defeated the Khazars in 737 (see Chapter 7), he resettled some of the Khazars between the Samur River and Shabaran (the capital of Shirvan in the lower Lakz lands of the present-day Azerbaijani Republic).[88] For instance, a village named Khazri was established along the middle Samur, at a location south of the fortress of Derbent and directly north of modern Azerbaijan. These Khazar settlers practiced Islam.

In 854, three hundred Muslim Khazar families left Khazaria and received assistance in resettling in Azerbaijan from Abu-Musa Bugha al-Kabir "the Elder," a Turkic ally of the Islamic Caliphate who served as the governor of Armenia and Azerbaijan.[89] This resettlement was recorded by al-Baladhuri in *Kitab al-Buldan* and by the *Georgian Chronicle*. Bugha founded a town, named Shamkur (Samkur), for these Khazars. Shamkur was located along the Kur River.

The majority of Azeris can trace their ancestry back to Turks of Oghuz origin, rather than to Khazars. In fact, the Azeri language is closely related to the Turkish spoken in the Republic of Turkey. Nevertheless, it is interesting to speculate on the ultimate fate of the descendants of these Azerbaijani Khazars.

KHAZARS IN THE NORTH CAUCASUS

A considerable number of Khazars settled in Derbent, a seaport city located in Daghestan, north of Azerbaijan. In 733 or 734, Maslama ibn 'Abd-al-Malik built a "mosque of the Khazar" in one of the seven districts of Derbent, and it served the Khazar Muslims who were living in the city.[90] It is likely that some Khazar Jews fled to Derbent after the Rus conquered Atil. The *Georgian Chronicle* discussed an invasion of "Khazars of Derbant," and the Persian poet Khaqani (circa 1106–1190) wrote about the defeat of an army from Derbent that consisted of Khazars, Alans, and Rus and had attempted to invade Shirvan.

A short passage in the *Tárik al-Bab* referred to a large migration of Khazars that occurred in 1064: "... the remnants of the Khazars, consisting of 3,000 households, arrived at the town of Qahtan from the Khazar territory. They rebuilt it and settled in it."[91] Qahtan is believed to have been located in the region of Qaytaq in Daghestan, north of Derbent, which is now inhabited by Kumyks (Kumuks).[92]

Many of these Khazars probably assimilated with other Turkic tribes and assumed new identities after the collapse of their kaganate and their subsequent immigration.

The Kumyks of the lowlands of Daghestan, between the Terek and the Samur Rivers (including the city of Makhachkala), speak a Kipchak Turkic language and claim to be descendants of the Khazars and the Cumans.[93] They adopted Islam in the eleventh century, but formerly believed in Tengri shamanism. Many scholars believe that the Kumyk town of Tarqu is located on the site of the Khazar city of Samandar (see Chapter 2). The Kumyk language even has some words of Hebrew origin. For example, *qaghal* (meaning "matzoh," "Passover," and "noise") comes from the Hebrew word *qahal* ("Jewish community or gathering").[94] One wonders whether the word gained much currency among the Khazars.

Other possible candidates for Khazar ancestry are the Karachays and the Balkars. Both groups are Muslims who speak closely-related Kipchak languages and live north of the Caucasus Mountains. According to Peter Golden, the Karachays and the Balkars descend from Khazars, Bulgars, and Cumans.[95]

Some writers, including Arthur Koestler, have conjectured that the Mountain Jews of Daghestan and Azerbaijan, who call themselves Djuhur or Chufut and speak an Iranian language called Tat, have Khazarian ancestry. However, the Mountain Jews probably descend from Persian Jews who came to the Caucasus in the fifth and sixth centuries.[96]

KHAZARS IN RUSSIA

There appears to be evidence that the Khazars still lived in Tmutorokan during the eleventh century. The *Rus'ian Chronicle* reported that Prince Mstislav of Tmutorokan was able to take control of Chernihiv in 1023 with the support of a "Khazar" army that included both Khazars and Kasogs. The army attacked Yaroslav, the prince of Kiev (reigned 1019–1054). Mstislav was able to maintain his possession of the Chernihiv region until his death in 1036. The *Rus'ian Chronicle* also spoke about a group of "Khazars" in Tmutorokan who imprisoned a certain Prince Oleg in 1079 and shipped him to Constantinople. However, Oleg returned in 1083 to kill these "Khazars." Minorsky suggested that these "Khazars" may have actually been Cumans (Polovtsi).[97]

Some scholars have contended that the Cossacks have Khazar origins. It is important to remember, however, that the Cossacks were a very mixed people, encompassing Russians and Ukrainians who mixed with Tatars, Cumans, and other steppe peoples. Solomon Grayzel suggested that some of the Jewish Khazars were baptized into Christianity but retained elements of Judaism:

> It is interesting to speculate whether the observance of the Sabbath among certain clans of Cossacks in the territory now known as the Ukraine, which the Russian Church was still

attempting to stamp out as late as the eighteenth century, was
an echo of the ancient Khazar influence.[98]

Some of the Khazars who still observed elements of Judaism
are said to have become the Grebentsk Cossacks—who were
also known as the Terek Cossacks, since some of them lived
near the Terek River.[99] The Grebentsy became influenced by
the north Caucasian cultures that surrounded them, especially
the traditions of the Chechens and the Nogays. They spent
their days hunting and harvesting grapes in lands that were
once part of the Khazar kaganate. George Gubaroff, a propo-
nent of the view that the Cossacks are Khazars, claimed that
the legendary ancestors of the Grebentsy were the
"Kazharovtsy" and contended that the ethnic name "Kazak"
(Cossack) may have derived from a combination of "Kazar"
and "Kasak."[100] The claim that the Grebentsy were Jewish
Khazars is offset by the alternative view that they were among
the Christian Slavs known as the "Old Believers."

Lev Gumilev, a Soviet archaeologist, theorized that the
Khazars remained in Sarkel (Byelaya Vyezha) and other localities along the middle and lower Don region of southern Russia until they were driven westward into Kievan Rus (i.e., near
Chernihiv) by the Cumans in 1117.[101] According to Gumilev,
these Khazars survived until the Mongol invasions. He proposed that these Khazars mixed with Slavs and became known
to Rus'ians as the "Brodniki." An alternative theory suggests
that the Brodniks descended from the Alans, not the Khazars.
The name "Brodniki" means "fishermen" or, alternatively,
"ramblers." The term "Brodniki" was first recorded in 1147.
The Brodniks belonged to communes along the Don, spoke
Rus'ian, and adhered to Orthodox Christianity, and yet were
distinct from the majority of Slavs. According to the
Novgorodian Chronicle, some of the Brodniks allied with the
Mongols and attacked a Rus'ian army in 1223 or 1224, killing many Rus at a fortification along the Kalka River. They
also threatened Hungary in 1254.[102] Gubaroff believed that
some of the Cossacks may descend from the Brodniks.

Gubaroff also said that a variety of Turkic tribes living along the Ros' River in around the eleventh century were called "Khazars" by chroniclers. These included the Black Caps (known as "Chernye Klobuki" in Russian and "Karakalpak" in Turkic), Torks, Porosyanians, Porchane, Berendei, Berendichi, Koui, and Torpety. Julius Brutzkus agreed that some of these tribes were probably remnants of the Khazars.[103] On the other hand, the Torks are generally considered to be an Oghuz rather than a Khazar tribe. Gubaroff remarked that Makarii, a sixteenth-century metropolitan and religious writer, referred to the people living in the River Don area on the shores of the Sea of Azov by the term "Kozary."[104] The Black Caps, Berendei, and Koui fought as soldiers against the Cumans in the late eleventh century. Brutzkus said that these Turkic tribes continued to live along both sides of the Dnieper near Kiev until the thirteenth century. Some of these tribes may have been remnants of the belligerent pagan Pechenegs.

One of the most famous medieval travelers' accounts is *History of the Mongols* by Friar Joannes de Plano Carpini, which was compiled between 1245 and 1247. Two versions of the text exist. During the course of his journeys in Kievan Rus and central Asia during the 1240s, Friar Joannes encountered Khazars who observed Christianity. For example, he noted that in the city of Ornas there lived many Christians, including Gazari, Ruthenians, and Alans.[105] The city of Ornas was governed by Muslims ("Saracens") and was astride "a river which flows through Iankint and the land of the Bisermins [the kingdom of Khwarizm] and runs into the sea . . . . " It seems that Ornas was located in central Asia. Macartney suggested that Ornas was an alternative name for the city of Gurganj. The prosperous city of Ornas was flooded when the Mongols dammed its river.

In another passage, Friar Joannes wrote that the Gazari were conquered by the Mongols.[106] Some of the Gazari lived south of Cumania, as did the Alans, Armenians, and Circassians, and according to Joannes all of these peoples were

Christians. These Gazari were probably descendants of Jewish Khazars who were forceably baptized. Yet, at least one tribe in southern Russia remained Jewish; the "Brutakhi who are Jews" were also mentioned by Joannes as victims of the Mongol conquests. Friar Joannes noted that the Brutakhi shaved their heads and lived south of Cumania. Paul Wexler considered the Brutakhi to be Jewish missionaries who were active in the "Cuman lands" of the Black Sea and Caspian Sea regions during the thirteenth century.[107] Nevertheless, the Brutakhi remain an unidentified and mysterious people since very little is known about them. It is not clear whether they were a Khazar, Cuman, or Judean tribe.

KHAZARS IN KAZAKHSTAN

After the fall of their kingdom, some of the Khazars went east. As mentioned in Chapter 8, a number of Khazars escaped to Siyah-Kuh on the Manghishlaq peninsula. What happened to these Khazar refugees? Some Kazakh historians believe that a number of Khazars settled along the Syr Darya and that some of the tribes in the Younger Horde (Kerderi, Berish, and Sherkesh) of western Kazakhstan were of Khazarian origin.[108] According to this view, the Khazars of Syr Darya were called "Kidarites" and, later, "Kerderites." Khazar origins have also been proposed for the Shekti tribe, which also was part of the Younger Horde.

It seems that in the thirteenth century the Turkic Khazars in Kazakhstan assimilated with other Turkic groups as well as with the Mongols, and consequently lost their ethnic identity. However, there still remain distinctive groups of Kazakhs who may be their progeny. For example, there are some modern-day Kazakhs who are called *Sary-Kazak* ("Yellow Kazakh") or *Kok-koz* ("Blue Eyes") because they have red hair, blue eyes, and white skin. For instance, some members of the Tobikti tribe are blue-eyed, and thousands of red-haired Kazakhs inhabit the western parts of the Kazakhstan near the Caspian

Sea. Thus, the Sary-Kazaks are presumably descendants of the Khazars or the Cumans.

It is hoped that further studies of culture and legends will help to determine the extent of any Khazar connection to western Kazakhstan.

KHAZARS IN OTHER PARTS OF THE WORLD

A number of Khazars immigrated to the Arabic regions of the Middle East, including Egypt and Iraq. Khazar soldiers served in an Abbasid army that fought the Byzantines circa 768.[109] Some Khazars even served as officers in the Arab Caliphate. Abu-Musa Bugha, the founder of the town of Shamkur in Azerbaijan, appears to have been a Khazar. Bugha took orders from Caliph Mutawakkil and allied with Muhammad ibn Khalid, ruler of Derbent. In the early 850s, Bugha broke the established order in the south Caucasus by attacking the Georgians, Abkhazians, Alans, Sanars, and Khazars; killing Armenian patricians as well as Ishaq ibn Ismail, the amir of Tbilisi; and exiling many other rulers from Transcaucasia to Iraq.[110] Ishaq ibn Kundajiq al-Khazari served as a general in the Caliphate during the wars between Caliph Mu'tamid (reigned 870–892) and the Tulunid governor of Egypt, Khumarawayh (ruled 884–896).[111] Takin ibn Abdullah al-Khazari served as governor of Egypt in the early tenth century.[112] A Muslim Khazar, Abdullah ibn Bashtu al-Khazari, served as Volga Bulgar khan Almush's envoy to the caliph Ja'far al-Muktadir and traveled from Baghdad to Bukhara with the diplomat Ahmad ibn Fadlan in the 920s. Muhammad ibn Raiq, a Muslim Khazar, served as *amir al-umara* (military chief) in the Abbasid Caliphate from 936–938 and 942–945.[113]

Benjamin of Tudela, when speaking of Egypt in the second half of the twelfth century, wrote: "Alexandria is a commercial market for all nations. Merchants come thither from all the Christian kingdoms." Among the places from which these merchants arrived were Croatia, England, France, India,

Italy, Russia, Yemen, and "Khazaria."[114] Benjamin gave no further indications of the identity of these "Khazarian" merchants. It is possible that the traders from "Khazaria" were non-Turkic Crimeans, and it is not clear whether or not they were Jews.

The Jewish Khazars were encountered by a prominent rabbi, Petakhiah ben Jacob, toward the end of his famous journey. Petakhiah was a German Jew, born in Regensburg (Ratisbon) and living in Prague, whose experiences were detailed in the travelogue *Sibbuv ha-Olam* (Journey Around the World) by Rabbi Judah the Pious bar Samuel in the late twelfth century. He began his travels in Bohemia in 1170 and returned to Central Europe in 1187. During his seventeen-year journey, he passed through Poland, the city of Kiev and the Dnieper, Crimea, Tartary (south Russia and the Caucasus), Armenia, and the Middle East and eastern Mediterranean.

Rabbi Petakhiah visited "the land of Kedar" around 1175 or 1180. Kedar apparently was the land east of the Dnieper. Petakhiah observed that the inhabitants of Kedar had no ships, but were skilled in archery and lived in steppe territories devoid of mountains. Herbert Zeiden identified the "Bnai Kedar" as the Cumans (Kipchak Turks).[115] Petakhiah found only "heretics" (apparently Karaites) in the land of Kedar because no Jews lived there.[116] These "heretics" did not have knowledge of the Talmud, and their prayers consisted exclusively of psalms. In fact, they were altogether unversed in rabbinical practices. On Sabbath day, they ate bread in the dark and stood still. After visiting Kedar, Rabbi Petakhiah traveled "at the extremity of the land of Khozaria" where seventeen Dnieper river tributaries existed. He passed between the Sea of Azov and the Caspian Sea, and then proceeded to enter Armenia before encountering Muslims.

Koestler claimed that the "heretics" interviewed by Petakhiah were Khazars living in the north of Crimea, while Schipper claimed that they were Karaites of the Tmutorokan area. Koestler's view is improbable, because there is no evidence that they were ethnic Khazars. It seems more likely that they were Karaites of Byzantine origin. Furthermore, "Kedar" does not necessarily refer to Khazaria, because it was probably a general term for nomads. In fact, the land of Kedar is considered to be separate from Khazaria in *Sibbuv ha-Olam*: "And a day's journey behind the land of Kedar extends a gulf [the Black Sea], intervening between the land of Kedar and the land of Khozaria."[117] This distinction is also apparent by another statement in the travelogue: "Khozaria has a language of its own; Togarma has a language of its own (they pay tribute to the King of Greece); and Kedar has a language of its own."[118]

Yet the rabbi eventually did have the opportunity to meet real Khazars, in a meeting that took place around the year 1185:

> Whilst at Baghdad he [Rabbi Petakhiah] saw ambassadors from the kings of Meshech (Khozaria), Magog is about ten days' journey thence. The land extends as far as the Mountains of Darkness. Beyond the Mountains of Darkness are the sons of Jonadab, son of Rechab.[119]

According to Dunlop, these Khazars " . . . had become Jews and been in communication with the Head of the Academy. They welcomed poor scholars to teach their children Torah and Talmud."[120]

NOTES

1. Alexander Scheiber, *Jewish Inscriptions in Hungary from the 3rd Century to 1686* (Budapest: Akadémiai, 1983), pp. 15, 21.

2. Raphael Patai, *The Jews of Hungary* (Detroit: Wayne State University Press, 1996), p. 29.

3. *An Ethnohistorical Dictionary of the Russian and Soviet Empires*, ed. James S. Olson (Westport, CT: Greenwood Press, 1994), p. 453.

4. István Fodor, *In Search of a New Homeland*, trans. Helen Tarnoy (Gyoma, Hungary: Corvina, 1982), p. 235.

5. See Sándor L. Tóth, "A nyolcadik törzs (Hogyan lett magyar a kabar?)," in *Száz rejtely a magyar történelemből*, ed. Ferenc Halmos (Budapest: Gesta, 1994), pp. 16–17.

6. István Fodor, *In Search of a New Homeland*, p. 238.

7. Attila Kiss, "11th Century Khazar Rings from Hungary with Hebrew Letters and Signs," *Acta Archaeologica Academiae Scientiarum Hungaricae* 22 (1970): 347.

8. György Györffy, *King Saint Stephen of Hungary*, trans. Peter Doherty (New York: Columbia University Press, 1994), p. 79.

9. István Herényi, "A magyar törzsszövetség törzsei és törzsfői," *Századok* 116:1 (1982): 68, 70. Herényi claimed that Zsid, Zsida, and Zsidó—i.e., "Jew"—were the names of documented tribal fragments amongst the Khazars.

10. László Makkai, "The Hungarians' Prehistory, Their Conquest of Hungary, and Their Raids to the West in 955," in *A History of Hungary*, ed. Peter F. Sugar (Bloomington, IN: Indiana University Press, 1990), p. 11; Douglas M. Dunlop, "The Khazars," in *The Dark Ages*, ed. Cecil Roth and I. H. Levine (New Brunswick, NJ: Rutgers University Press, 1966), p. 348.

11. It is possible that Anonymus was referring to goat herders, since that is the meaning of the word *kozar* in the Slavic languages (see Gyula Pauler and Sandor Szilágyi, *A magyar honfoglalás kútföi* (Budapest, Nap, 1995), p. 408). On the other hand, Hansgerd Göckenjan suggested that "Cozar" was actually an ethnonym for the Khazars (see Hansgerd Göckenjan, *Hilfsvölker und Grenzwächter im mittelalterlichen Ungarn* (Wiesbaden, West Germany: Franz Steiner, 1972), p. 39). If so, Anonymus' account confirms other reports about the occupation of the northern and eastern sections of Hungary, plus lands in present-day Slovakia, by the Kabars, although the Khazars also settled in other parts of Hungary. Göckenjan said that Anonymus was familiar with the local tradition about Khazar settlements from residents of the upper Tisza. However, other scholars regard Anonymus as an unreliable source since he recorded oral traditions that could be legendary rather than factual.

12. Douglas M. Dunlop, "The Khazars," in *The Dark Ages*, p. 348.

13. Ibid.

14. Carlile A. Macartney, *The Magyars in the Ninth Cen-*

tury (Cambridge, England: Cambridge University Press, 1930), p. 231.

15. György Györffy, *King Saint Stephen of Hungary*, p. 27.

16. Alexander A. Vasiliev, *The Goths in the Crimea* (Cambridge, MA: The Mediaeval Academy of America, 1936), p. 100.

17. György Györffy, *King Saint Stephen of Hungary*, p. 19.

18. Alexander Scheiber, *Jewish Inscriptions in Hungary from the 3rd Century to 1686*, p. 75.

19. Attila Kiss, "11th Century Khazar Rings from Hungary with Hebrew Letters and Signs," p. 347. The Ellend cemetery also contained coins minted between 1000 and 1063. Kiss pointed out that rings containing interesting characters (possibly runes) were also unearthed at other Hungarian sites, although they may be Pecheneg or Cuman rings. Some of the rings appear to contain Hebrew-, Roman-, Turkic-, and Greek-style letters. They have been dated to the tenth and eleventh centuries. According to Kiss, the Khazar rings are unlike Roman-era inscriptions from Hungary (see Kiss, p. 344).

20. Douglas M. Dunlop, *The History of the Jewish Khazars* (New York: Schocken, 1967), p. 94.

21. Alexander A. Vasiliev, *The Goths in the Crimea*, p. 99.

22. Károly Czeglédy, "From East to West: The Age of Nomadic Migrations in Eurasia," *Archivum Eurasiae Medii Aevi* 3 (1983): 115.

23. Zvi Ankori, *Karaites in Byzantium* (New York: Ams Press, 1968), p. 73.

24. Hansgerd Göckenjan, *Hilfsvölker und Grenzwächter im mittelalterlichen Ungarn*, pp. 40–41.

25. Ibid., p. 41.

26. *An Ethnohistorical Dictionary of the Russian and Soviet Empires*, ed. James S. Olson, p. 314; *Magyar zsidó lexikon*, ed. Péter Ujvári (Budapest: Pallas, 1929), p. 510.

27. Alfred H. Posselt, *Geschichte des chazarisch-jüdischen Staates* (Vienna: Vereines zur Förderung und Pflege des Reformjudentums, 1982), p. 54; Arthur Koestler, *The Thirteenth Tribe* (New York: Random House, 1976), p. 143.

28. See Sándor L. Tóth, "Kabarok (kavarok) a 9. századi magyar törzsszövetségben," *Századok* 118:1 (1984): 92–113.

29. *Magyar zsidó lexikon*, ed. Péter Ujvári, p. 309; Nathan Ausubel, *Pictorial History of the Jewish People* (New York: Crown, 1953), p. 130.

30. S. Dagoni, "When a Jewish Kingdom Ruled Southern Russia," in *The Jewish People's Almanac*, ed. David C. Gross (New York: Hippocrene, 1994), p. 431.

31. Hansgerd Göckenjan, *Hilfsvölker und Grenzwächter im mittelalterlichen Ungarn*, p. 40. Simon Szyszman theorized that the Hungarian king Samuel Aba (ruled 1041–1044) was a chief of Kabar origin (see his "Le roi Bulan et le problème de la conversion des Khazars," *Ephemerides Theologicae Lovanienses* 33 (1957): 74–75).

32. Douglas M. Dunlop, "The Khazars," in *The Dark Ages*, p. 356.

33. *Magyar zsidó lexikon*, ed. Péter Ujvári, p. 510.

34. Alfred H. Posselt, *Geschichte des chazarisch-jüdischen Staates*, p. 44.

35. I would like to thank Ken Ottinger, a descendant of the Turkic Jews of Sfîntu Gheorghe, for sharing this folklore with me.

36. Edward D. Rockstein, "The Mystery of the Székely Runes," *The Epigraphic Society Occasional Papers* 19 (1990): 176. Four supplemental letters (a, f, h, l) were derived from the Greek script.

37. This is claimed by László Makkai in his "The Hungarians' Prehistory, Their Conquest of Hungary, and Their Raids to the West in 955," p. 10.

38. Lajos M. Ligeti, "The Khazarian Letter from Kiev and Its Attestation in Runiform Script," *Acta Linguistica Academiae Scientiarum Hungaricae* 31 (1981): 10.

39. László Makkai, "The Hungarians' Prehistory, Their Conquest of Hungary, and Their Raids to the West in 955," p. 13.

40. *The Illustrated Atlas of Jewish Civilization*, ed. Martin Gilbert (New York: Macmillan, 1990), p. 77.

41. David Bezborodko, *An Insider's View of Jewish Pioneering in the Glass Industry* (Jerusalem: Gefen, 1987), p. 63.

42. Samuel V. Kurinsky, *The Glassmakers* (New York: Hippocrene, 1991), p. 338.

43. Norman Davies, *God's Playground*, vol. 1 (New York: Columbia University Press, 1982), p. 79.

44. Joseph R. Rosenbloom, *Conversion to Judaism* (Cincinnati: Hebrew Union College Press, 1978), p. 113.

45. Kazimierz Piechotka and Maria Piechotka, *Wooden Synagogues*, trans. Rulka Langer (Warsaw: Arkady, 1959), p. 9.

46. Salo W. Baron, *A Social and Religious History of the Jews*, vol. 3 (New York: Columbia University Press, 1957), p. 338.

47. Jacob Litman, *The Economic Role of Jews in Medieval Poland* (Lanham, MD: University Press of America, 1984), p. 89; Paul Wexler, *The Ashkenazic Jews* (Columbus, OH: Slavica, 1993), p. 92; Paul Wexler, "The Reconstruction of Pre-Ashkenazic Jewish Settlements in the Slavic Lands in the Light of Linguistic Sources," *Polin—A Journal of Polish Jewish Studies* 1 (1986): 11.

48. See Moshe Altbauer, "Jeszcze o rzekomych 'chazarskich' nazwach miejścowych na ziemiach polskich," *Onomastica* 13 (1968): 120–128.

49. Samuel V. Kurinsky, *The Glassmakers*, pp. 340–341.

50. Alfred H. Posselt, *Geschichte des chazarisch-jüdischen Staates*, p. 45.

51. See Adolph Neubauer, "Egyptian Fragments," *The Jewish Quarterly Review* 9 (1897): 26–29.

52. Douglas M. Dunlop, *The History of the Jewish Khazars*, p. 256. The phrase "Wilderness of the Nations" derives from Ezekiel 20:35. Another messianic movement, in the middle of the twelfth century, was led by a Khazar Jew named Menahem ben Solomon, son of Solomon ben Duji. Menahem studied the Halakhah, Torah, and Talmud in Babylonia, according to Benjamin of Tudela. He changed his name to David al-Roy and planned to capture Jerusalem and restore the Jewish exiles to sovereignty in the Holy Land. See Arthur Koestler, *The Thirteenth Tribe*, pp. 136 –137.

53. Paul Wexler, *The Ashkenazic Jews*, pp. 113, 132.

54. Neal Ascherson, *Black Sea* (New York: Hill and Wang, 1995), p. 233.

55. Vladimir F. Minorsky, *A History of Sharvan and Darband in the 10th–11th Centuries* (Cambridge, England: W. Heffer and Sons, 1958), p. 149.

56. Paul Wexler, *The Ashkenazic Jews*, p. 131. Herbert G. Zeiden offers some alternative Turkic etymologies for *yarmulka* in his latest article, "Khazar/Kipchak Turkisms in Yiddish: Words and Surnames," *Yiddish* 11:1–2 (1998): 85–86.

57. Herbert G. Zeiden, "Davenen: A Turkic Etymology," *Yiddish* 10:2–3 (1996): 96 –97. Alternative theories propose that *davenen* derives from Hebrew or the Pontic dialect of Greek. On the Greek theory, see Daniel E. Gershenson, "Yiddish 'davenen' and the Ashkenazic Rite: Byzantine Jewry and the Ashkenazim," *Yiddish* 10:2–3 (1996): 85–86.

58. Daniel E. Gershenson, "Yiddish 'davenen' and the Ashkenazic Rite," p. 91. The form *bayrak* is found in Crimean Tatar and Turkish.

59. In Turkish, however, *balaban* means "bittern," a heron-like bird.

60. Qaplan Girai I ruled the Crimean Khanate from 1707 to 1708, then again from 1713 to 1716, and also from 1730 to 1736. Qaplan Girai II ruled during 1770. A word for "tiger" in Old Turkic was *tunga* or *tonga*. An alternative theory holds that Kaplan designates the Kohanim, since it means "priest" or "chaplain" in German and Czech and derives from a Latin root.

61. The Seljuk sultan circa 1067 was named Alp-Arslan.

62. Yusuf Khass Hajib, *Wisdom of Royal Glory*, trans. Robert Dankoff (Chicago: University of Chicago Press, 1983), p. 48.

63. Julius Brutzkus, "The Khazar Origin of Ancient Kiev," *Slavonic and East European Review* 22 (1944): 123.

64. Paul Wexler, *The Ashkenazic Jews*, pp. 108, 139.

65. Paul Wexler, "The Reconstruction of Pre-Ashkenazic Jewish Settlements . . . ," pp. 8–9.

66. Paul Wexler, *The Non-Jewish Origins of the Sephardic Jews* (Albany, NY: State University of New York Press, 1996), p. 206. Nisi, the name of one of the Khazar kings, derived his name from *Nisan* as well.

67. Nathan Ausubel, *Pictorial History of the Jewish People*, p. 138.

68. Douglas M. Dunlop, *The History of the Jewish Khazars*, p. 262; Benjamin Pinkus, *The Jews of the Soviet Union* (Cambridge, England: Cambridge University Press, 1988), p. 4.

69. Samuel V. Kurinsky, *The Glassmakers*, p. 338.

70. Thomas S. Noonan, "The Khazar Economy," to appear in *Archivum Eurasiae Medii Aevi* 9.

71. *Readings in Russian History*, eds. Alexander V. Riasanovsky and William E. Watson, vol. 1 (Dubuque, IA: Kendall/Hunt, 1991), pp. 27–28. The story of the Khazar delegation to Vladimir in 986 originates from the *Nestor Chronicle*, which seems to have been written no earlier than 1099. These Khazars lived in the "Zhidove" section of Kiev, near the Jewish Gate.

72. Henrik Birnbaum, "On Jewish Life and Anti-Jewish Sentiments in Medieval Russia," in *Essays in Early Slavic Civilization*, ed. Henrik Birnbaum (Munich: Wilhelm Fink, 1981), p. 244.

73. Benjamin Pinkus, *The Jews of the Soviet Union*, p. 4.

74. Kazimierz Piechotka and Maria Piechotka, *Wooden Synagogues*, p. 48.

75. Vsevolod L. Vikhnovich, "From the Jordan to the Dnieper," *Jewish Studies (Mada'e ha-Yahadut)* 31 (1991): 19–20. The view is sometimes expressed that these tombstones belonged to the Karaites, but evidence suggests that only the tombstones from the fifteenth century onward were those of Karaites.

76. Ibid, p. 23.

77. The letter from Cairo is mentioned in Henrik Birnbaum, "On Jewish Life and Anti-Jewish Sentiments in Medieval Russia," p. 231. In 1031, Yehudah ha-Kohen referred to Kievan Rus as the "Greek Canaan" (see Jacob Litman, *The Economic Role of Jews in Medieval Poland*, p. 93). In the twelfth century, Benjamin of Tudela noted that the Russian or Bohemian Jews of his time called the land of the Slavs "Canaan" (see Benjamin of Tudela, *The Itinerary of Benjamin of Tudela*, trans. Marcus N. Adler (Malibu, CA: Joseph Simon/Pangloss Press, 1987), p. 139).

78. Solomon Grayzel, *A History of the Jews* (New York: Meridian, 1984), p. 388.

79. Paul Wexler, "The Reconstruction of Pre-Ashkenazic Jewish Settlements . . . ," p. 4.

80. Henrik Birnbaum, "On Jewish Life and Anti-Jewish Sentiments in Medieval Russia," p. 231.

81. Douglas M. Dunlop, *The History of the Jewish Khazars*, p. 230.

82. Ibid., p. 262.

83. Joseph R. Rosenbloom, *Conversion to Judaism*, p. 113.

84. W. E. D. Allen, *The Ukraine* (New York: Russell and Russell, 1963), pp. 8–9. The Jewish historian Cecil Roth also believed that Ashkenazi Jews with Turkic physical features are Khazars (see Cecil Roth, *A Short History of the Jewish People* (London: Horovitz, 1969), p. 288). Some historians have written that Jews with brachycephalic skulls are probably descendants of the Khazars.

85. Raphael Patai and Jennifer Patai, *The Myth of the Jewish Race*, rev. ed. (Detroit: Wayne State University Press, 1989), p. 72.

86. Benjamin of Tudela, *The Itinerary of Benjamin of Tudela*, p. 70.

87. Douglas M. Dunlop, *The History of the Jewish Khazars*, p. 120.

88. Vladimir F. Minorsky, *Hudud al-'Alam (The Regions of the World)* (London: Luzac & Co., 1937), p. 455.

89. Thomas S. Noonan, "Did the Khazars Possess a Monetary Economy? An Analysis of the Numismatic Evidence," *Archivum Eurasiae Medii Aevi* 2 (1982): 246.

90. Thomas S. Noonan, "Why Dirhams First Reached Russia: The Role of Arab-Khazar Relations in the Development of the Earliest Islamic Trade with Eastern Europe," *Archivum Eurasiae Medii Aevi* 4 (1984): 265.

91. Vladimir F. Minorsky, *A History of Sharvan and Darband in the 10th–11th Centuries*, p. 51.

92. Peter B. Golden, *Khazar Studies*, vol. 1 (Budapest: Akadémiai, 1980), p. 85. Qaytaq, also spelled Xaydaq, is an alternative name for Jidan.

93. Lars Funch and Helen L. Krag, *The North Caucasus* (London: Minority Rights Group, 1994), p. 22.

94. Paul Wexler, "The Reconstruction of Pre-Ashkenazic Jewish Settlements . . . ," p. 10.

95. Peter B. Golden, *An Introduction to the History of the Turkic Peoples* (Wiesbaden, Germany: Otto Harrassowitz, 1992), p. 391.

96. Lars Funch and Helen L. Krag, *The North Caucasus*, p. 23.

97. Vladimir F. Minorsky, "A New Book on the Khazars," *Oriens* 11 (1959): 142.

98. Solomon Grayzel, *A History of the Jews*, p. 257.

99. Blanch Lesley, *The Sabres of Paradise* (New York: Carroll & Graf, 1960), p. 108.

100. George V. Gubaroff, *Cossacks and Their Land*, trans. John N. Washburn (Providence, RI: Cossack American National Alliance, 1985), pp. 193, 205–206.

101. Lev N. Gumilev, "New Data on the History of the Khazars," *Acta Archaeologica Academiae Scientiarum Hungaricae* 19 (1967): 84.

102. Vladimir F. Minorsky, *A History of Sharvan and Darband in the 10th–11th Centuries*, p. 113.

103. Julius Brutzkus, "The Khazar Origin of Ancient Kiev," p. 122. The Black Caps of medieval Russia may or may not be associated with the present-day Karakalpaks who live in Uzbekistan, because "Karakalpak" is a generic name referring to black-colored headgear.

104. For discussion, see George V. Gubaroff, *Cossacks and Their Land*, pp. 188–190.

105. *The Mongol Mission*, ed. Christopher Dawson (New York: Sheed & Ward, 1955), p. 29.

106. Ibid., p. 41.

107. Paul Wexler, *The Ashkenazic Jews*, pp. 199–200.

108. Beimbet B. Irmukhanov, *Kazakstan: istoriko-publitsisticheskiy vzglyad* (Almaty, Kazakhstan: Olke, 1996), p. 37.

109. Thomas S. Noonan, "Why Dirhams First Reached Russia . . . ," p. 234.

110. Vladimir F. Minorsky, *A History of Sharvan and Darband in the 10th–11th Centuries*, pp. 19, 25, 161.

111. Douglas M. Dunlop, *The History of the Jewish Khazars*, p. 61.

112. Ibid., p. 190.

113. *Great Dates in Islamic History*, ed. Robert Mantran (New York: Facts on File, 1996), p. 34.

114. Benjamin of Tudela, *The Itinerary of Benjamin of Tudela*, p. 134.

115. Herbert G. Zeiden, "Davenen: A Turkic Etymology," p. 99.

116. A translation of Petakhiah's visit to Kedar is given in *Jewish Travellers*, ed. Elkan N. Adler (London: George Routledge & Sons, 1930), p. 66.

117. Ibid., p. 65.

118. Ibid., p. 67.

119. Ibid., p. 83.

120. Douglas M. Dunlop, *The History of the Jewish Khazars* p. 220.

10

THE PHENOMENON OF PROSELYTISM

It was not only the Khazars who became Jewish. This chapter explores Iranian, Slavic, African, Middle Eastern, and other Turkic proselytes. Some of the Alans and Cumans appear to have adopted Judaism under the influence of the Khazars.

JUDAISM AMONG THE AVARS

The Avars were a Turko-Mongolian people who had an influence on European affairs in the sixth, seventh, and eighth centuries. As in the case of the Khazars, the Avars ruled a large multiethnic empire, known as the Avar Empire or the Avar Kaganate. The supreme Avar ruler was called the kagan. His wife was called the khatun. His deputies were the yugur and the tudun. The Avars also had tarkhans.

The Avars were originally shamanists. They were great warriors as well as artists. The Avars created bronze belt plaques and buckles, harness hooks, ornaments, carpets, and artwork depicting animals, plants, and geometric patterns. Avar military leaders owned gold-plated swords and quivers, while warriors owned silver-plated ones. The Avars did not mint their own coins.[1] They used a runic script for inscriptions, but probably belonged to an oral tradition since no Avarian documents have been discovered.[2]

Samur (Sam-Ör), kagan of the Avars, conquered the Pannonian plain in the sixth century. By 560, the Avars controlled the territory from the Volga to the mouth of the Danube. In 562, the Avars conquered as far west as the River Elbe region. The Slavs of the Elbe were ruled by the Avars until 605.

Many of the Avars intermingled with their neighbors. Indeed, some Avars were Slavicized. Mixed Avar-Slav graves existed in modern-day Slovakia, Moravia, and Austria; mixed Germanic-Avar settlements existed in Bavaria; and mixed Avar-Slav-Germanic graves existed in Slovenia.[3]

The Avar kagan Bayan (reigned 565–602) began to attack the Byzantines in 582. The Avars assembled an army of considerable strength, numbering many thousands of soldiers. Avar forces plundered and ravaged much of the Balkans during the early seventh century. The Byzantine emperor Heraclius signed a peace treaty with the Avars around 622, and the Byzantine Empire paid tribute to the Avars.[4] However, the Avars, in collaboration with Slavs and Bulgars, attacked the city of Constantinople for several days in late July and early August of 626.

However, the Avars would not dominate central Europe much longer. By 650 their territory was reduced in size to include only the area from the lower and middle Danube to the Carpathians, along with some lands west of the middle Danube. In the second half of the eighth century, a terrible drought fell upon the Avar Empire, causing widespread famine. Neither the Avar commoners nor the nobles were immune to this disaster. Even worse events were to follow.

The Avars allied with Tassilo III, the duke of Bavaria, whose reign had begun in 748. When he was removed from power in 787 or 788, the Avars invaded Bavaria but were repelled by the Franks. The emperor of the Franks, Charlemagne, absorbed Bavaria into his realm and began direct attacks upon the Avars in 791. He established a strike force to go against the Avars, consisting of King Pepin (his son), Duke John of Istria, a bishop, and many other officials and nobles. The strike force plundered an Avar fortification and seized a large quantity of booty, as well as 150 prisoners.[5] As Charlemagne approached other Avar fortifications in the autumn of 791, the Avar garrisons fled. According to the *Annales Mosellani*, this Frankish expedition devastated much of Avaria, yet Avaria was not completely crushed.[6]

In 795, Eric, the *margrave* (prince) of Friuli, sent out an army under the leadership of Wonomyr, a Slav, which took a great many treasures from the Alföld region of Avaria.

The Avar kaganate began to fall apart. In early 796, according to *Annales regni Francorum*, an Avar tudun came to Aachen to submit to Emperor Charlemagne's authority, and he was baptized into Christianity. In the same year, King Pepin led a large expedition against the Avars in the Alföld and won a tremendous victory.[7] The Avar chief Zodan, along with many other Avars, submitted to Frankish control in November 803.

Annales regni Francorum stated that the Avar khan Theodorus, a convert to Christianity, came to Emperor Charlemagne's court in early 805 and asked him to grant his people a territory on or near the Kis Alföld in upper Pannonia extending from Szombathely in the south to Petronel in the north. The khan explained to Charlemagne that his people were being attacked by Slavs and could no longer survive in their existing Avarian homeland.[8] Charlemagne accepted Theodorus' request and allowed the Avar people to settle on the far eastern edge of Austria near the Rába and Danube rivers, but Theodorus died not long afterward. The new Avar khan, Abraham (reigned 805–?), was baptized and given limited autonomy as the Frankish client over the new Avar territory.

Annales regni Francorum recorded that the Avars were quarreling with the Slavs of the Danube in the year 811. The Avar khan and tudun, as well as the opposing Slavic leaders, arrived in the Frankish court to explain the situation, and the Franks soon sent an expedition into Pannonia to try to end the dispute. Thereafter the Avars disappeared from historical documentation.

In 1972, 263 graves were discovered near the village of Chelarevo, in the Vojvodina district of present-day Serbia. The site appears to verify the existence of intimate ties between Turkic Avars or Khazars and observers of the Jewish faith in the years following the destruction of the Avar Empire. Some of the graves included horse skeletons, decorated horse harnesses, armor, and yellow ceramics.[9] More important, Jewish motifs have been found on at least seventy of the brick fragments excavated from the graves. The Jewish symbols on the fragments include menorahs, shofars, etrogs, candle-snuffers, and ash-collectors.[10] One of the brick fragments, which was placed over the grave of Yehudah, has a Hebrew inscription that reads, "Yehudah, oh!"[11] The skulls in the Chelarevo graves had Mongolian features.[12] These findings led the archaeologists R. Bunardžić and S. Živanović to conclude that a Judaized Mongolian people lived near the site.

Bunardžić considered the Chelarevo burials to be Avar in origin, and he estimated that they date from the late eighth century to the early ninth century. The linguist Paul Wexler also characterized the graves as Avarian.[13] However, carbon-14 dating of bone samples from the double burial 244–244A suggests that they date from the year 969 ± 66 years.[14] István Erdélyi therefore concluded that the burials may originate from the period when the Magyars and the Kabars first settled in the Carpathian Basin—i.e., the late ninth century or the early tenth century:

> One can conjecture that this burial ground belonged to the Kabar tribes which joined the Hungarians at the time when

they discovered their fatherland. Some of the Kabars, arriving from Khazaria, apparently kept their Judaic religion.[15]

Vsevolod Vikhnovich, an expert on Khazar history, agreed with Erdélyi's suggestion that the people buried at Chelarevo were Kabars.[16]

JUDAISM AMONG THE CUMANS

Another Turkic people, the Cumans, also may have become Jews. The Cumans were called Polovtsy ("yellowish, sallow") by the Rus'ians, Kunok by the Magyars, and Comani by Europeans, but they were also known as Kipchak Turks. In the ninth and tenth centuries, the Cumans lived in the steppes of Asia near the Irtysh River, but in the early eleventh century they trekked westward and arrived near the Volga. They dominated the Russian and Ukrainian steppes from the mid-eleventh century to the early thirteenth century, demanding tribute from many peoples. Cumania included the flat steppelands between the Dnieper, Don, Volga, and Ural (*Yayik*) Rivers.

In the eleventh century, the Cumans began to live in the valleys along the middle and lower Donets. The Cuman horde led by Khan Blush arrived at the periphery of Kievan Rus and negotiated a peace settlement with the Rus'ians. Additionally, the Cumans defeated the Pechenegs and drove them westward. The initial harmony between the Rus'ians and the Cumans did not last long. The Rus'ians launched their first expedition against the Cumans in the early eleventh century. They marched toward the shores of the Sea of Azov, where the hordes of khans Urusoba, Altunopa, and Belduz were residing. Urusoba and Altunopa both were killed in combat, as were many other khans. The victorious Rus'ians seized cattle, sheep, horses, camels, and other possessions from the Cumans.[17] The Cumans recovered from these blows only several decades later. By the end of the eleventh century and the start of the twelfth century, khans Bonyak and Tugorkin

(Tugarin) had once again transformed the Cumans into a formidable military force. However, Tugorkin was killed during
a march against the Rus'ians.

The Cumans also went on several expeditions to Poland.
The *Chronicle of Gallus* reported that in 1100 or 1101, three
divisions of Cuman soldiers marched as far west as the left
hand of the Vistula River in central Poland and stole many
items, but that they were defeated by Polish troops.[18] In 1135,
Cumans destroyed the town of Wiślica, which was located
along the Nida River in southern Poland.

Soldiers from Kievan Rus, under their ruler Vladimir
Monomakh, defeated the Cumans in 1111.[19] However, the
Cumans continued to rule the steppes until about 1223. In
the middle of the twelfth century, the Cumans ruled over the
lands between the Dnieper and the Volga, as far north as the
territory between the Sula and Orel Rivers, and as far south
as Cherson, Tmutorokan, and the north Caucasus.

In the late twelfth century, Khan Konchak led a powerful
military organization along the Tora and Don Rivers, and the
Rus'ians were no longer able to defeat the Cumans. Igor
Svyatoslavich, prince of Novgorod-Severski, led two expeditions
against the Cumans in 1184 and 1191 but failed both times.[20]

The Cumans were ultimately conquered by the Mongol
invaders. In the spring of 1223, the Cumans and Rus'ian
armies were soundly defeated by the Mongols at the River
Kalka, in the steppes along the Azov shore. Many of the
Cumans escaped into the Carpathian region and became subjects of the Hungarian king.[21] Other Cumans migrated to
Egypt and became the sultan's guards, known as Mamluks.[22]
The remainder of the Cumans remained in the steppes. In
the fourteenth century, the Arab writer al-Omari wrote that
the Cumans intermarried with the Mongols of the Golden
Horde.[23]

Recently, a few scholars have suggested that some of the
Cumans became Jews. David Nicolle, for example, wrote: "In
additional [sic] to the Khazar Turks' well-known conversion

to Judaism, part of the Turkish Qipchaq tribe also converted to Judaism in the mid-12th century."[24]

The hypothesis that Judaism existed among the Cumans is questionable, since it is known that shamanism was practiced by many, if not most, of the Cumans. The Persian poet Nizami (circa 1141–1203) described in one of his poems how the Cumans worshipped their ancestors and predecessors by kneeling down before stone statues and leaving sacrificial animals (such as sheep and horses) beside the statues.[25] The traveler William de Rubruck verified this practice when he wrote (in 1253) that the Cumans built stone statues over the graves of the dead, each of which had a large engraved image of the dead person holding a drinking cup over the stomach.[26] The Cuman statues faced the East. A number of these statues have survived to the present day, and they have been examined by archaeologists.

There are, however, a few facts that may be presented in favor of the hypothesis of Jewish Cumans. The sons of the Cuman prince Kobiak were given the Jewish names Isaac and Daniel.[27] The Brutakhi missionaries mentioned in the travelogue of the Italian friar Joannes de Plano Carpini (see Chapter 9) may have converted some of the Cumans to Judaism. Furthermore, the Cuman words *shabat* and *shabat kün* (meaning "Saturday") are related to the Hebrew word *Shabbat*, meaning "Sabbath."[28] The Jewish influences upon the Cumans may have resulted from intermarriage between the Khazars and the Cumans in the mid-eleventh century, as Peter Golden has suggested.[29] Perhaps Cumanic rule over a loose confederation of tribes in southern Russia may be seen as a continuation of the Khazarian tradition.

As to physical appearance, the ethnonym Polovtsy is sometimes interpreted as meaning that the Cumans had blond hair. Whether any of the blond-haired Jews of eastern Europe are descended from the Cumans cannot be ascertained as of yet. It is certain, however, that many Cumans adopted Christianity, and thus live among Christian populations to this day.

JUDAISM AMONG THE ALANS

The Alan people (also known as *As, Os,* and *Yasians*), ancestors of the Ossetians, were descendants of Sarmatians. They spoke an Iranian language. Alania, the homeland of the Alans, was located north of the Caucasus Mountains. Their capital city was called Maghas.

The Alans converted to Orthodox Christianity in around 915. However, they rejected Christianity in around 932, according to al-Masudi, and expelled the bishops and priests who had been sent to them by the Byzantine emperor.[30] A number of the Alans soon adopted the Jewish faith of their Khazar neighbors, as recorded by the *Schechter Letter:*

> [But in the days of Benjamin] the king, all the nations were stirred up against [Khazaria], and they besieged the[m with the aid of] the king of Maqedon . . . only the king of Alania was in support of [the people of Khazaria, for] some of them were observing the Law of the Jews.[31]

Duke Svyatoslav of Kievan Rus conquered the Alans in the year 965. The Alans were again conquered, this time by the Mongols, between 1221 and 1223. Some of the Alans settled in Moldova,[32] while other Alans lived in the Cherson and Chufut-Kale regions of the Crimea in the thirteenth and early fourteenth centuries.[33]

The ultimate fate of the Alans who converted to Judaism went unrecorded. It has been suggested that the Judaized Alans mixed with other Jews of the Caucasus to form part of the population of Mountain Jews.[34]

EUROPEAN CONVERTS TO JUDAISM

According to many scholars, Judaism was propagated widely as early as the first century. In Matthew 23:15, the apostle Matthew reported that the Pharisees traveled by land and by sea in pursuit of proselytes. Furthermore, the first-century Jewish historian Josephus wrote that there were many converts to

Judaism in the Roman Empire. It was common for Roman women to convert after marrying Jews. About ten percent of the population of the Roman Empire was Jewish by about the start of the common era.[35] This significant percentage is often attributed to the spread of Judaism among non-Jews.

Martin Goodman, however, challenged the theory that many converts were sought by Jews in the first century. Rather, it was only in the second and third centuries that some rabbis called for an active mission to non-Jews, according to Goodman:

> The missionary hero in search of converts for Judaism is a phenomenon first attested well after the start of the Christian mission, not before it. There is no good reason to suppose that any Jew would have seen value in seeking proselytes in the first century with an enthusiasm like that of the Christian apostles.[36]

Goodman proposed that Matthew 23:15 refers to the conversion of existing Jews to the beliefs of the Pharisee sect, rather than to the conversion of non-Jews to Judaism.[37] He also wrote that it is possible that the vast majority of early conversions to Judaism were performed because a non-Jewish woman planned to marry a Jewish man.[38]

In ancient times, many gentiles had an informal association with Judaism. These gentiles were granted the title "God-fearers" by the Jews. God-fearers lived in such places as Romania, Greece, and Asia Minor. An early third-century Jewish Greek inscription from a synagogue in Aphrodisias (southwest Anatolia) demonstrates that some non-Jews had accepted part of the Jewish way of life.[39] Although the God-fearers attended synagogue services, they did not formally convert to Judaism.

When the Roman Empire officially adopted Christianity, conversion to Judaism became prohibited. In 315, Emperor Constantine I issued the first Roman edict forbidding Jews to seek converts. In 339, Emperor Constantine II issued a policy stating that property would be confiscated from any Jew who assisted a Christian to convert.[40] Yet, Judaizing movements continued to spring up in the following centuries in many lands.

Judaism became so popular in ninth-century Bulgaria that Bulgarian proselytes converted others to Judaism as well, according to a query letter composed in 866 by King Boris I of Bulgaria.[41] Pope Nicholas I "the Great" (reigned 858–867) wrote, in Reply #10 of his *Responsa Nicolai ad consulta Bulgarorum* to the king, that he was also aware of how Jewish preachers were active in Judaizing the Bulgarian populace. In particular, the pope complained about how Judaizers encouraged non-Jews to abstain from work on Saturdays.[42] Nikolaj Kochev suggested that Balkan slaves also became Jews, encouraged by Jewish laws under which Jewish-owned slaves who adopted Judaism were freed after seven years of servitude.[43]

Jews were active in seeking converts on the Iberian peninsula. Evidence suggests that African slaves owned by Jews in Spain and Morocco converted to Judaism. Jews were proselytizing in Granada (in Andalusia, southern Spain) as early as the fourth century.[44] Because of the existence of a fairly large conversion phenomenon in Spain, Jews were obliged to take appropriate steps. For this reason, it was necessary for Rabbi Shlomo ben Adret of Barcelona (1230–1310) to indicate the order of the blessings to be said when converts were initiated into the Jewish community.[45] Christian authorities initiated measures to try to stem the tide of conversion, and by the eleventh or twelfth century they had largely succeeded in halting widespread proselytism in Spain. Yet, even as late as the fourteenth and fifteenth centuries, there were still Spanish church edicts and royal proclamations that tried to prevent Jews from owning non-Jewish slaves and to stop Christians from converting to the Jewish faith.[46] In his book *The Non-Jewish Origins of the Sephardic Jews,* Paul Wexler put forth the theory that the Sephardic Jews of Spain and Portugal were descended primarily from Arabs, Berbers, and Romance-language-speaking Europeans who adopted Judaism and mixed with a small number of Palestinian Jews.

A Catholic priest in Mainz, Germany, became a proselyte in 1012.[47] A Norman priest in southern Itlay converted to Judaism in 1102 and adopted the name Obadiah. In the 13th century, a French monk converted and adoped the name Abraham ben Abraham. He was captured and burned after fleeing to Germany.

In the twelfth century, Judaized Vlachs who lived in the highlands of Wallachia, north of Greece, gave themselves Jewish names and did not observe Christianity, according to Benjamin of Tudela's travelogue. The Judaized Vlachs were described as a fierce and autonomous people who were engaged in theft. Benjamin wrote that some people considered the Vlachs to be Jews.[48]

Most of the recorded cases of conversion to Judaism come from twelfth- and thirteenth-century France and Germany. Many rabbis in those countries belonged to the Tosafist school of rabbinical theology and strongly supported conversion to Judaism, considering it a divine commandment. The Tosafists succeeded in bringing many Europeans into the Jewish community. For example, proselytes during the Middle Ages in Pontoise (northern France), Lunel (southern France), Hungary, and many other places became quite dedicated to the study of Torah and Talmud. Many specific instances of Tosafist-sponsored conversion have been recorded. A Tosafist named Abraham ha-Ger was a convert to Judaism who believed that proselytes observe Jewish laws better than "born Jews."[49] A convert lived and studied Talmud in the home of Rabbi Yitzhak ben Asher ha-Levi, a Tosafist in Speyer (a German city along the Rhine).[50]

The Tosafist rabbis struggled with the issue of whether converts should consider themselves members of the people of Israel and whether they could use phrases declaring their membership in the Israelite nation during prayer. Some, such as Rabbi Yitzhak ben Samuel of Dampierre, used the Palestinian Talmud to show that converts shared equal status with "born Jews" regarding the heritage of Israel, whereas others (such as Rabbi Jacob Tam of Rameru) declared that converts were not entirely equal and thus could not lead the saying of blessings.[51] Tosafist rabbis also dealt with issues surrounding ownership of houses, land, and other possessions following the death of a convert.

How many Christians, in total, converted to Judaism in France and Germany? Detailed records of the numbers of converts are not available, but Ben Zion Wacholder estimated—based on the existing documentation—that hundreds of individuals converted during the twelfth and thirteenth centuries.[52]

The many medieval anti-Jewish laws that prohibited slave conversion and intermarriage between Jews and Christians demonstrate that among Christians the fear of proselytism was widespread. It was not until around the eleventh to thirteenth centuries that widespread conversion to Judaism ceased. The decrease in Jewish proselytism in Europe was directly connected to the harsh laws and persecutions created by Christians. European church and government policies against conversion to Judaism intensified, starting in around 1215.[53] Yitzhak Males of Toulouse (France) was executed in 1278 for his participation in proselytizing efforts.

Salomon of Üregh, a Hungarian Jew, converted his slave girl to Judaism in the early thirteenth century.[54] When the Hungarian city of Buda was under Turkish rule (1526–1686), it was common for Jews to own Christian slaves and subsequently to convert them to Judaism and marry them.[55]

Judaizing in Russia occurred even as late as the late fifteenth and early sixteenth centuries, but it was eventually suppressed. In 1539, a Polish proselyte from Kraków was burned to death. Converts to Judaism in the first half of the eighteenth century in Dubno (Ukraine), Vilnius (Lithuania), and other parts of eastern Europe also were massacred. For example, in the small town of Sverovoch, a retired naval captain named Alexander Vosnitzyn decided to convert to Judaism and was circumcised, but as a result he was publicly burned in Saint Petersburg in July 1738 to deter others from converting.

Conrad Victor, a German professor at the University of Marburg, moved to Salonika and converted to Judaism in the beginning of the seventeenth century, adopting the name Moses Prado. Some Bohemian Hussites took up Judaism in the seventeenth century. They adopted the circumcision rite and began to observe the Jewish Sabbath.

There was also an eighteenth-century Catholic in Kletzk, Lithuania named Martin Nicolai Radziwill who adopted the Jewish faith.[56] He learned Hebrew, studied the Torah and Talmud, and adhered to Jewish laws—including those pertaining to the observance of the Sabbath.

THE SABBATARIANS

The Sabbatarian movement was an example of the appeal of Jewish traditions to large numbers of non-Jewish peoples. The Sabbatarians were Unitarian Christians in Transylvania who adopted elements of Judaism. For instance, they adhered to kosher laws and celebrated Jewish holidays, and their day of rest was Saturday rather than Sunday.[57]

The Sabbatarian movement began in the late sixteenth century when an influential Székely nobleman named Andreas Eőssi and his Transylvanian followers began to observe the Jewish Sabbath and the other commandments of the Torah. After Simon Péchi (1575–1642) created a Sabbatarian prayerbook, it became a very attractive belief system in the region, and about twenty thousand Székelys converted to Sabbatarianism in the late sixteenth century.

The leaders of the sect were executed in 1639 by Transylvanian governmental authorities. As a result, Sabbatarianism diminished, and only some people in certain villages remained committed to the ideology. The Székelys of Bözödujfalu stayed faithful to Sabbatarianism over the years and officially converted to rabbinical Judaism in 1869.[58] Five years later, they constructed a synagogue.

THE SUBBOTNIKI

The Subbotniki ("Sabbath worshippers") of Russia are sometimes considered to be descendants of the Khazars who
adopted the Slavic language and the Orthodox Christian religion while retaining aspects of Jewish identity. However, it
seems that the Subbotniki are actually ethnic Russians whose
beliefs combined Christianity with Judaism. They believe that
Jesus was a prophet, but not a divinity. Apparently, the
Subbotniki originated in the late seventeenth century—well
after the fall of Khazaria.

After Czar Nicholas I (reigned 1825–1855) exiled the Russian Molokani sect to the Caucasus, they came into contact
with Subbotniki missionaries, and many of them thus also
adopted the Judaized Subbotniki teachings. Subbotniki worshippers pray in Russian, rather than Hebrew, but many of
their beliefs—including observing the Sabbath on Saturday
rather than Sunday—reflect their Judaized status. Many
Subbotniki adopted Hebrew names.

The example of the Subbotniki demonstrates the attraction
of Jewish beliefs and practices to large numbers of Slavs in recent centuries.

WEXLER'S THEORY OF PROSELYTISM
AMONG THE WEST SLAVS

In his book *The Ashkenazic Jews*, Paul Wexler proposed a
Sorbian origin for German and eastern European Jews. His
theory is based primarily on cultural and linguistic grounds,
but is not supported by historical documentation. Wexler
claimed that Yiddish words have similarities with Upper
Sorbian.[59] However, many Yiddish words derive from other
forms of Slavic as well, including Russian and Polish. Wexler
also claimed that Yiddish shares a verbal prefix similarity with
Slavic.[60] In essence, Wexler characterized Yiddish as a form of
Slavic:

Yiddish—in contrast to its massive German vocabulary—has a native Slavic syntax and sound system—and thus must be classified as a Slavic language; Yiddish has a Slavic syntax and phonology since it was a form of the West Slavic language Sorbian which became re-lexified to High German. A massive German lexicon cannot make Yiddish German, just as the massive Franco-Latin component of Modern English gives no grounds for declaring that English has ceased to be a Germanic language, and has moved over to the Romance camp.[61]

Needless to say, this hypothesis is highly controversial.

It is known that some Jews were slaveowners in the early medieval period. It is also known that some of Germany's Slavs became slaves. Any Slavs who were slaves to Jews would have converted to Judaism, as it was a common practice for slaves owned by Jews to convert. The Sorbs, who are West Slavs and today live in Brandenburg and Saxony in eastern Germany, have never had their own independent nation. Furthermore, the Sorbs—as well as the West Slavic Polabians—were still pagans in the late tenth century. The nationless, pagan Sorbs thus would have been prime candidates for conversion to Judaism, according to Wexler.

In my opinion, there is no reason to limit the conversion phenomenon to the Sorbs of eastern Germany. Converting to Judaism was a feasible choice wherever the general population was still pagan, as in Bulgaria, Poland, and Lithuania. Poland was officially Christianized only around 966, when King Mieszko I, founder of the Piast dynasty, was baptized. Moreover, Lithuania was the last country in Europe to accept Christianity. Lithuania officially became a Catholic country in 1387 when Grand Duke Jagiello accepted the faith, but most Lithuanian peasants remained pagans for several more centuries.[62]

Wexler attempted to ascribe to Ashkenazic customs a Sorbian or other Slavic origin. Among these customs are:

1. The Jewish practice of mounting protective mezuzah amulets on doorposts of homes. The mezuzah is a

parchment with two passages from the Book of
Deuteronomy inscribed on it. A mezuzah is placed in a
decorative case prior to being mounted. Wexler compared this practice to Sorbian horseshoes, as well as to
other Slavic (e.g., Czech) practices.[63] However, the use
of the mezuzah among Jews dates from ancient times,
and is mentioned in the Talmud.

2. The tradition of performing certain routines—like lick-
ing a child's forehead and spitting three times—as protection against the so-called "evil eye." This tradition was
common to both Sorbs and Jews.[64] However, the "evil
eye" was guarded against by Oriental Jews, who were not
of European origin, as well as by many other peoples,
such as Italian sailors.

3. The tradition of slaughtering a rooster as an offering.
It was both a Slavic and a Jewish practice.[65] However,
the Jewish slaughtering practice (*kapparot*)—performed
on the eve of Yom Kippur—is mentioned in the writings of the Gaonim and was also practiced in Spain, and
is not necessarily Slavic in origin.

4. The Jewish practice of giving two names to a person,
one secular and one religious. This is parallel to Slavic
tradition.[66]

5. The arrangement of marriages by a brokering process
handled by males. This was common among both Slavs
and eastern European Jews.[67]

6. Both Jews and pagan Slavs practiced many religious ceremonies at home rather than at the temple.[68] However,
as Wexler himself stated, the Jewish home ceremonies
(e.g., the Pesach seder, the lighting of the menorah during Hanukkah, etc.) are extremely ancient.

7. The Jewish tradition of breaking a glass at weddings in
order to ward off evil spirits. This may have a pagan origin.[69]

8. The *tashlikh* ceremony of washing away one's sins and
emptying one's pockets during the afternoon of Rosh

Hashanah. It has parallels with medieval Italian Christian customs, as well as with Slovak and Hungarian customs, and may be of non-Jewish origins.[70]

9. Jewish funeral practices in eastern Europe. These had parallels not only with Sorbs, but also with South Slavs, Poles, Moravians, and Germans.[71]

I do not see how any of these customs can be attributed exclusively to Sorbian influence. The vast majority of cultural similarities and Slavic words in Yiddish cited by Wexler may be explained just as easily by a connection between the Ashkenazic Jews and Polish, Czech, Slovak, Ukrainian, or Polabian cultures and languages. Just because a particular Jewish custom may be of pagan origin does not necessarily mean that it is West Slavic. More important, none of Wexler's cultural and linguistic arguments proves that Sorbs ever converted to Judaism in large numbers. Wexler's suggestion that the Sorbs and the Polabians were the primary ancestors of the Ashkenazic Jews is thus unable to be substantiated. On the other hand, it is correct to assume that Slavs in general were part of the Ashkenazic ethnogenesis, as were Turkic tribes.

CONVERTS IN ADIABENE

History presents several examples of other territories that, like Khazaria and ancient Judea and Israel, were once under Jewish sovereignty. In these kingdoms, the rulers and the people embraced Judaism.

Two of the kings of Adiabene, members of the royal family, and a number of the people became Jews in the first century C.E.[72] The kingdom of Adiabene was located east of the Tigris River between the Great Zab and Little Zab Rivers, and was part of the Assyrian section of the Parthian Empire. Today, the area encompasses part of northern Iraq. The capital of Adiabene was Arbela.

In *Antiquities of the Jews*, compiled circa 93 or 94 C.E., Josephus wrote that Monobazus I,[73] king of Adiabene, married his sister, Helena. Monobazus I and Queen Helena had two sons, Izates and Monobazus (later Monobazus II), but Monobazus I also had other sons by other wives. However, Izates was the king's favorite son, so he was accorded many honors. He was sent to the palace of Abennerig, king of Charax-Spasini. Izates and Abennerig became good friends, so Izates married Abennerig's daughter Samacha and was given some measure of ruling power. After his sojourn in Charax-Spasini, Izates was given control over the land of Carrae,[74] where the remains of Noah's ark were kept. Izates remained in Carrae until his father's death.

During Izates' residence in Carrae, a Jewish merchant named Ananias (Hananya) interested the women of Izates' harem in the Jewish religion. Not long afterward, Ananias also converted Izates to Judaism. Meanwhile, Helena was also converted to Judaism, although by a different Jew; she thus began to observe the Jewish rituals. Yet, the members of the Adiabenite aristocracy maintained their belief in the Zoroastrian religion.[75]

When Monobazus I died, it became necessary to appoint the new ruler of Adiabene. Since Izates was abroad, his older brother Monobazus was chosen as the new king, receiving his father's ring and diadem, but shortly afterward the "favorite son" Izates returned to Adiabene and took control of the government. Ananias accompanied Izates and visited the royal court of Arbela in the year 40 C.E.

Since Izates, the new king of Adiabene, wanted to embrace Judaism in its entirety, he thought that it was necessary to be circumcised. His mother Helena objected to this, voicing concerns that he would come into disfavor among his subjects—who had not yet adopted Judaism—if he was circumcised and knowledge of his Jewish beliefs became public. His tutor Ananias also persuaded Izates to delay circumcision for the time being. Nevertheless, Izates still wanted to be circumcised. Eleazar, a Jew from Galilee, met the king and urged him to be circumcised so as to meet the requirements of Jewish law.

With Eleazar's encouragement, a surgeon performed the circumcision on Izates.

Helena and Ananias remained concerned that Izates would lose his status as king if the people of Adiabene learned that he had adopted a foreign religion. However, Josephus pointed out that the conversion to Judaism actually helped Izates to retain his power:

> But it was God himself who hindered what they feared from taking effect; for He preserved both Izates himself and his sons when they fell into many dangers, and procured their deliverance when it seemed to be impossible, and demonstrated thereby that the fruit of piety does not perish as to those that have regard to Him, and fix their faith upon Him only.[76]

After her initial shock when she learned of Izates' circumcision, Helena saw how Adiabene remained at peace and how Izates continued to be respected by subjects and foreigners alike. She thus became content with his decision, and desired to visit Jerusalem to worship at the Holy Temple. When Helena arrived in Jerusalem, she learned that the people in the city were suffering from famine, so out of kindness she helped to import corn and dried figs to Judea. Izates, also being a compassionate man, sent large amounts of money to Jerusalem's leading men. Rabbinical sources, including the Tosefta, Mishnah, and Palestinian Gemara, added that Helena arranged for the establishment of a tall sukkah in Lydda.[77] She contributed a golden lamp and an inscribed golden plate to the Temple in Jerusalem.

Five of Izates' sons were educated in Jerusalem, where they learned the Hebrew language and studied Jewish scholarship. Monobazus, the brother of King Izates, and his relatives also wanted to embrace Jewish customs. When the non-Jewish nobility of Adiabene learned this, they angrily plotted against Izates, calling upon Abia, king of Arabia, to war against the royal house. Izates' army successfully defended Adiabene against the Arab invaders, and when Abia found himself surrounded by the Adiabenite army, he committed suicide. Despite Abia's defeat, the Adiabenite nobility remained opposed to the Izates regime's adherence to Judaism. They urged Vologases, king of Parthia, to kill Izates. King Vologases declared war on Izates, and a large army was sent to Adiabene. Josephus wrote that Izates prayed to God, asking Him to defend him in battle, and God answered his prayers, since an expedition was sent to destroy Parthia. Vologases was forced to retire to his own country to attend to the problems there, and so Izates was saved.

The great King Izates, friend of Judea, died around 58 C.E., and Helena died soon afterward. Izates and Helena were buried in Jerusalem in three pyramids called "Tomb of the Kings." The pyramids were commissioned by Monobazus II, Izates' older brother, who was installed as Adiabene's new king.

Following a strong precedent, Monobazus II also decided to convert to Judaism, as did many of his relatives and associates. The Tosefta recorded that members of the royal house of Monobazus II affixed mezuzahs to staffs and carried these with them when they traveled, placing them in inns where they stayed overnight.[78] The Tosefta, Mishnah, and Palestinian Gemara noted that Monobazus II contributed money to the Jewish Temple to ensure that the vessels used during Yom Kippur services had golden handles.

Many of the non-royal Adiabenites seem also to have become Jews. The names of the Adiabenite Jews Jacob Hadyaba and Zuga (Zuwa) of Hadyab have been preserved.[79]

The Jewish kings of Adiabene were regularly involved in political and military affairs. In 61 C.E., Monobazus II sent troops to Armenia to try to thwart an invasion of Adiabene.[80] Two years later, he was in attendance at a peace settlement between Parthia and Rome. During the war of Judea against the Roman Empire (66–70 C.E.), the Adiabenite royal family supported the Judean side. A fire destroyed the Palace of Queen Helena.[81] In *Wars of the Jews*, written circa 78 or 79 C.E., Josephus wrote that the Adiabenite Jews Kenedeus and

Monobazus (relatives of Monobazus II) attempted to defend Jerusalem, but perished in the war against the Romans.[82] The sons and relatives of the Adiabenite king were captured and sent to Rome as hostages by Roman co-Emperor Titus.

According to Paul Kahle, there were many Jews in the city of Arbela even after the establishment of bishops and the spread of Christianity in Adiabene.[83]

The last king of an independent Adiabene was Meharaspes, who ruled in around 115. In around the year 116, Adiabene became part of Assyria, a province of the Roman Empire, when Trajan of Mesopotamia invaded it. However, in 117, Hadrian ended Roman control over Adiabene.

The ultimate fate of the Adiabenite Jews is not entirely certain, but Itzhak Ben-Zvi claimed that they migrated to Georgia and Armenia.[84] If so, the Armenian Jews who migrated to Khazaria may have been, at least in part, Adiabenites.

CONVERTS AMONG SEMITIC TRIBES OF GREATER ISRAEL

The Adiabenites adopted Judaism because of a sincere interest in the religion. By contrast, the Itureans and Idumeans (Edomites), Semitic tribes of the Middle East, were forceably converted to Judaism during the second century B.C.E.

Josephus recorded that the army of John Hyrcanus, the High Priest of Judea (reigned 134–104 B.C.E.), took possession of Dora and Marissa, which were cities in Idumea. After conquering the Idumeans, Hyrcanus let the Idumeans stay in their land on the condition that they would be circumcised and observed the Jewish laws.[85] In this way, the Idumeans, descendants of Esau, became Jews by force rather than by choice.

Hyrcanus' son and successor to the priesthood, Judah Aristobulus (reigned 104–103 B.C.E.), converted the Itureans.

The historical record appears to indicate that the Idumeans and the Itureans mingled with the Judeans and celebrated the Jewish festivals along with them.

CONVERTS IN YEMEN

Jews lived in Yemen as early as the first century C.E., according to surviving historical records.

Several Himyarite kings embraced the Jewish religion.[86] The first of these, Yassirum Yohre'am of Himyar, the king of Saba (*Sheba* in Hebrew), and Dhu Raidan, adopted Judaism in the year 270 C.E. Kings 'Amr-Shlomo ben David (reigned 325–330) and Malki Kariba Juha'min (reigned 378–385) were also Jews. Christianity was introduced to Himyar by the evangelist Theophilus in the middle of the fourth century. Theophilus founded three churches in the kingdom. However, during the same century, a small number of former Christians in Yemen adopted Judaism.[87]

Jewish sages from Mecca and Yathreb converted King Abu Kariba As'ad (ruled circa 385–420) to Judaism toward the end of his rule. The conversion of this king was memorialized in Arab ballads.[88] The Himyarite army also adopted Judaism as its official religion. According to the early fifth-century writer Philostorgius, both Judaism and pagan cults were practiced among the people of Himyar. The sixth-century writer Theodorus Lector wrote that the pagan Himyarites left paganism and were Judaized by a queen of Saba.

King Martad Ilan (reigned 495–515) and his successor, King Yusuf Ash'ar Dhu Nuwas (reigned circa 515–525), were also Judaized. After Dhu Nuwas became a convert to Judaism, he spread the religion among the Arab people in Yemen. He also destroyed the Christian churches in Zafar and Al-Makha.

When Dhu Nuwas and his army attacked the city of Najran in October 523, the king demanded that the Christians living in the city convert to Judaism, or die. They refused to convert, so the Himyarite army massacred approximately twenty thousand of them. Other Christians—in particular, the Byzantines and the Abyssinians—were outraged by this incident and took military action against Dhu Nuwas. The *negus* (king) of Abyssinia, Kaleb Ela Asbeha, sent seventy thousand men to Himyar with Commander Aryat at the helm. Aryat's

Abyssinian forces won a battle against the Himyarites toward the end of 523. The decisive Abyssinian victory against the Himyarites came in 525 when Commander Abraha attacked Dhu Nuwas' army. King Dhu Nuwas killed himself by plunging his horse into the sea and drowning.[89]

After the death of Dhu Nuwas (the last Himyarite king in Yemen), the Abyssinians conquered and settled the whole of Yemen. The religious climate changed dramatically. The Abyssinians tried to convert the Yemenites to Christianity, and Abraha built a magnificent cathedral called al-Qadis. The final shift in religious affiliation came in 628, when Islamic rulers took control of Yemen and transformed the country into a Muslim society.

The Arab converts to Judaism probably intermingled with city-dwelling Israelite Jews who had come to Yemen. Some of the Yemenite Jews later resettled in Cochin, India.

CONVERTS IN ETHIOPIA

The Jews of Ethiopia are known as the Beta Israel ("House of Israel") and the Falashas ("Foreigners"). The Ethiopian Jews may descend in part from Jews from the Himyarite kingdom in Yemen. It seems that the Ethiopian Jews also descend from Agau proselytes, since they closely resemble other Ethiopians. Wexler thought that Yemenite Jewish immigrants may have been responsible for the spread of Judaism in Ethiopia as early as the third to fifth centuries.[90]

Sections of Abyssinia were ruled by Jews during the Middle Ages. The so-called Falashas, descended from members of the Agau tribe who converted to Judaism, conquered and destroyed the city of Aksum in the tenth century. Thus, in 937, the Falasha queen Judith usurped the Ethiopian throne. According to legend, Queen Judith was a Jew. Judith ruled over the whole country until 977, when she was overthrown by Tekla Haimanot. The Christian Agau dynasty known as the Zagwe thus came into power, and retained control until 1270.

Several Christian princes in the provinces of Sallamt and Semien converted to Judaism in the fifteenth century and contributed to the military strength of the Falashas. Zar'a Ya'eqob (reigned 1438–1468), the Christian *negus* (emperor) of Ethiopia, engaged in battle against these Jewish rebels.[91] The Falashas killed many of the Amhara people and enjoyed military successes against Zar'a Ya'eqob's army. Zar'a Ya'eqob's successor, Emperor Ba'eda Maryam (reigned 1468–1478), eventually was able to crush the Falashas.

CONVERTS IN NORTH AFRICA

Proselytism was largely responsible for the growth of Jewish communities in Tunisia, Algeria, and Morocco.

In the seventh century, a large number of Spanish Jews fled their Visigoth oppressors. Some of these Spanish Jews settled in the Sahara Desert region of North Africa and actively proselytized Berber tribes. The close connection between Jews and Berbers was recorded by many medieval writers, such as the eleventh-century Spanish poet Abu Bakr ibn 'Ammar.[92] However, the first historian to mention Judaized North Africans was al-Idrisi, a twelfth-century Moroccan geographer who wrote about Berbers of the Jewish faith as well as Jewish proselytizing efforts in the western Sudan.

The fourteenth-century Tunisian historian 'Abd-ar-Rahman ibn Khaldun wrote that it was possible that some of the Berbers adopted Judaism, such as the Berber tribe Jarawa, which lived in the Aurès Mountains region of northeastern Algeria.[93] The Jarawa queen was called the Kahina (meaning "Soothsayer"). Her full name was Kahya al-Kahina. According to ibn Khaldun, Caliph 'Abd-al-Malik sent the governor of Egypt, Hasan, to North Africa in the Arab year 49 A.H. (about 669 C.E.) to conquer additional territory, but he was soundly defeated by the Kahina. For several years, the Kahina ruled over a wide expanse of land extending from Tripoli in northwestern Libya to Tangiers in northern Morocco.[94]

In the 690s or 700s, the Kahina was killed in battle by Governor Hasan's regrouped Arab forces, and her tribe was defeated and lost its independence. The Arabs thus completed their conquest of North Africa. The Jarawa tribe dispersed, with some of them migrating to the Melilla region in northeastern Morocco. The majority of the Berbers were forced to convert to Islam. Among the Jewish tribes forced to adopt Islam were the Uled Jari people of the Touggourt Oasis in Algeria, the Daggatun tribe that lives between the Sudan and Timbuktu, and Tunisian and Moroccan Berbers.[95] The Daggatuns were tent-dwelling Berber Jews of the Sahara oases who shared many customs with the Tuaregs and other Berber tribes, but also retained some Jewish traditions.

The Rif Jews of northern Morocco are believed to have descended from Berber converts to Judaism.[96]

NOTES

1. István Erdélyi, "The Avars," in *Peoples That Vanished*, ed. P. Puchkov, trans. Ye. Voronov (Moscow: Nauka, 1989), p. 99.

2. Ibid., p. 100.

3. Paul Wexler, *The Ashkenazic Jews* (Columbus, OH: Slavica, 1993), pp. 192–193.

4. George Ostrogorsky, *History of the Byzantine State* (New Brunswick, NJ: Rutgers University Press, 1969), pp. 100–101.

5. Charles R. Bowlus, *Franks, Moravians, and Magyars* (Philadelphia: University of Pennsylvania Press, 1995), p. 49.

6. Ibid., p. 51.

7. Ibid., pp. 55–56.

8. Ibid., p. 57.

9. István Erdélyi, "Kabari (Kavari) v Karpatskom Basseyne," *Sovietskaya Arkheologiya* 4 (1983): 174. Some of the horses were buried to the left of the decreased men, while others

were buried to the right of them. There was, in addition, a separate burial for horses only.

10. Alexander Scheiber, *Jewish Inscriptions in Hungary from the 3rd Century to 1686* (Budapest: Akadémiai, 1983), p. 55; Vsevolod L. Vikhnovich, "From the Jordan to the Dnieper," *Jewish Studies (Mada'e ha-Yahadut)* 31 (1991): 19.

11. Alexander Scheiber, *Jewish Inscriptions in Hungary from the 3rd Century to 1686*, pp. 55–56.

12. István Erdélyi, "Kabari (Kavari) v Karpatskom Basseyne," p. 179. The Khazars, on the other hand, were largely non-Mongolian in type, although some Mongolian types were among them (see Chapter 1).

13. Paul Wexler, *The Ashkenazic Jews*, p. 195. See idem., pp. 196–198, for an interesting discussion of various Balkan and Slavic words referring to Jews, Avars, and Khazars (e.g., Romanian *Jidov*, Russian *Zhidovin*, Slovenian *óber*) that carry the secondary meaning of "giant." Wexler interprets these words as confirming that both the mighty Avars and Khazars had become Jews. This interpretation would explain how Jews could be viewed as powerful military adversaries rather than as a weak subordinate population. Whereas the Khazar conversion to Judaism is well documented (see Chapter 6), the suggestion that the Avars converted to Judaism requires further verification. Khan Abraham was baptized into Christianity in the Fisha River and was given the name Abraham at that time, so it has *no* Jewish significance.

14. István Erdélyi, "Kabari (Kavari) v Karpatskom Basseyne," p. 176.

15. Ibid., p. 179.

16. Vsevolod L. Vikhnovich, "From the Jordan to the Dnieper," p. 19.

17. Svetlana A. Pletnyova, "The Polovtsy," in *Peoples That Vanished*, ed. P. Puchkov, trans. Ye. Voronov (Moscow: Nauka, 1989), p. 26.

18. Edward Tryjarski, "Some Early Polish Sources and their Importance for the History of the Altaic World," *Journal of Asian History* 3:1 (1969): 38.

19. Nicholas V. Riasanovsky, *A History of Russia*, 5th ed. (New York: Oxford University Press, 1993), p. 40.

20. Svetlana A. Pletnyova, "The Polovtsy," in *Peoples That Vanished*, p. 31.

21. István Fodor, *In Search of a New Homeland*, trans. Helen Tarnoy (Gyoma, Hungary: Corvina, 1982), p. 197. Descendants of the Cumans still live in Hungary.

22. Svetlana A. Pletnyova, "The Polovtsy," in *Peoples That Vanished*, p. 32.

23. Ibid., p. 33.

24. David Nicolle, *Medieval Warfare Source Book*, vol. 2 (London: Arms & Armour Press, 1996), p. 260.

25. Svetlana A. Pletnyova, "The Polovtsy," in *Peoples That Vanished*, p. 28.

26. Ibid.

27. Arthur Koestler, *The Thirteenth Tribe* (New York: Random House, 1976), p. 134.

28. Peter B. Golden, "Khazaria and Judaism," *Archivum Eurasiae Medii Aevi* 3 (1983): 153. In Chuvash, the corresponding words for "Saturday" are *shamat* and *shamatkun*; in Karaim, *shabat-k'un'*; in Karachay-Balkar, *shabat kün*. The word *kun* means both "day" and "sun" in Turkic languages. Significantly, Karachay-Balkar and Karaim are both descended from Kipchak Turkic (see Table 4–1). For an interesting discussion of Hebrew loan-words in Chuvash (including *shamat, shamatkun*, and *shamat pasare*), see Ia. F. Kuz'min-Yumanadi, "O gebraizmax v chuvashskom yazike," *Sovietskaya Tyurkologiya* No. 2 (1987): 68–76.

29. Peter B. Golden, "Khazaria and Judaism," p. 154.

30. Vladimir F. Minorsky, *A History of Sharvan and Darband in the 10th–11th Centuries* (Cambridge, England: W. Heller & Sons, 1958), p. 156.

31. Norman Golb and Omeljan Pritsak, *Khazarian Hebrew Documents of the Tenth Century* (Ithaca, NY: Cornell University Press, 1982), pp. 113, 115.

32. George Vernadsky, *A History of Russia*, vol. 1 (New Haven, CT: Yale University Press, 1948), p. 133.

33. Alexander A. Vasiliev, *The Goths in the Crimea* (Cambridge, MA: The Mediaeval Academy of America, 1936), pp. 166–167.

34. Salo W. Baron, *A Social and Religious History of the Jews*, vol. 3 (New York: Columbia University Press, 1957), p. 208.

35. Dennis Prager, "Judaism Must Seek Converts," in *Readings on Conversion to Judaism*, ed. Lawrence J. Epstein (Northvale, NJ: Jason Aronson, 1995), p. 91.

36. Martin D. Goodman, "Jewish Proselytizing in the First Century," in *The Jews Among Pagans and Christians in the Roman Empire*, ed. Judith Lieu, John North, and Tessa Rajak (London: Routledge, 1992), p. 75.

37. Ibid., pp. 60–61.

38. Ibid., pp. 65–66.

39. See Joyce M. Reynolds and Robert F. Tannenbaum, *Jews and God-Fearers at Aphrodisias: Greek Inscriptions with Commentary* (Cambridge, England: Cambridge Philological Society, 1987).

40. Egon Mayer, "Why Not Judaism?" in *Readings on Conversion to Judaism*, ed. Lawrence J. Epstein (Northvale, NJ: Jason Aronson, 1995), p. 102.

41. Paul Wexler, *The Ashkenazic Jews*, p. 213.

42. Nikolaj Kochev, "The Question of Jews and the So-Called Judaizers in the Balkans from the 9th to the 14th Cen-

tury," *Bulgarian Historical Review* 6 (1978): 63–64. Naturally, the Judaizers also challenged the alleged divinity of Jesus (see idem., p. 68).

43. Ibid., pp. 66–67.

44. Paul Wexler, *The Non-Jewish Origins of the Sephardic Jews* (Albany, NY: State University of New York Press, 1996), p. 41.

45. Ibid., p. 48.

46. Ibid., p. 49.

47. Dennis Prager, "Judaism Must Seek Converts," in *Readings on Conversion to Judaism*, p. 92.

48. Benjamin of Tudela, *The Itinerary of Benjamin of Tudela*, trans. Marcus N. Adler (Malibu, CA: Joseph Simon/ Pangloss Press, 1987), p. 68.

49. Ben Zion Wacholder, "Attitudes Toward Proselytizing in the Classical Halakah," in *Readings on Conversion to Judaism*, ed. Lawrence J. Epstein (Northvale, NJ: Jason Aronson, 1995), p. 19. Other proselytes in Christian countries also changed their names to Abraham.

50. Ben Zion Wacholder, "Cases of Proselytizing in the Tosafist Responsa," *Jewish Quarterly Review* 15 (1960–1961), pp. 297–298.

51. Ibid., p. 302.

52. Ibid., p. 313.

53. Ben Zion Wacholder, "Attitudes Toward Proselytizing in the Classical Halakah," in *Readings on Conversion to Judaism*, p. 26.

54. Raphael Patai and Jennifer Patai, *The Myth of the Jewish Race*, revised edition (Detroit: Wayne State University Press, 1989), p. 85.

55. Raphael Patai, *The Jews of Hungary* (Detroit: Wayne State University Press, 1996), pp. 176–177.

56. Masha Greenbaum, *The Jews of Lithuania* (Jerusalem: Gefen, 1995), p. 58.

57. Raphael Patai, *The Jews of Hungary*, p. 157.

58. Ibid., pp. 159–160.

59. Paul Wexler, *The Ashkenazic Jews*, p. 68.

60. Ibid., p. 54.

61. Ibid., p. 5.

62. Nancy Schoenburg and Stuart Schoenburg, *Lithuanian Jewish Communities* (Northvale, NJ: Jason Aronson, 1996), p. 6.

63. Paul Wexler, *The Ashkenazic Jews*, pp. 167–168.

64. Ibid., p. 154.

65. Ibid., pp. 171–172, 210.

66. Ibid., p. 120.

67. Ibid., pp. 209–210.

68. Ibid., p. 210.

69. Ibid., pp. 162–163.

70. Ibid., pp. 169–171.

71. Ibid., pp. 174–175.

72. Flavius Josephus, *The Complete Works of Josephus*, trans. William Whiston (Grand Rapids, MI: Kregel, 1981), pp. 415–418.

73. However, the Midrash called Monobazus I by the name Talmai instead (see Bernard J. Bamberger, *Proselytism in the Talmudic Period* (New York: Hebrew Union College Press, 1939), p. 227).

74. At first, Izates was governor of Corduene, located just north of Adiabene.

75. Paul E. Kahle, *The Cairo Geniza* (London: Oxford University Press, 1947), p. 185.

76. Flavius Josephus, *The Complete Works of Josephus*, p. 416.

77. Bernard J. Bamberger, *Proselytism in the Talmudic Period*, p. 228.

78. Ibid.

79. Richard Gottheil, "Adiabene," in *The Jewish Encyclopedia*, vol. 1 (New York: Ktav, 1901–1906), p. 192.

80. Ibid., p. 191.

81. Mireille Hadas-Lebel, *Flavius Josephus* (New York: Macmillan, 1993), p. 172.

82. Flavius Josephus, *The Complete Works of Josephus*, p. 495.

83. Paul E. Kahle, *The Cairo Geniza*, p. 189.

84. Itzhak Ben-Zvi, *The Exiled and the Redeemed*, trans. Isaac A. Abbady (Philadelphia: The Jewish Publication Society of America, 1961), pp. 50–51.

85. Flavius Josephus, *The Complete Works of Josephus*, p. 279.

86. Itzhak Ben-Zvi, *The Exiled and the Redeemed*, pp. 251–252.

87. Nikolaj Kochev, "The Question of Jews and the So-Called Judaizers in the Balkans from the 9th to the 14th Century," p. 63.

88. Philip K. Hitti, *History of the Arabs*, 8th ed. (New York: St. Martin's Press, 1963), p. 60.

89. Ibid., p. 62. Much of the story of Dhu Nuwas seems like it could have been fictionalized with a pro-Christian slant. Some now suggest that the claim that Dhu Nuwas persecuted Christians was invented as justification for increased Christian intervention in the region.

90. Paul Wexler, *The Non-Jewish Origins of the Sephardic Jews*, p. 29.

91. Steven Kaplan, *The Beta Israel (Falasha) in Ethiopia* (New York: New York University Press, 1992), p. 59.

92. Paul Wexler, *The Non-Jewish Origins of the Sephardic Jews*, p. 41.

93. Haim Z. Hirschberg, "The Problem of the Judaized Berbers," *Journal of African History* 4:3 (1963): 317.

94. Ibid., p. 318.

95. Ibid., p. 336; Nathan Ausubel, *Pictorial History of the Jewish People* (New York: Crown, 1953), pp. 225–227.

96. Maurice Fishberg, *The Jews* (London: Walter Scott, 1911), p. 145.

11

EASTERN AND CENTRAL EUROPEAN JEWS AFTER THE TENTH CENTURY

This chapter gives an overall demographic survey of the development of Jewish communities in the lands that became part of the Russian, Polish-Lithuanian, and Austrian-Hungarian Empires. Surviving historical data indicates that the eastern and central European Jews are not merely descendants of western Jews, but also, in large measure, descendants of Jews from farther East, including the Jews of Khazaria. While it is impossible to establish the precise percentage of German and Bohemian Jews versus the percentage of Khazarian and Byzantine Jews in the old Russian shtetl populations, evidence suggests that the Khazarian Jews may represent about twenty-five percent of Ashkenazi Jewry and as much as sixty percent of Ukrainian Jewry.

THE ORIGINS OF THE ASHKENAZIM

The history of Jewish settlement in eastern Europe is a combination of several phenomena. First, there was the influx of

Jews from the Middle East who settled in the Crimea during Roman times. The fate of these early Crimean communities is unknown, but it is possible that there was a continuity between them and later Crimean Jewish populations. Second, the renewed persecutions of Jews during the medieval period—especially from the eighth to the tenth centuries—brought about new migrations of Jews from Europe and Asia to present-day Ukraine and southern Russia. Third, many Khazars, Alans, Slavs, and other peoples converted to Judaism, and later resettled in Hungary, Poland, and Kievan Rus. The fourth major factor in the creation of large Jewish communities in eastern Europe was the resettlement of Jews from southern and eastern Germany, Bohemia, Austria, and other parts of central Europe. These Jews arrived in Poland in large numbers starting in the mid-thirteenth century, and in Belarus by the late fourteenth century, bringing with them the Yiddish language and culture. Many scholars believe that Yiddish-speaking Jews from central Europe continued to establish new lives in the East as late as the early seventeenth century. After 1648, however, the general direction of migration seems to have shifted westward, with many Polish Jews moving to central and western Europe. The culmination of this westward trend was in the 1880s to 1920s, when millions of eastern European Jews immigrated to the United States and Canada.

The Yiddish cultural tradition was only the latest in a succession of Jewish cultures in eastern Europe, spanning nearly two thousand years. Many Jewish historians recognize this fact. Benjamin Harshav, for example, wrote:

> The label "Ashkenazi" does not necessarily mean that all Ashkenazi Jews came from Germany but that they adopted the cluster of Ashkenazi culture which included the specific Ashkenazi religious rite and the German-based Yiddish language. Thus, it is plausible that Slavic-speaking Jewish communities in Eastern Europe (which existed there from early times) became dominated in the sixteenth century by Ashkenazi culture and adopted the Yiddish language.[1]

A similar view was held by Nathan Ausubel:

> . . . the hitherto Slavonic character of Polish-Jewish culture was rapidly transformed into a Yiddish-speaking one. Polish Jews adopted the Ashkenazic rites, liturgy, and religious customs of the German Jews as well as their method of Torah and Talmud study and the use of Yiddish as the language of oral translation and discussion. By the 16th century, except for inevitable regional variations, a homogeneous Jewish culture had crystalized.[2]

The linguist Max Weinreich called the Slavic speech of the eastern European Jews "Eastern Knaanic" and proposed that the Knaanic-speaking Jews intermingled with the Yiddish-speaking Jews in around the fourteenth and fifteenth centuries.[3] In Chapter 9, I suggested that the Knaanic Jews were originally Khazars who had mixed with Slavs. The first intermingling—between Khazars and Slavs in Kievan Rus—led to the almost complete disappearance of Turkic cultural remnants from Khazaria. The second intermingling—between Knaanic Jews and German Jews—led to the dominance of Yiddish over Slavic. Today a similar process is going on: Most American Jews no longer learn to speak Yiddish, since they have adopted the English language as a replacement.

JEWS IN MEDIEVAL UKRAINE

As I noted in Chapter 9, Jews lived in Kievan Rus in significant numbers as early as the tenth century. In Kievan Rus, the Khazarian Jews were forced to adjust to the dominant role of non-Jewish princes, administrators, and priests in daily life. Yet, despite persistent persecutions and tragedies, Jewish identity survived.

Intolerance and hatred began to be directed toward Jews following the Rus'ian conversion to Orthodox Christianity in 988. The religion of the Rus'ian people was dictated by the Kievan princes and, later, the Moscovite czars, and Judaism was officially discouraged. This situation led to frequent problems, which grew in intensity as the years progressed. In the early period (until 1495), however, the Jews in Ukraine were relatively free from discrimination, since they could live almost anywhere and often married non-Jewish Slavs.

The city of Kiev remained the center of an important Jewish community during the Middle Ages. Jews were mentioned in early Rus'ian law codes, and the Rus'ian laws against moneylending were primarily directed against Jews and other merchants.[4] Rus'ian Jews participated in an eleventh-century assembly of anti-Karaite Jews that was held in Constantinople or Salonika.[5] During the same century, Jewish narratives were being translated into Old Rus'ian, including *Sefer Yosippon* (a Hebrew historical treatise from Italy) and *History of the Jewish War* by Josephus Flavius.[6] According to Benjamin Pinkus, this confirms that among the Kievan Jews "at least some of them were fluent in Slavic."[7] Pinkus also pointed out that in 1124 the Rus'ian Jews produced a commentary on the Pentateuch, entitled *Sefer Rushia*, under the guidance of German Jews.

The Hypatian edition of the *Rus'ian Primary Chronicle*, composed in about 1425, described the first recorded pogrom against Jews in the land of Rus. According to this account, in 1113 residents of Kiev looted the mansion of Putyata, a high official, and then turned against the Jews.[8] This uprising became so serious—to the extent that monasteries were being looted and the royal family was being threatened—that Prince Vladimir of Pereyaslav was forced to attend to matters in Kiev. After the revolts and rioting had ceased, Vladimir was installed as the new Kievan ruler.

The *Kievan Chronicle* mentioned the existence of a "Jewish Gate" and a "Golden Gate" in Kiev under the years 1146 and *sub anno* 1151.[9] The "Jewish Gate" was located in the northeastern corner of Kiev.

In the second half of the twelfth century, there were several rabbis in Kiev and Chernigov (Chernihiv), and thriving Jewish communities existed in both cities. The rabbis in Kiev maintained ties with Babylonian and German Jews. For example, Rabbi Moses of Kiev wrote to the Gaon of Baghdad, Rabbi Samuel ben Ali, during the twelfth century.[10] However, the level of Jewish learning in Kievan Rus at the close of the century was not as great as in western and central Europe, as indicated by a letter composed in around the year 1200 by Rabbi Eliezer ben Yitzhak of Bohemia:

> ... in most localities of Poland, Russia, and Hungary there are no students of Torah; because of their poverty, the communities hire any competent man they can to serve as their reader, judge, and school teacher.[11]

Similarly, Rabbi Petakhiah's travelogue indicated that the Khazar Jews asked (circa 1185) the Babylonian Jews to send them teachers to provide instruction in the Jewish law (see Chapter 9). There were not enough religious teachers and cantors in eastern Europe until around the sixteenth century. For this reason, Rus'ian Jewish students from Kiev and Chernigov often traveled to the West in order to be trained at the excellent yeshivas in western Germany, London, and Toledo.[12]

Maurice Samuel, an expert on Yiddish, proposed that the comparatively low level of Jewish learning in eastern Europe is a likely reason for the transition from Slavic to Yiddish:

> One factor in the disappearance of *loshn knaan* from among Jews must have been the cultural backwardness of early Russian Jewry. It had no schools of its own and sent its young men to the west, to France and Germany, to obtain a Jewish education, just as pious American Jews used to send their sons to European yeshivas. . . .[13]

However, Samuel thought that it was "possible, even probable, that some of the Slavic words today found in Yiddish also occurred in *loshn knaan*. . . ." In any case, it is clear that Yiddish was not the original mother tongue of the Rus'ian Jews, but rather was imported from the West. The superior scholarship of German Jewry came to dominate eastern Europe, leading many scholars to erroneously conclude that the Ukrainian Jews were almost entirely descended from western Jews.

The western sections of Ukraine were also settled by Jews during this time. A document from circa 1171 reported that Benjamin, a Jew from Volodymyr Volynskyi (a town in the Volhynia province near the present-day Polish border), traded in Cologne (Köln).[14] Jews lived in urban centers in western Ukraine during the reign of Daniel Romanovich, prince of Volhynia (1221–1264) and Galicia (1238–1264).[15] It is said that Daniel invited German Jews to settle in Galicia.

The Mongol invasion of Kievan Rus had major consequences for both Jews and non-Jews. The Jewish communities of Kiev and Volodymyr Volynskyi were destroyed during the 1240s. The level of destruction in Kiev was especially considerable. When Friar Joannes de Plano Carpini visited Kiev only a few years after its destruction, he found that only about two hundred homes remained in the once-grand city.[16] Yet, it is not necessarily the case that the Mongol invasion decimated the Jewish populations in Kievan Rus entirely. Henrik Birnbaum postulated that, in the mid-thirteenth century, many Kievan Jews left Kiev and moved to Galicia and Volhynia, where they met and mixed with German Jews, while others moved to the Crimea.[17] In fact, it seems that most Jewish settlements in eastern Europe survived the Mongol conquests. Moreover, Jews resettled in Kiev starting in 1259.[18] The *Galician-Volhynian Chronicle* recorded that Jews mourned when Prince Vladimir Vasil'kovich of Volhynia died (around 1289).

During the following centuries, the Ukrainian Jewish population rose considerably in numbers, partly because of a natural increase and partly because of migrations from Poland and Lithuania.[19] From 1569 to 1654, much of Ukraine was under Polish rule. Unfortunately, Jewish-Christian relations in Ukraine began to deteriorate substantially. After 1648, the rapid expansion of the size of Ukrainian Jewry was halted.

In 1648, tens of thousands of Jews living in Ukraine and Galicia were slain by the Cossacks, who were led by the *hetman* Bohdan Khmielnitzki. Some Jewish communities, such as those in Ostrog and Lublin, were entirely wiped out. After the Cossacks captured the city of Nemirov in the late spring of 1648, they slaughtered numerous Jews. Some of Nemirov's Jews escaped and sought refuge in the walled city of Tulchin. However, the Cossacks eventually reached Tulchin and killed its Jews. Thousands of Jews were also killed in Kiev, Pereyaslav, Lubny, Piryatin, Lokhnitz, Polonnoye, and other towns. Some Jews survived by converting to Orthodox Christianity. Others were held captive by Tatars, brought to the Crimea, and sold into slavery.

Religious persecutions and anti-Jewish laws prevented the majority of Jews from residing within "Russia proper." Russian czar Ivan IV "the Terrible" (reigned 1533—1584) opposed Jewish settlement in the Russian Empire, and required Russian Jews to convert to Christianity or else face death.[20] In 1563, approximately three hundred Jews of Polotsk were drowned in the Dvina River for refusing to convert to Christianity.[21] Czar Fyodor III (reigned 1676–1682) excluded Jewish traders from Muscovite Russia. Czar Peter "the Great" (reigned 1682–1725) also hated Jews intensely. When Ukraine was acquired by the Russian Empire, Jews were allowed to remain there, but their ability to visit and trade in Moscow was severely limited. In the 1790s, Empress Catherine (reigned 1762–1796) issued a decree preventing Jews from settling in "Russia proper." The restrictive boundaries of the Russian Empire's Pale of Settlement, created between 1773 and 1776, symbolized this discrimination. Only beginning in 1917 could most Jews reside in the Russian heartland.

THE EARLY JEWS OF POLAND

Small numbers of Jews lived in Poland toward the close of the Khazar epoch. Around 965, Ibrahim ibn Yakub, a Jewish traveler from Catalonia, indicated the existence of a Jewish community in the western Slavic lands.[22] Similarly, the tenth-century scholar Kalonimus ben Shabtai wrote that Jews lived in the western Slavic territories and Hungary.[23]

Jewish life in Poland existed on a virtually continuous basis since the eleventh century. One of the first documentary indications of a Jewish community in Poland was the report of Rabbi Yehudah ben Meir ha-Kohen of Mainz, who indicated that, in 1031, the Rus captured a number of Jews from Przemysl.[24] Western Jews migrated to Poland as early as 1098, as indicated by such accounts as that of the chronicler Cosmas of Prague, who wrote that Bohemian Jews settled in Poland following the Crusades.[25] The tolerant rulers of Poland explicitly invited Jews to settle in their land as early as 1133. A large number of Jews settled in Kraków in the twelfth century, working as merchants and tax farmers, and some of them became mintmasters to Polish princes. In around 1150 Jews owned the town of Mały Tyniec, but it was purchased by Piotŕ Wlast.[26] In 1200, the village of Sokolników (near Wroclaw) was owned by two Jews, Joseph and Khaskel. Jewish peasants who tilled the soil on the lands of Count Henryk I around Bytom circa 1227 were required to hand over ten percent of their harvest to the bishop of Wroclaw.[27] It is also known that Jews lived in the Warsaw Duchy town of Płock by 1237.[28]

The Mongol conquest of eastern Europe affected Polish Jewry just as it affected Rus'ian Jewry. Many regions of Poland were ravaged, and many Jews were slaughtered. The city of Kraków was destroyed in 1241, but was rebuilt in 1257. Starting in 1241, Polish Jews—possibly of Khazar origin—fled to Silesia, Moravia, Bohemia, and Austria, and mixed with German Jews who had typical Germanic names.[29]

After the Mongol conquest, renewed invitations for Jewish settlement were made in depopulated Poland. In 1264, Duke Boleslav V "the Pious" (reigned 1227–1279) secured rights for Jews in a written charter, the *Statute of Kalisz*. Among the rights enumerated in Boleslav's charter were: the right for Jews to be able to practice Judaism; the right to travel freely; the right to worship in a synagogue; trading rights; and the right to own property. Important provisions prohibited the kidnapping of Jewish children, established the equality of the amount of customs duties charged to both Jews and Christians for transporting goods, and instituted the requirement for a fine to be paid by anyone who threw stones at a synagogue. The charter also instructed Christians to help their Jewish neighbors when they were in need.[30]

The first seeds of intolerance came to Poland in the thirteenth century, when three Christian synods in Polish towns adopted anti-Jewish resolutions: in Kalisz in 1264, in Wroclaw in 1267, and in Łęczyca in 1285.[31] These Church Council resolutions were enacted in response to Boleslav's charter.

Despite the anti-Jewish sentiments of the church, many Polish rulers remained friendly to Polish Jews. In 1344, Kazimierz III "the Great" (reigned 1333–1370) reaffirmed Boleslav's charter and added further protections for Jews.

New Jewish communities continued to emerge in Poland during the thirteenth, fourteenth, and fifteenth centuries. For instance, Jews resided in the city of Warsaw by 1414.[32] According to Jacob Litman, many of the Jews who settled in Poland during this period came from southern Germany (including Nuremberg), Austria (including Vienna), Moravia, and Silesia.[33] The Jewish populations in Poznan, Kalisz, Kraków, and Wroclaw were probably in the main descended from German, Moravian, and Bohemian Jews. However, there is no evidence that Jews from the Rhineland (western Germany) came to Poland. This may explain why Yiddish—the language of the last wave of Jewish immigrants to Poland—has more affinities with eastern German dialects (especially Bavarian) than with southwestern German dialects.[34]

In the early fifteenth century, anti-Jewish documents, outbreaks, and accusations prevailed among the Christians of Kraków and other parts of Poland, indicating a shift in attitude from the earlier tolerance of Jews. The rulers of Poland soon adopted anti-Jewish attitudes as well. For instance, the Polish king Sigismund III (reigned 1587–1632), overlord of Ukraine as well as Poland, issued an edict in February 1619 that prevented Jews from owning real estate in the city of Kiev.[35]

In 1519, the Jews of Poland created an autonomous legislative authority, known as the Council of the Four Lands. The Council passed many ordinances to govern the financial affairs of Polish Jews. The Council also collected taxes from Jews for handing over to the Polish government.[36] It was disbanded in 1764.

Polish Jews were engaged in a wide range of professions. Some of them were blacksmiths, silversmiths, tailors, bakers, tax collectors, candlestick makers, fur traders, and scribes.

JEWS IN LITHUANIA AND BELARUS

Farther to the east of Poland were large Jewish settlements in the Lithuanian-Belarusian lands that included significant vestiges of Jewish Khazars. Medieval Lithuania, at one point, also included much of Ukraine, including the Kiev district, where Khazars also lived.

The Jewish settlements in Belarus were founded by the early twelfth century; those in Lithuania were founded by the thirteenth century. Some historians, however, speculated that Khazar Jews from the Crimea arrived in Lithuania in the early eleventh century. According to the account of the Jewish trader Ibrahim ben Jacob, Jews lived in Hrodna (Grodno in Russian, Gardinas in Lithuanian) by 1128 and in Kaunas (Kovno) by 1280.[37] The mysterious documents about the establishment of a Khazar glass factory (see Chapter 9) may prove that Jewish Khazars lived in Hrodna even earlier. Gedminias, the king of Lithuania from 1316 to 1341, encouraged Middle Eastern, Bukharan, and German Jews to settle in Lithuania.[38] Nancy and Stuart Schoenburg suggested that the earliest Jews to settle in Lithuania were invited because they had a reputation as excellent soldiers.[39]

The Grand Duchy of Lithuania expanded in size starting in the mid-thirteenth century, and by the fifteenth century was at its maximum extent, reaching from the Black Sea to the Baltic Sea. Lithuanian Grand Duke Algirdas (reigned 1345–1377) acquired much territory, including Volhynia, Kiev, Chernigov, and part of Smolensk. Thus, the Jews of Ukraine came under Lithuanian control.

In 1386, Grand Duke Jagiello (reigned 1377–1392 in Lithuania, 1386–1434 in Poland), son of Algirdas, married Jadwiga, the queen of Poland, thus forming a personal union between Lithuania and Poland. Jagiello was baptized into Christianity. In his decree of 1432, Jagiello mentioned the existence of Jews in Volhynia, Kraków, and Lviv (Lwów in Polish).[40]

Grand Duke Vytautas "the Great" (reigned 1392–1430) extended Lithuania's borders as far south as the Black Sea and incorporated the remainder of Ukraine and Belarus. In 1388 and 1389, Vytautas granted legal and religious rights to the Jews living in Hrodna, Brest, and Troki. Vytautas furthermore invited Crimean Jews and Karaites to settle in Lithuania. The new Jewish settlers contributed greatly to Lithuania's economy, and Vytautas' reign is remembered as a time when Lithuanian Jewry prospered greatly.

Polish-Lithuanian Grand Duke Kazimierz IV (reigned 1440–1492 in Lithuania, 1446–1492 in Poland), son of Jagiello, further helped Lithuanian Jewry to flourish, despite the objections of Catholics. The Lithuanian Jews of this period were speaking the Belarusian, Tataric, and Yiddish languages.

By the fifteenth century, many new Jewish communities had taken root in Lithuanian cities and towns, including Keidan, Palanga, and Slobodka.[41] Salo Baron estimated that about 30,000 Jews lived in the Polish-Lithuanian realm by the late fifteenth century.[42]

Grand Duke Alexander (reigned 1492—1506 in Lithuania, 1501–1506 in Poland), son of Kazimierz IV, did not share his father's tolerant attitude toward Jews. In 1495, Alexander issued an edict expelling all Jews from Lithuania. Fortunately, he revoked this edict in 1503, since Lithuania needed Jews for their financial and trading expertise. A number of Jews from Portugal and Spain arrived in Lithuania by the sixteenth century.

By the 1530s, the Lithuanian Jews founded the Council of the Land of Lithuania as a counterpart to the related institution in Poland, the Council of the Four Lands.[43]

Jews lived in Vilnius (which later became the most important Jewish center in Lithuania) under the protection of the law beginning in 1593.[44]

The Lithuanian Jewish communities were spared from the Khmielnitzki massacres, and many Ukrainian Jews fled northward to Lithuania to escape the Cossacks.

Some Jews in Lithuania were fluent in "Russian" rather than Yiddish or German as late as the seventeenth century.[45] In my opinion, they were probably among the purest descendants of the Khazars of Kievan Rus, having kept the *loshn knaan* for several centuries beyond the time that every other Jewish community had embraced Yiddish.

JEWS IN HUNGARY

During the late Middle Ages, Hungary remained the home of many thousands of Jews of Khazar origin. The early Hungarian Jews were highly religious and carefully observed the Sabbath and all holidays.

Unfortunately, the early Hungarian Jewish communities did not leave behind documents, so most of the available information about their existence comes from governmental documents. It is known that Jews lived in the city of Esztergom by around 1050 and in Buda by 1217.[46]

As early as the eleventh century, anti-Jewish sentiments began to take hold among the Christian leaders of Hungary. Hungarian nobles and religious leaders who took part in the Council of Szabolcs wrote anti-Jewish laws in 1092. The council said that the Jews' working implements were to be taken from them if they worked on a Sunday, and furthermore said that Christian women and slaves were to be taken from all Jews who owned them.[47] Several years later, King Kálmán (reigned 1095–1116) issued his own series of anti-Jewish laws. Kálmán's anti-Jewish restrictions included provisions on moneylending and purchases of merchandise, and also prevented Jews from buying or selling any Christian slaves.[48] Since Jews were no longer allowed to use these slaves for agricultural work, they were forced to abandon agriculture and involve themselves more heavily in other professions, most notably moneylending. Despite continued restrictions on the types of professions Jews could be involved in, Hungarian Jews remained tax collectors and coin minters throughout the thirteenth century.[49]

The situation changed for the better under King Béla IV (reigned 1235–1270). Béla IV wanted Jews from Germany and elsewhere to settle in Hungary. Thus, he decreed in December 1251 a series of thirty-one rights for Jews, concentrating on judicial procedures. Under these protections, a Jew was to pay the same level of customs duties as any other person would pay; Christians who wounded or killed a Jew were punished and required to pay money in compensation; anyone who disturbed a synagogue was required to pay a fine to the Jews; kidnapping of Jewish children was not permissible; and no one was allowed to force Jews to violate their religious prohibition of work during Jewish holidays.[50] Endre III (reigned 1290–1301), the last king of the Árpád dynasty, stated in writing that the Jews living in the city of Pressburg (Bratislava) "should enjoy the same freedoms as the other citizens."[51]

In the following centuries, the Hungarian rulers once again adopted harsh anti-Jewish attitudes. King Lajos I (reigned 1343–1382) tried to convert the Jews to Catholicism, but when this did not work, all Hungarian Jews were expelled from his kingdom. The expelled Jews went to Austria and Bohemia, according to the chronicler János Túróczi. Some of the expelled Jews from northern and northeastern Hungary went to

Poland.[52] Although Jews were readmitted to Hungary around 1364 and many returned, some of them chose to stay in Austria. Jews once again formed communities in Pressburg, Buda, Sopron, and elsewhere throughout the kingdom of Hungary. They were joined by some French-speaking Jewish refugees who had left France in 1394, as was recorded by the traveler Bertrandon de la Broquinière.[53]

JEWS IN HISTORIC ROMANIA

The lands historically belonging to Romania are now divided into three separate political divisions: Most of Bessarabia is part of the modern nation of Moldova; North Bukovina and South Bessarabia are part of Ukraine; and South Bukovina, Wallachia, and western Moldavia are part of Romania. The Jews from historic Romania are closely related to Hungarian and Ukrainian Jews, and thus may have some Khazarian origin.

The early history of Jews in this region is somewhat obscure, because of sparse documentation. It seems that some of the Hungarian Jews expelled by Lajos I arrived in Wallachia during the 1360s. Jewish refugees from Spain arrived in Wallachia after 1492.

Jewish communities were established in Iasi by the fifteenth century, in Suceava by the early sixteenth century, and in Ploesti by the second half of the seventeenth century. Some Polish and Ukrainian Jews fled to Moldova in 1648–1649 to escape the Khmielnitzki massacres. Jewish settlers continued to arrive from Poland and Ukraine in the following centuries.

The Moldovan Jews contributed to the development of trade, crafts, and finance in Moldova.

THE KRYMCHAKS

Although the Ashkenazi Jews formed the dominant population of Jews in eastern Europe, distinctive communities of Jews developed.

By the late thirteenth century, Jews lived in the Crimean Tatar capital of Solkhat (later called Eski-Krim, but today known as Staryi Krim). A large number of Jews continued to live in the coastal Crimean city of Kaffa (Feodosia) until the fifteenth century, when most of the Crimean Jews moved to Lithuania.[54]

By the sixteenth century, the Krymchak sect emerged as the major Jewish population in Crimea. The Krymchaks were rabbinical Jews who adopted the Tatar language between the late fourteenth century and the early sixteenth century. Their dialect was based primarily on Crimean Tatar, although they also used some Hebrew words. However, the Krymchaks read Hebrew in the Sephardic pronunciation rather than the Ashkenazic pronunciation.[55] The Krymchaks used the Hebrew alphabet until 1936 and Cyrillic thereafter.

It has been suggested that the Krymchaks may be a remnant of the Khazars, but this does not seem to be the case. According to Anatoly Khazanov, the Krymchaks may have descended in part from the early Greek-speaking Jews of the Crimea.[56] It is known that the Krymchaks also descended from many other Jewish emigrants from Europe (especially Spain and Italy) and the Middle East (especially Persia and Turkey).[57]

Krymchaks lived in many Crimean towns—in particular, Bakhchisarai, Karasu Bazar (modern Belogorsk), Eski-Krim, Kaffa, Kerch, Mangup, Sevastopol, Simferopol, Yalta, and Yevpatoria. Small groups of Krymchaks later settled outside of the Crimea: in Odessa (Ukraine), Temryuk (southern Russia), and Taman (southern Russia). Most of the Krymchaks worked as craftsmen and merchants, although some were gardeners and vineyard keepers.

Krymchak culture was similar to the Crimean Tatar culture. The Krymchaks' dances, recipes, clothing, and homes resembled those of their Tatar neighbors.

Linguistically, the Krymchak language was most closely related to Crimean Tatar, the extinct Belarusian-Lithuanian Tatar language, the nearly-extinct Karaim language spoken by the

Jewish Karaite sect, and the Kumyk and Karachay-Balkar languages of the north Caucasus.[58] All of these languages are members of the Kipchak (Cumanic/Pontic) branch of the Turkic languages (see Table 4–1). The Khazars, on the other hand, appear to have spoken an Oghuric form of Turkic (see Chapter 4). Thus, there appears to be no evidence that Krymchak (or the related Karaim) was the language of the Jewish Khazars.

In the early twentieth century, many Krymchaks adopted the Russian language. About 70 percent of Krymchaks were murdered by the Nazis and their collaborators during the German occupation of the Crimea in 1941 and 1942. Remnants of the Krymchaks survive in the Crimea, Russia, Israel, and the United States. The Krymchak language, however, is now essentially extinct.

THE CRIMEAN AND LITHUANIAN KARAITES

Karaism was founded by 'Anan ben David, a member of the exilarch family, around 760 or 761, and gained adherents in Egypt, Palestine, Mesopotamia, and Asia Minor, some of whom later migrated northward into eastern Europe. The Karaites have always been a distinctive sect separate from mainstream Judaism. The Karaites adhered strictly to the written word of the Torah and rejected the Mishnah, the Talmud, and all aspects of Oral Law. Unlike rabbinical Jews, the early Karaites did not kindle lights on the evening of the Sabbath, and generally spent it in the dark and without the warmth of a fire. However, the Karaite leader Menahem ben Joseph Bashyazi permitted the kindling of Sabbath candles in around 1440, and his example was followed by Karaites who lived in Lithuania, Poland, Crimea, and Turkey. Additionally, the Karaites did not use the standard Jewish calendar.

The first definite evidence of Karaism in eastern Europe dates from the 1180s, when Rabbi Petakhiah met "heretics" in the "land of Kedar" (see Chapter 9). The earliest known

Karaite settlements on the Crimean peninsula date from 1278.[59] Zvi Ankori, an expert on Karaite history, was of the opinion that the Karaites probably did not settle in eastern Europe before the twelfth century.[60] It is clear that the Karaites arrived in the Crimea only after rabbinical Jews had already built up major settlements there. The Crimean Karaites were traders and crafters.

In the fourteenth century, the Lithuanian Grand Duke Vytautas resettled three hundred Crimean Karaite families in Troki so that they would guard the Troki castle.[61] Crimean Karaites also settled in Panevezys, a city north of Troki, during this time.[62] The Karaite-speaking communities of Lithuania and nearby Poland are now nearly extinct.

Many scholars suggested that the Karaites were the direct descendants of the Khazars. One of the advocates of this view was Ananiasz Zajaczkowski, a Turkologist of Karaite origin, who wrote: "The Karaims fully deserve to be called the rightful successors of Khazarian culture." [63] Zajaczkowski alleged that Karaite missionaries converted many Turkic tribes (such as Khazars and Cumans) in the steppes surrounding the Black and Caspian Seas. To bolster his argument, he cited the *Great Soviet Encyclopedia* of 1957, which claimed that the Khazar rulers embraced Karaism.

Zajaczkowski also explained that numerous Persian and Arabic words exist in the Karaim language. He assumed that these words were acquired in multicultural Khazaria.[64] There is, however, the possibility that such words were adopted by the Karaites during their former residence in the Middle East. Zajaczkowski expanded his linguistic argument by mentioning that the Karaites speak a Kipchak dialect but use Hebrew as a liturgical language. He tried to explain this by the Khazars' adoption of the Hebrew script but retention of a Turkic language.

Other scholars have asserted that Khazarian legends and cuisine were passed on to the Crimean Karaites. These include the desserts *hazar helvasi* ("Khazar halva") and seven-layered cheesecake, and Karaite songs that include folkloric references to the Khazars.[65] The problem here is that we do not know any medieval Khazarian recipes, and songs about Khazars are inconclusive as far as ethnic origin is concerned, since the Khazars were also well-known to Russians, Crimean Tatars, Mountain Jews, Circassians, and other non-Khazar groups.

To adequately address the question of whether Karaites are Khazars, it is necessary to refer to documentary evidence. The adherence of the Khazars to the Talmud and Mishnah was indicated by *King Joseph's Reply* (see Chapter 6), and Talmud study in Khazaria was also reported by the *Chronicle of Elchanan the Merchant* (see Chapter 1). Abraham ibn Daud explicitly stated in *Sefer ha-Qabbalah* that the Khazars he met in Spain were rabbinical (see Chapter 9), and the Khazars in the twelfth century who asked Iraqi Jews for assistance in teaching their children the Talmud clearly were mainstream Jews and not Karaites (see Chapter 9). We also recall that the wording of the *Kievan Letter* indicated that the Khazars who lived in Kiev were rabbinical (see Chapter 6). Their descendants, who tried to convince Prince Vladimir of Kiev to adopt their faith, likewise professed mainstream rabbinical Judaism rather than the belief of a small sect (see Chapter 9). These facts reveal that the Khazars' belief system was incompatible with Karaism, which from the beginning rejected the Talmud and Mishnah. There is, in fact, no documentation whatsoever indicating Khazar adherence to Karaism.[66]

It is also significant that tenth-century Karaites condescended and criticized the Khazars for being proselytes and thus, in their view, illegitimate *mamzerim* ("bastards") (see Chapter 6). This type of scorn would not have been directed by Karaites toward other Karaites.

There appear to be no aboriginal Khazar traditions among the Karaites. The Byzantine Karaites adopted Tataric surnames only by the fifteenth century when they fell under Turkish rule.[67] Even the Tataric language which the Karaites adopted was not Khazarian. As already mentioned, the Karaites of eastern Europe, like the Krymchaks, spoke a Kipchak dialect, while most of the Khazars spoke Oghuric rather than common Turkic. Oghuric and Kipchak are two different variants of Turkic, just as English, German, and Swedish are distinctive Germanic languages.

Finally, it must be stressed that the heretical Karaites who lived in the land of Kedar toward the end of the twelfth century probably were not Khazars (see Chapter 9). Scholars have sometimes erroneously presumed that these heretics, who sat in the dark on Sabbath, were Khazars, without considering the distinction between Khozaria and Kedar in Rabbi Petakhiah's travelogue.

The acclimation of the Crimean and Lithuanian Karaites to the Turkic realm does not seem to reflect a Khazar origin. "Clearly," remarked Philip Miller, "the case for the Khazar origins of the Crimean Karaites is not a strong one." [68] The origin of the Karaites is thus to be found in the Middle East (although the Karaites may have intermarried with Crimean Tatars), as Karaism was not professed in Crimea or eastern Europe until after Khazaria's decline and fall. The claim that Karaite anti-Talmudists of Middle Eastern origin have a connection with talmudic Khazar scholars of the steppe whom they criticized is untenable.

CONCLUSIONS

In Chapter 10, I examined the evidence concerning the widespread phenomenon of conversion to Judaism in premodern Europe. Given this evidence, it is possible to establish a direct kinship between Jews and their non-Jewish neighbors. Many Jews may be descended from Slavs (such as Belarusians, Poles, and Russians), as well as from Germans, Austrians, Gypsies, and many other peoples. At the same time, it is probable that there is a small underlying Israelite-Judean component among Ashkenazi Jews.

Many issues must be addressed in order to solve the mystery of Ashkenazic origins. One of these issues is the origin of the ethnic name *Ashkenaz*. In ancient times, the Scythians were called Ashguzai (Ashkenaz).[69] The geographic location of the Ashkenaz, based on references in the Torah, may be centered around southern Russia, Armenia, and Asia Minor. The Ashkaênoi (*Askaê or Askai*) were the people also known as Phrygians or Mysians (Meshech).[70] Their god was named Mên Askaênos. A lake, as well as other places in Mysia, Phrygia, and Bithynia, were called Ascania. Additionally, Askênos or Askaios referred to towns and rivers in Mysia, Phrygia, Bithynia, Pisidia, Aeolis, Troas, and several islands in the Aegean.[71] All of these places are in the western part of modern Turkey.[72] The Askênos also lent their name to the legendary hero Ascanius, who was said to be an ethnic Askênos. Allen Godbey postulated that the Jews who inhabited southern Russia in early times were Scythian converts and were known as Ashkan or Ashkênos Jews.[73] Whatever the case may be, Ashkenaz originally meant Iranian peoples and the lands they inhabited.

Saadiah Gaon considered the Khazars to represent the kingdoms of Minni (Mannai), Ararat (Urartu), and Ashkenaz, who, according to the scriptures, were going to destroy Babel.[74] According to the mid-tenth-century *Jami' al-Alfaz* by the Karaite David ben Abraham al-Fasi, Ashkenaz may be equal to the Khazars or the Franks.[75] It should also be pointed out that Ashkenaz did not become a definite Jewish designation for Germany until the eleventh century. During previous centuries, the term appears to have been applied to multiple ethnic groups. But the author Eusebius wrote that he thought that the Teutonic (Germanic) peoples were the Ashkenaz, and this view was later adopted by the Jews of medieval Europe.[76] Among the first Jewish writers to associate Ashkenaz with Germany were Rashi (eleventh century) and Benjamin of Tudela (twelfth century).

To summarize, the term Ashkenaz referred at first to Iranian, Armenian, Phrygian, and Mysian territories, then to Khazarian and Slavic lands, and later to German lands. It can therefore be postulated that a tribal group called Ashkenaz chose Judaism, mingled with the Israelites, and formed part of the northward migrations of Byzantine, Armenian, and Persian Jews into Khazaria. The Ashkenaz of eastern Europe then intermarried with the Khazar Turks, who were descended from Togarmah. The fact that the Ashkenazim retain their ancient Scythian tribal name appears to suggest a continuity with the Jews of Khazaria, as well as with the Jews of the ancient Middle East.

The Byzantine rites among Ashkenazic Jews may also be explained by northward migrations, since the Khazars mixed with Greek-speaking Jews (*Romaniotes*) who had originally come from the Byzantine Empire, i.e., the Balkans and Asia Minor (see Chapter 6). Byzantine Jews and Ashkenazic Jews have religious traditions in common. Ashkenazic Jews and Romaniotes both include the liturgical hymns of the Byzantine poet Eleazar ha-Qalir in rituals during the Ninth of Ab, Yom Kippur, and Rosh Hashanah.[77] These hymns are not in general use among any other Jewish group. The *Kievan Letter* used the style of rhyme that ha-Qalir had developed;[78] this demonstrates a direct link between the Khazar Jews of Kiev and the immigrants to Khazaria from Byzantium. Additionally, Ashkenazic Jews uniquely share with Greek-speaking Jews certain phrases recited during prayer, such as the verse "Living and Existent God, may He reign over us forever and ever!"[79] There are even some Yiddish words of Greek origin, such as *kile* ("hernia"), which derives from the Greek *kêlê*.[80]

Another important issue is the type of German that formed the Yiddish language. According to the linguist Robert King, Yiddish did not originate in Rhineland Germany. Rather, Yiddish is similar only to the east central and Bavarian dialects of German. King identified three major structural features in common between central German and Yiddish, and nine major features in common between Bavarian and Yiddish.[81] Both Dovid Katz and Robert King independently proposed that the Jews of the city of Regensburg, with their high level of culture and scholarship, may be the group that developed

Yiddish.[82] This provides a partial solution to the question of Ashkenazic origins. That is to say, many Polish Jews have some distant ancestors who lived in Germany.

A final issue concerns whether there is a continuity between medieval Khazar Jewry (including Jews of Turkic, Romaniote, Armenian, Persian, and Iraqi origins) and modern eastern European Jewry. It would not be reasonable to accept Bernard Weinryb's view that the early Jewish settlements in Crimea and Poland disappeared without any remaining descendants.[83] As we have seen, the Khazars professed standard Judaism and can rightly be called Jews from the eastern frontier of Europe, or simply "eastern European Jews"; and the Khazars still continued to exist after the destruction of their kingdom by the Rus'ians. I will argue that there was no geographic gap or time gap of any significance separating the Khazar Jews from the later Jewish settlements in eastern Europe. To reiterate, documentary evidence suggests that the Khazar and eastern Jews lived in the Kiev region, among others, continuously since the ninth century. After moving to Kievan Rus, they adopted the Slavic language and became known as "Rus'ian" or "Canaanite" Jews. The Jews from central Europe who moved eastward into Poland as early as 1096 to 1098 and then spread into Belarus and Ukraine met these Canaanite Jews and assimilated with them.

A good example of the continuity of Jewish population may be seen in the city of Hrodna. It was, as indicated earlier, one of the first towns in Poland-Lithuania that was settled by a large number of Jews—apparently by Khazars in the ninth or tenth century. There was only one major break in the continuity: Jews were expelled from Hrodna in 1495, but returned in 1503. The Jews of Hrodna were spared from the Khmielnitzki massacres in 1648.

Another example of continuity is found in Kiev, which had Khazar settlement as early as the ninth century. In around 930, the *Kievan Letter* was composed; in 945, the "Kozare" district in Kiev was reported; in 986, Khazar Jews met Prince Vladimir in Kiev; in 1018, the "Khazaria" district in Kiev was reported. Although a disruption in the community occurred in the 1240s with the Mongol invasion, many Kievan Jews escaped to other regions and perhaps eventually returned to their home city. In any event, a large portion of the Kievan Khazars (and the Khazars of Chernigov as well) continued to live in eastern Europe even after being displaced, but they gradually lost their identity as Khazars and became simply "Jews" (in Yiddish, *Yidn*).

The notion that the large numbers of Khazars in Europe simply vanished is not in accord with the facts. The evidence suggests that the Khazars of Ukraine and Belarus did not embrace Christianity or some other religion, but remained believers in Judaism. When Yiddish became the dominant language of eastern European Jews in the fourteenth and fifteenth centuries, the assimilation of the formerly Slavic-speaking Khazars into the overall Jewish community was completed.

The adoption of Judaism by Khazars, Alans, Slavs, Cumans, Berbers, and other peoples was not an insignificant process to be mentioned only in passing. Rather, conversion and intermarriage have been major factors in the development of Jewish communities in Yemen, Ethiopia, Tunisia, the Middle East, the Caucasus, and central and eastern Europe. In addition to the conversion of volunteers and slaves, sons and daughters of non-Jewish men became Jews as the result of rape or the keeping of concubines.[84] As a result of widespread conversions, today's Jews do not represent a distinct "race" or a homogeneous ethnicity. Even the ancient Hebrews were heterogeneous and multiracial, mixing with Egyptians, Amorites, Hittites, and numerous other tribes.

As for why most of the descendants of Khazars no longer designated themselves as Khazars or descendants of Togarmah, we must remember that converts are required by Jewish law to become part of the overall Jewish community and are considered to be the children of Abraham. The convert is said, by Talmudic scholars, to be like a newborn child, in possession of a new soul, and any relatives he or she had before conversion are no longer considered his or her relatives.[85] Judaism's prayers and holidays also emphasize a connection to the ancient land of Israel—not to Khazaria. As Jacob Agus wrote:

> When non-Jewish groups accepted the Jewish faith, they also embraced the myth of Hebraic descent. . . . Even the Khazars who were converted to Judaism in the light of history regarded themselves as somehow of the "seed" and the "blood" of ancient Israel. They belonged at least in part to the tribe of "Simeon" or the "half-tribe Menasseh." [86]

It should be added that the descendants of Khazars did not attach the appellation "ha-Kuzari" to their Hebrew names, because it was not officially recognized by Jewish authorities (even though "ha-Kohen" and "ha-Levi" are). Thus, the Khazar converts began the process by which they would eventually forget their Turkic origins when they embraced Judaism.

SUMMARY

Let us now summarize the main points brought forth in this book:

Chapter 1 traced the Turkic ethnogenesis of the Khazar ethnic group and the creation of the Khazar Empire.

Chapter 2 chronicled the establishment and settlement of important cities, towns, and villages in the empire, such as Sarkel, Atil, and Kiev, which supported large Jewish populations.

Chapter 3 described the role of the Khazar government officials in the affairs of state.

Chapter 4 noted how the Khazars actively engaged in fishing, farming, and artwork and contributed greatly to the economic development of their empire.

Chapter 5 examined the high level of international trading activity in eastern Europe during the Khazar era.

Chapter 6 detailed the evidence for the Khazars' conversion to the standard form of Judaism after being influenced by Jews from the Hellenistic and Islamic spheres. The Khazars intermarried with these Jews and created a synthesis of the Jewish and Turkic worlds.

Chapter 7 described the intricate web of diplomatic relations between the Khazars and their neighbors—at times fragile links that erupted into renewed episodes of violence, as in the case of relations with the Byzantines and the Alans.

Chapter 8 outlined the eventual fall of the Khazar Empire at the hands of the Rus'ians and the Byzantines.

Chapter 9 used historical and archaeological evidence to show that Khazar Jews were among the early settlers in Ukrainian, Hungarian, and Polish towns.

Chapter 10 showed that the Khazars' adoption of Judaism was part of a larger, widespread trend in the medieval world—a trend that also embraced Berbers, Arabs, Spaniards, Germans, and many others. The Jewish people has been enriched by the addition of non-Israelite elements for three thousand years.

Finally, Chapter 11 demonstrated that Jewish communities existed on a continuous basis in eastern Europe from early medieval times.

After considering the strong evidence for cultural, linguistic, and ethnic ties between eastern Ashkenazic Jews and the Khazar Jews, as well as the equally strong evidence for Jewish migrations into eastern Europe from the south and west, one can come to only one conclusion: that the eastern European Jews are descended from both Khazars and other converts, as well as from Judeans. The fact that most of our people descend from converts does not diminish our Jewish status, since all converts share equally in the Jewish heritage.

The Khazars were an extraordinary part of the Jewish experience—and memory of them must never again be forgotten. As the twenty-first century dawns, those of us who are

Ashkenazic Jews have the right, as well as the obligation, to rediscover and reclaim our unique, mixed heritage. Many of us are, indeed, heirs to the great Khazar Empire that once ruled the Russian steppes.

NOTES

1. Benjamin Harshav, *The Meaning of Yiddish* (Los Angeles and Berkeley: University of California Press, 1990), pp. 5–6.

2. Nathan Ausubel, *Pictorial History of the Jewish People* (New York: Crown, 1953), p. 133.

3. Henrik Birnbaum, "On Jewish Life and Anti-Jewish Sentiments in Medieval Russia," in *Essays in Early Slavic Civilization*, ed. Henrik Birnbaum (Munich: Wilhelm Fink, 1981), p. 232.

4. Ibid., pp. 226–227, 230.

5. Shmuel Ettinger, "Kievan Russia," in *The Dark Ages*, ed. Cecil Roth and I. H. Levine (New Brunswick, NJ: Rutgers University Press, 1966), p. 320.

6. Henrik Birnbaum, "On Jewish Life and Anti-Jewish Sentiments in Medieval Russia," p. 225.

7. Benjamin Pinkus, *The Jews of the Soviet Union* (Cambridge, England: Cambridge University Press, 1988), p. 5.

8. Henrik Birnbaum, "On Jewish Life and Anti-Jewish Sentiments in Medieval Russia," p. 222.

9. Ibid., p. 223.

10. Ibid., p. 234.

11. Salo W. Baron, *A Social and Religious History of the Jews*, vol. 10 (New York: Columbia University Press, 1965), p. 31.

12. Itzhak Schipper, "Rozwój ludności Żydowskiej na ziemiach Dawnej Rzeczypospolitej," in *Żydzi w Polsce Odrodzonej*, ed. A. Hafftka, Itzhak Schipper, and A. Tartakower (Warsaw, 1936), p. 28.

13. Maurice Samuel, *In Praise of Yiddish* (New York: Cowles, 1971), p. 29.

14. Itzhak Schipper, "Dzieje gospodarcze Żydów Korony i Litwy w czasach przedrozbiorowych," in *Żydzi w Polsce Odrodzonej*, ed. A. Hafftka, Itzhak Schipper, and A. Tartakower (Warsaw, 1936), p. 116.

15. John D. Klier, *Russia Gathers Her Jews* (DeKalb, IL: Northern Illinois University Press, 1986), p. 24.

16. *The Mongol Mission*, ed. Christopher Dawson (New York: Sheed & Ward, 1955), p. 30.

17. Henrik Birnbaum, "On Jewish Life and Anti-Jewish Sentiments in Medieval Russia," pp. 232–233, 253.

18. Herman Rosenthal, "Kiev," in *The Jewish Encyclopedia*, vol. 7 (New York: Ktav, 1901–1906), p. 488.

19. Shmuel Ettinger, "Jewish Participation in the Settlement of Ukraine in the Sixteenth and Seventeenth Century," in *Ukrainian-Jewish Relations in Historical Perspective*, ed. Howard Aster and Peter J. Potichnyj (Edmonton, Alberta, Canada: Canadian Institute of Ukrainian Studies Press, 1990), p. 26.

20. *Karaite Separatism in Nineteenth-Century Russia*, ed. Philip E. Miller (Cincinnati: Hebrew Union College Press, 1993), p. 3.

21. Henrik Birnbaum, "On Jewish Life and Anti-Jewish Sentiments in Medieval Russia," p. 241.

22. Paul Wexler, "The Reconstruction of Pre-Ashkenazic Jewish Settlements in the Slavic Lands in the Light of Linguistic Sources," *Polin* 1 (1986): 4.

23. Ibid., pp. 4, 12.

24. Salo W. Baron, *A Social and Religious History of the Jews*, vol. 3 (New York: Columbia University Press, 1957), p. 219.

25. Jacob Litman, *The Economic Role of Jews in Medieval Poland* (Lanham, MD: University Press of America, 1984), p. 95; *Encyclopedia of Jewish History*, ed. Ilana Shamir and Shlomo Shavit (New York: Facts on File, 1986), p. 80.

26. Itzhak Schipper, "Dzieje gospodarcze Żydów Korony i Litwy w czasach przedrozbiorowych," in *Żydzi w Polsce Odrodzonej*, p. 111.

27. Ibid., pp. 111–112.

28. Salo W. Baron, *A Social and Religious History of the Jews*, vol. 10, p. 37.

29. Jacob Litman, *The Economic Role of Jews in Medieval Poland*, pp. 97–98.

30. A translation of Duke Boleslav's 1264 charter may be found in *Scattered Among the Nations*, ed. Alexis P. Rubin (Northvale, NJ: Jason Aronson, 1995), pp. 88–89.

31. Salo W. Baron, *A Social and Religious History of the Jews*, vol. 10, p. 33.

32. Ibid., p. 32.

33. Jacob Litman, *The Economic Role of Jews in Medieval Poland*, p. 98.

34. Paul Wexler, *The Ashkenazic Jews* (Columbus, OH: Slavica, 1993), p. 61.

35. Michael F. Hamm, *Kiev* (Princeton, NJ: Princeton University Press, 1993), p. 118.

36. Nancy Schoenburg and Stuart Schoenburg, *Lithuanian Jewish Communities* (Northvale, NJ: Jason Aronson, 1996), pp. 17–18.

37. Masha Greenbaum, *The Jews of Lithuania* (Jerusalem: Gefen, 1995), p. 353. However, most Jews were forbidden from permanently residing in Kaunas during the fifteenth and sixteenth centuries. Some Jewish traders from Ukraine and Poland lived there temporarily during Grand Duke Vytautas' reign (1392–1430).

38. Ibid., pp. 4–5.

39. Nancy Schoenburg and Stuart Schoenburg, *Lithuanian Jewish Communities*, p. 10.

40. Salo W. Baron, *A Social and Religious History of the Jews*, vol. 10, p. 46.

41. Nancy Schoenburg and Stuart Schoenburg, *Lithuanian Jewish Communities*, pp. 116, 222, 293.

42. Salo W. Baron, *A Social and Religious History of the Jews*, vol. 10, p. 36.

43. Nancy Schoenburg and Stuart Schoenburg, *Lithuanian Jewish Communities*, p. 17.

44. Ibid., pp. 348–349.

45. *A Historical Atlas of the Jewish People*, ed. Eli Barnavi (New York: Schocken, 1992), p. 118.

46. Raphael Patai, *The Jews of Hungary* (Detroit: Wayne State University Press, 1996), pp. 31, 34.

47. Ibid., p. 41.

48. Ibid., pp. 42–43. King Kálmán's government also passed restrictions on the Muslim Bulgars living in Hungary.

49. Hungarian Jewish mintmasters, like their counterparts in Poland, engraved Hebrew letters on the coins they pro-

duced (see Alexander Scheiber, *Jewish Inscriptions in Hungary from the 3rd Century to 1686* (Budapest: Akadémiai, 1983), p. 77).

50. Raphael Patai, *The Jews of Hungary*, pp. 48–49.

51. Ibid., p. 39.

52. Ibid., p. 56.

53. Ibid., p. 72.

54. Benjamin Pinkus, *The Jews of the Soviet Union*, p. 6.

55. Anatoly M. Khazanov, *The Krymchaks* (Jerusalem: The Marjorie Mayrock Center for Soviet and East European Research, 1989), p. 27.

56. Ibid., p. 8.

57. Ibid., p. 13.

58. Peter B. Golden, "Turkic Languages," in *Encyclopedia of Asian History*, vol. 4 (New York: Charles Scribners' Sons, 1988), p. 154.

59. Henrik Birnbaum, "On Jewish Life and Anti-Jewish Sentiments in Medieval Russia," p. 235.

60. Zvi Ankori, *Karaites in Byzantium* (New York: Ams Press, 1968), p. 60.

61. Nancy Schoenburg and Stuart Schoenburg, *Lithuanian Jewish Communities*, pp. 315–316.

62. Ibid., p. 224.

63. Ananiasz Zajaczkowski, "Khazarian Culture and its Inheritors," *Acta Orientalia Academiae Scientiarum Hungaricae* 12 (1961): 306. Sheraya Markovich Shapshal (1873–1961), the Chief Rabbi (*hakham*) of the Lithuanian Karaites of Troki in the late 1920s and 1930s, also declared that his people were descendants of the Khazars.

64. Ibid., p. 304. Indeed, the Khazars did adopt some words originally of Persian origin, such as *baghatur*, *chater*, and *tarkhan*.

65. W. Zajaczkowski, "The Karaites in Eastern Europe," in *Encyclopedia of Islam*, new ed., vol. 4 (Leiden, Netherlands: E. J. Brill, 1993), pp. 608–609.

66. Zvi Ankori, *Karaites in Byzantium*, p. 66.

67. Ibid., p. 59. The Greek vocabulary in the Karaim language may testify to their roots in Byzantium.

68. *Karaite Separatism in Nineteenth-Century Russia*, ed. Philip E. Miller (Cincinnati: Hebrew Union College Press, 1993), p. 7.

69. Vladimir F. Minorsky, *A History of Sharvan and Darband in the 10th–11th Centuries* (Cambridge, England: W. Heffer & Sons, 1958), p. 104. *Ashknz* appears to have been a scribal error for *Ashguz* or *Ashguza*, which in turn may be equivalent to the Greek word Skuthai, meaning "Scythians." The Scythians were an Iranian group.

70. Allen H. Godbey, *The Lost Tribes, A Myth* (Durham, NC: Duke University Press, 1930), p. 293. According to Godbey (idem., p. 294), the Askênos or Askaê people arrived in Asia Minor from Thrace circa 1900 B.C.E. and gradually moved eastward, trading in Tyre, Kuë, and Hittite towns. By the tenth century B.C.E., the Askênos were active in Armenia and southwest Colchis.

71. Ibid., p. 293.

72. In fact, Bithynia is the region along the Sangarius (Sakaria) River, around the modern-day city of Izmit, which is the same region where Yitzhak ha-Sangari—the Jewish missionary to the Khazars—apparently originally resided.

73. Allen H. Godbey, *The Lost Tribes, A Myth*, pp. 268, 294.

74. Arthur Koestler, *The Thirteenth Tribe* (New York: Random House, 1976), p. 182. In Jeremiah 51:27, the peoples of Urartu, Mannai, and Ashkenaz were summoned against Babylon.

75. Douglas M. Dunlop, "The Khazars," in *The Dark Ages*, ed. Cecil Roth and I. H. Levine (New Brunswick, NJ: Rutgers University Press, 1966), p. 350.

76. Allen H. Godbey, *The Lost Tribes, A Myth*, p. 295. Hasdai ibn Shaprut called the King of Germany *Melekh Ashkenaz* in his letter to King Joseph.

77. Daniel E. Gershenson, "Yiddish 'davenen' and the Ashkenazic Rite: Byzantine Jewry and the Ashkenazim," *Yiddish* 10:2–3 (1996): 84.

78. See Norman Golb and Omeljan Pritsak, *Khazarian Hebrew Documents of the Tenth Century* (Ithaca, NY: Cornell University Press, 1982), pp. 10–11.

79. Daniel E. Gershenson, "Yiddish 'davenen' and the Ashkenazic Rite: Byzantine Jewry and the Ashkenazim," p. 85.

80. Ibid., p. 89.

81. Robert D. King, "Migration and Linguistics as Illustrated by Yiddish," in *Reconstructing Languages and Cultures*, ed. Edgar C. Polemé and Werner Winter (Berlin: Mouton de Gruyter, 1992), pp. 426–428.

82. Ibid., pp. 434–436.

83. As was argued in Bernard D. Weinryb, *The Beginnings of East European Jewry in Legend and Historiography* (Leiden, Netherlands: E. J. Brill, 1962), pp. 56–57.

84. Paul Wexler, *The Ashkenazic Jews*, p. 185.

85. Bernard J. Bamberger, *Proselytism in the Talmudic Period* (New York: Hebrew Union College Press, 1939), p. 63.

86. Jacob B. Agus, *The Meaning of Jewish History*, vol. 1 (New York: Abelard Schuman, 1963), pp. 42–43.

Appendix: A Timeline of Khazar History

5th century

circa 434–452—Akatzirs are subjects of the Huns.

circa 455—Jews from Armenia and Persia begin to immigrate to the north Caucasus.

6th century

circa 505–525—Sabirs immigrate to the north Caucasus and the Volga valley.

circa 570–630s—Western Turkish Empire rules over the Khazars.

7th century

626–630—Byzantine Empire allies with the Khazars.

628 or 629—Khazars conquer the Georgian city of Tbilisi.

circa 630s—Western Turkish Empire falls apart.

630–642—Khan Kubrat rules Great Bulgaria in southern Russia.

642–652—First Arab-Khazar War.

642—Arab troops attack Khazaria for the first time.

650–1016—Khazaria exists as a distinct, independent political entity.

650—Khazars' territorial expansion drives some Bulgars westward.

651–652—Khazars defeat invading Arab troops and retain control over Balanjar.

671—Jews reside on the Taman peninsula in large numbers.

683–685—Khazars invade Transcaucasia and inflict much damage.

8th century

circa 703 or 704—Byzantine emperor Justinian II marries Theodora, a royal Khazar.

705–711—Justinian II fights the Khazars and attempts to destroy Cherson.

711—Khazars play a role in instituting Philippicus as the new emperor of Byzantium.

714—Arabs seize Derbent and its fortress.

717—Khazars attempt to invade Azerbaijan.

722–737—Second Arab-Khazar War.

723 or 724—Arabs destroy the city of Balanjar.

723 or 724—Samandar becomes the new Khazar capital.

circa 723–944—Jews move to Khazaria from the Middle East because of anti-Jewish persecutions.

730—Khazar commander Barjik leads 300,000 Khazar troops through the Darial Pass to invade Azerbaijan.

730—At the Battle of Ardabil, the Khazars defeat an entire Arab army.

731–732—Khazars briefly recapture Derbent.

731—Said ibn Omar al-Harashi leads an Arab army to penetrate Khazar-held fortresses in Azerbaijan and free prisoners from the Khazars.

731—Maslama ibn 'Abd-al-Malik kills the Khazar kagan's son in battle.

732—Arabs permanently acquire Derbent.

732 or 733—Byzantine emperor Constantine V marries Khazar princess Chichek (Irene).

733 or 734—Maslama ibn 'Abd-al-Malik builds a mosque for Khazars in Derbent.

737—Khazar capital transferred from Samandar to Atil.

737—Arabs force the Khazar kagan to convert to Islam. Muslim Khazars are resettled in Azerbaijan.

759 or 760—Khazar kagan Baghatur's daughter marries the Arab governor of Armenia.

762–764—Khazars, led by As Tarkhan, conquer Transcaucasia.

775–780—Leo IV "the Khazar" rules the Byzantine Empire.

circa 780s—Leo II, grandson of a Khazar kagan, rules Abkhazia.

9th century

circa 820–840—Khazars found Sambata (part of Kiev) and establish a garrison there.

circa 830s–862—Khazarian Kabars rebel against the king of Khazaria.

circa 830s—First Rus Kaganate is established.

circa 833–838—Sarkel fortress is built by Khazars and Byzantines.

circa 842 or 843—Caliph Al-Wathiq sends mathematical expert Muhammad ibn Musa al-Khwarizmi to the palace of the Khazar king.

circa 852—The renegade Khazar leader Bugha "the Elder," directed by the caliph, attacks the Khazars and exacts poll taxes from them.

854—Muslim Khazars settle in Shamkur, Azerbaijan.

860—Khazar people report being persuaded by Muslims and Jews to abandon shamanism and accept monotheism.

860—Saint Cyril visits Cherson and learns Hebrew.

861—Saint Cyril debates in the Khazar court against Rabbi
Yitzhak ha-Sangari and a Muslim mullah.

861—Khazar king Bulan, the nobility, and some of the common people convert to Judaism.

circa 860s–870s—Khazar king Obadiah builds synagogues and schools.

864—*Expositio in Matthaeum Evangelistam* is first written record of the Khazars' Judaism.

circa 875–925—Khazars build a glass factory in Hrodna (present-day Belarus).

885—Most of the eastern Slavs become united.

894—Magyar prince Levente leads Kabar troops against Bulgaria.

895–896—Some Khazarian Kabars settle in Transylvania and Hungary along with the Magyars.

10th century

901—Unsuccessful attack by Khazars upon Derbent.

circa 913—In a major battle with the Khazars, thousands of Rus'ian ship voyagers perish.

922—Khazar kagan closes down a Muslim minaret in Atil in retaliation for the destruction of a Jewish synagogue in the Middle East.

circa 930–988—Khazars use the square Hebrew script for writing.

circa 930—*Kievan Letter* written by rabbinical Khazar Jews of Kiev.

circa early 930s—Khazar king Aaron allies with the Alans, who adopt Judaism.

circa early 930s—King Aaron's son, Joseph, marries the Alan king's daughter.

932—King Aaron allies with the Oghuz.

circa late 930s—Khazar baliqchi Pesakh defeats the Rus'ians.

circa 947—Croatian Jews Saul and Joseph meet Mar 'Amram, a scholarly Khazar Jew.

circa 948–949—*Schechter Letter* is written by a Khazar Jew in Constantinople.

circa 954—Hasdai ibn Shaprut's literary secretary writes a letter to Khazar king Joseph.

circa 955—*King Joseph's Reply* reaches Hisdai in Spain.

circa 955–970—Duke Taksony invites Khazar Jews to Hungary.

956–1048—Jewish Khazars erect tombstones in the Chufut-Kale cemetery on Crimea.

circa 964—Pechenegs seriously threaten Khazaria.

965—Prince Svyatoslav of Kiev conquers and seizes Sarkel.

circa 965–967—Khazar kagan momentarily converts to Islam for political reasons.

circa 967—Rus'ians seize Atil, the Khazar capital.

circa 969—Khazar refugees escape to Baku and islands in the Caspian and become Muslims.

986—Khazar Jews discuss Judaism with Prince Vladimir in Kiev.

988—Prince Vladimir of Kiev accepts the Christian religion.

11th century

circa 1000–1300—Some Khazars in Kievan Rus are Slavicized and adopt the East Slavic language.

1016—Khazar kagan Georgius Tzul is captured by the Rus'ians.

1016—Khazar Jews move to Lithuania.

1018—Khazar Jews remain in city of Kiev.

1023—"Khazars" ally with Prince Mstislav of Tmutorokan.

1064—Khazars settle in Qahtan, north Caucasus.

1079–1083—"Khazars" still live in Tmutorokan.

1096—Rabbi Nissim says that seventeen communities of Khazars enter the "Wilderness of the Nations."

12th century

circa 1100–1150—Jewish Khazars settle in central Romania.

1106—Khazar general Ivan commands Rus'ian army.

1113—Anti-Jewish riots erupt in Kiev.

1117—"Khazars" settle near Chernigov.

1120–1140—Yehudah ha-Levi writes *Sefer ha-Kuzari*.

1154—Kalizian warriors of the Balkans, originally from Khazaria, retain Judaic beliefs.

1161—Abraham ibn Daud notes that he has met Khazar Jewish scholars in Toledo, Spain.

1185—Rabbi Petakhiah ben Jacob sees Khazar Jews in Baghdad.

13th century

1206—*Ta'rik-i Fakhr al-Din Mubarak Shah* says that Khazar Jews use a form of the Cyrillic script for writing.

circa 1242—A theory suggests that an Endzher-ruled Daghestani Khazar kingdom existed until this year.

circa 1245–1247—Christian Khazars are encountered by Friar Joannes de Plano Carpini.

14th century

circa 1300–1500—Descendants of Jewish Khazars in eastern Europe adopt the Yiddish language.

1309—Hungarian clergy declares that Catholics cannot marry "Khazars."

1349–1360—Hungarian Jews, partly of Khazar origin, resettle in Poland and Austria.

GLOSSARY

ak Khazarian for "white." The upper classes (i.e., royalty and nobility) in the Khazar Empire were called "Ak-Khazar." Alternative spelling: aq.

alp Turkic for "hero."

amir Arabic title for "ruler, prince" in Muslim countries. Alternative spelling: emir.

at Khazarian for "horse." Alternative spelling: alas-at.

Atil Khazarian term for the River Volga; also the name of the Khazars' capital city along the Volga; apparently from *as* ("great") + *til* ("river"). Alternative spellings: Itil, Ityl, 'Til.

babaghuq Khazarian title for an elected "father of the city."

baghatur Khazarian for "brave warrior." Alternative spelling: bogatur.

baliqchi Khazarian for "fisherman"; from *baliq* ("fish") + *chi* ("profession"). Appointed provincial governors were given this title. Alternative spellings: bolushchi, balgitzi, balquitzi.

Bar Khazarian term for the Dnieper River. Alternative spelling: Var.

bek Turkic title for the king who leads the army and affairs of state. Alternative spellings: beg, peg, peh, pekh, bey.

bulan Khazarian for "elk." Alternative spelling: bolan.

chater Khazarian for "tent."

chichek Khazarian for "flower." This word was used as a feminine personal name in Khazaria. Alternative spellings: chichak, chichäk.

Duna Khazarian term for the Danube River.

el-teber Hunnic and Turkic title for a local king. Alternative spellings: el-tebir, yiltavar, ilut'uer.

er Khazarian for "man." Alternative spellings: ar, är, ör.

eristavi Georgian title for "prince."

ev Khazarian and Turkic for "settlement, home."

gorodishche Russian for "hill fort."

gyula Magyar title for the king who leads the army and affairs of state. Alternative spellings: jula, dzsula.

Hagar Khazarian term for Hungary.

javishgar Khazarian title for the kender's deputy. Alternative spelling: jawshyghr.

kabar Khazarian or Magyar for "rebel" or "ethnic mixup." The Kabars were a dissident group of Khazars who left the empire and resettled in Hungary in the ninth century.

kagan Turkic title for "great (sacral) king, supreme judge." Alternative spellings: kaghan, khaghan, qaghan, khaqan, khakan.

kaganate the realm ruled by a kagan.

kara Khazarian for "black." The lower classes (i.e., commoners) in the Khazar Empire were called "Kara-Khazar." Alternative spelling: qara.

kel Khazarian for "fortress." Alternative spelling: kil.

kende Magyar title for their sacral king.

kender Khazarian title for "sub-king," i.e., third-in-command. Alternative spelling: kundur.

khatun Avar and Khazarian for "queen" or "princess." Alternative spellings: katoun, chatoun.

kilich Turkic for "sword, saber." Alternative spelling: qilich.

kizil Turkic for "red." Alternative spelling: qizil.

kniaz' Russian title for "prince."

kök Turkic for "blue." The Western Turkish Kaganate was ruled by the Kök Türks. Alternative spelling: gök.

kurgan Turkic and Russian for "burial mound."

metropolitan A bishop in the Eastern Orthodox Church, ranked just below the patriarch.

oq Old Turkic for "arrow." Two tribal confederations, one among the Bulgars and the other among the Magyars, were called the On-Oghur, i.e., "ten arrows."

ostikan Armenian title for "governor."

qam Khazarian or Turkic for "priest, shaman."

qut Turkic for "heavenly good fortune, charisma." The Turks believed that a ruling kagan bestowed qut upon his kaganate.

Romaniote Term for a Greek (especially Byzantine) Jew. Alternative spelling: Romaniot.

sam Khazarian for "high, top"; used in many Khazar town names.

saq, sar Khazarian for "white" or "gray." These two words were contractions of *sarigh*.

sarigh Turkic for "yellow." Occasionally also meant "white."

tabib Oghuric Turkic for "medicine man, shaman."

talyga Khazarian for "wagon, chariot."

tamga Turkic term for tribe or clan symbols, which often were engraved on pottery and stones. The Khazars continued to use tamgas even after their conversion to Judaism.

tarkhan Khazarian title for "army commander, local governor or chief."

tengri Turkic for "sky"; the name of the shamanists' Sky god. Alternative spelling: tängri.

törü Old Turkic for "traditional (customary) law." Alternative spelling: turah.

tudun Avar and Khazarian title for "provincial governor." Alternative spellings: titano, titanus, thodanus.

Varshan Khazarian term for the Sulak River and the surrounding mountains. Alternative spellings: Warsan, Varach'an.

voievoda Old Russian title for "military commander."

yaligh Old Turkic for "bow."

yer-sub Turkic for "earth-water"; from *yer* ("earth, soil") + *sub* ("water"). Tengri shamanists believed in an earth-water god whom they called simply Yer-sub. Alternative spelling: Yir-sub.

yurt Russian term for a sturdy, portable, dome-shaped tent often made partly of felt and used by nomadic Eurasian peoples, including the early Khazars. Alternative spellings: yurta (Central Asian Turkic), ger (Mongolian).

BIBLIOGRAPHY

Articles

Arbman, Holger. "Einige orientalische Gegenstände in den Birka-Funden." *Acta Archaeologica* 13 (1942): 303–315.

Bálint, Csanád. "Some Archaeological Addenda to P. Golden's Khazar Studies." *Acta Orientalia Academiae Scientiarum Hungaricae* 35:2–3 (1981): 397–412.

Bazin, Louis. "Pour une nouvelle hypothèse sur l'origine des Khazar." *Materialia Turcica* 7/8 (1981–1982): 51–71.

Brutzkus, Julius. "The Khazar Origin of Ancient Kiev." *Slavonic and East European Review* 22 (1944): 108–124.

Butler, Francis. "The Representation of Oral Culture in the *Vita Constantini*." *Slavic and East European Journal* 39:3 (1995): 367–384.

Chekin, Leonid S. "The Role of Jews in Early Russian Civilization in the Light of a New Discovery and New Controversies." *Russian History/Histoire russe* 17:4 (Winter 1990): 379–394.

————. "Samarcha, City of Khazaria." *Central Asiatic Journal* 33:1–2 (1989): 8–35.

Colarusso, John. "Two Circassian Tales of Huns and Khazars." *The Annual of the Society for the Study of Caucasia* 4–5 (1992–1993): 63–75.

Czeglédy, Károly. "Khazar Raids in Transcaucasia in 762–764 A.D." *Acta Orientalia Academiae Scientiarum Hungaricae* 11 (1960): 75–88.

————. "A Terhin-i ujgur rovásirásos felirat török és magyar történeti és nyelvészeti vonatkozásai." *Magyar Nyelv* 87 (1981): 461–462.

————. "From East to West: The Age of Nomadic Migrations in Eurasia." *Archivum Eurasiae Medii Aevi* 3 (1983): 25–125.

Edwards, Mike. "Searching for the Scythians." *National Geographic* 190:3 (Sept. 1996): 54–79.

Erdélyi, István. "Kabari (Kavari) v Karpatskom Basseyne." *Sovietskaya Arkheologiya* 4 (1983): 174–181.

————. "Megvan a Kazár Atlantisz!" *Napjaink* (March 17, 1993): 24.

Gershenson, Daniel E. "Yiddish 'davenen' and the Ashkenazic Rite: Byzantine Jewry and the Ashkenazim." *Yiddish* 10:2–3 (1996): 82–95.

Gil, Moshe. "The Radhanite Merchants and the Land of Radhan." *Journal of the Economic and Social History of the Orient* 17:3 (1976): 299–328.

Golden, Peter Benjamin. "Imperial Ideology and the Sources of Political Unity Amongst the Pre-Činggisid Nomads of Western Eurasia." *Archivum Eurasiae Medii Aevi* 2 (1982): 37–76.

————. "The Question of the Rus' Qağanate." *Archivum Eurasiae Medii Aevi* 2 (1982): 77–97.

————. "Khazaria and Judaism." *Archivum Eurasiae Medii Aevi* 3 (1983): 127–156.

————. "A New Discovery: Khazarian Hebrew Documents of the Tenth Century." *Harvard Ukrainian Studies* 8:3–4 (December 1984): 474–486.

Gumilev, Lev Nikolaevich. "New Data on the History of the Khazars." *Acta Archaeologica Academiae Scientiarum Hungaricae* 19 (1967): 61–103.

Hankó, Ildikó. "A kazár főváros rejtéje." *Napjaink* (March 17, 1993): 25.

Herényi, István. "A magyar törzsszövetség törzsei és törzsfői." *Századok* 116:1 (1982): 62–92.

Hirschberg, Haim Zeev. "The Problem of the Judaized Berbers." *Journal of African History* 4:3 (1963): 313–339.

Jakobson, Roman. "Minor Native Sources for the Early History of the Slavic Church." *Harvard Slavic Studies* 2 (1954): 39–73.

Kaplan, Frederick I. "The Decline of the Khazars and the Rise of the Varangians." *American Slavic and East European Review* 13 (1954): 1–10.

Kiss, Attila. "11th Century Khazar Rings from Hungary with Hebrew Letters and Signs." *Acta Archaeologica Academiae Scientiarum Hungaricae* 22 (1970): 341–348.

Kochev, Nikolaj. "The Question of Jews and the So-Called Judaizers in the Balkans from the 9th to the 14th Century." *Bulgarian Historical Review* 6 (1978): 60–79.

Ligeti, Lajos Munkái. "The Khazarian Letter from Kiev and Its Attestation in Runiform Script." *Acta Linguistica Academiae Scientiarum Hungaricae* 31 (1981): 5–18.

MacLennan, Robert S. "In Search of the Jewish Diaspora: A First-Century Synagogue in Crimea?" *Biblical Archaeology Review* 22:2 (March/April 1996): 41–51, 69.

Martinez, A. P. "Gardizi's Two Chapters on the Turks." *Archivum Eurasiae Medii Aevi* 2 (1982): 109–217.

Minorsky, Vladimir Fedorovich. "A New Book on the Khazars." *Oriens* 11 (1959): 122–145.

Noonan, Thomas S. "Did the Khazars Possess a Monetary Economy? An Analysis of the Numismatic Evidence." *Archivum Eurasiae Medii Aevi* 2 (1982): 219–267.

———. "Russia's Eastern Trade, 1150–1350: The Archaeological Evidence." *Archivum Eurasiae Medii Aevi* 3 (1983): 201–264.

————. "Why Dirhams First Reached Russia: The Role of Arab-Khazar Relations in the Development of the Earliest Islamic Trade with Eastern Europe." *Archivum Eurasiae Medii Aevi* 4 (1984): 151–282.

————. "The Khazar Economy." To appear in *Archivum Eurasiae Medii Aevi* 9.

Peeters, Paul. "Les Khazars dans la Passion de S. Abo de Tiflis." *Analecta Bollandiana* 52 (1934): 21–56.

Petrukhin, Vladimir Iakovlevich. "The Normans and the Khazars in the South of Rus' (The Formation of the 'Russian Land' in the Middle Dnepr Area)." *Russian History/Histoire russe* 19 (1992): 393–400.

————. "The Early History of Old Russian Art: The Rhyton from Chernigov and Khazarian Tradition." *Tor* 27:2 (1995): 475–486.

Pines, Shlomo. "A Moslem Text Concerning the Conversion of the Khazars to Judaism." *Journal of Jewish Studies* 13 (1962): 45–55.

Pritsak, Omeljan. "An Arabic Text on the Trade Route of the Corporation of Ar-Rus in the Second Half of the Ninth Century." *Folia Orientalia* 12 (1970): 241–259.

————. "The Khazar Kingdom's Conversion to Judaism." *Harvard Ukrainian Studies* 3:2 (Sept. 1978): 261–281.

Rockstein, Edward D. "The Mystery of the Székely Runes." *The Epigraphic Society Occasional Papers* 19 (1990): 176–183.

Senga, T. "The Toquz Oghuz Problem and the Origin of the Khazars." *Journal of Asian History* 24:2 (1990): 57–69.

Shaw, Stanford Jay. "Christian Anti Semitism in the Ottoman Empire." *Belleten C.* 54:68 (1991): 1073–1145.

Szyszman, Simon. "Le roi Bulan et le problème de la conversion des Khazars." *Ephemerides Theologicae Lovanienses* 33 (1957): 68–76.

Tóth, Sándor Laszló, "Kabarok (kavarok) a 9. századi magyar törzsszövetségben." *Századok* 118:1 (1984): 92–113.

Tryjarski, Edward. "Some Early Polish Sources and Their Importance for the History of the Altaic World." *Journal of Asian History* 3:1 (1969): 34–44.

Vikhnovich, Vsevolod L. "From the Jordan to the Dnieper." *Jewish Studies (Mada'e ha-Yahadut)* 31 (1991): 15–24.

Wacholder, Ben Zion. "Cases of Proselytizing in the Tosafist Responsa." *Jewish Quarterly Review* 15 (1960-1961): 288–315.

Werbart, Bozena. "Khazars or 'Saltovo-Majaki Culture'? Prejudices about Archaeology and Ethnicity." *Current Swedish Archaeology* 4 (1996): 199–221.

Wexler, Paul. "The Reconstruction of Pre-Ashkenazic Jewish Settlements in the Slavic Lands in the Light of Linguistic Sources." *Polin—A Journal of Polish Jewish Studies* 1 (1986): 3–18.

Ya'ari, Ehud. "Skeletons in the Closet." *The Jerusalem Report* (Sept. 7, 1995): 26–30.

Zajaczkowski, Ananiasz. "Khazarian Culture and Its Inheritors." *Acta Orientalia Academiae Scientiarum Hungaricae* 12 (1961): 299–307.

Zeiden, Herbert Guy. "Davenen: A Turkic Etymology." *Yiddish* 10:2–3 (1996): 96–99.

Zuckerman, Constantine. "On the Date of the Khazars' Conversion to Judaism and the Chronology of the Kings of the Rus Oleg and Igor." *Revue des Études Byzantines* 53 (1995): 237–270.

Books

Adler, Elkan Nathan, ed. *Jewish Travellers.* London: George Routledge and Sons, 1930.

Agus, Jacob Berhard. *The Meaning of Jewish History.* Vol. 1. New York: Abelard Schuman, 1963.

Aharoni, Reuben. *Yemenite Jewry: Origins, Culture, and Literature.* Bloomington, IN: Indiana University Press, 1986.

Allen, William Edward David. *The Ukraine—A History.* New York: Russell and Russell, 1963.

Ankori, Zvi. *Karaites in Byzantium: The Formative Years, 970–1100.* New York: Ams Press, 1968.

Ascherson, Neal. *Black Sea.* New York: Hill and Wang, 1995.

Ashtor, Eliyahu. *The Jews of Moslem Spain.* Vol. 1. Trans. Aaron Klein and Jenny Machlowitz Klein. Philadelphia: The Jewish Publication Society, 1992.

Ausubel, Nathan. *A Treasury of Jewish Folklore.* New York: Crown, 1948.

———. *Pictorial History of the Jewish People.* New York: Crown, 1953.

Bamberger, Bernard J. *Proselytism in the Talmudic Period.* New York: Hebrew Union College Press, 1939.

Barnavi, Eli, ed. *A Historical Atlas of the Jewish People.* New York: Schocken, 1992.

Baron, Salo Wittmayer. *A Social and Religious History of the Jews.* Vol. 3. New York: Columbia University Press, 1957.

———. *A Social and Religious History of the Jews.* Vol. 10. New York: Columbia University Press, 1965.

Bartha, Antal. *Hungarian Society in the 9th and 10th Centuries.* Trans. K. Balazs. Budapest: Akadémiai, 1975.

Barthold, Wasilii Vladimirovich. *Turkestan Down to the Mongol Invasion.* 3rd ed. Trans. H. A. R. Gibb and T. Minorsky. London: Messrs. Luzac and Co., 1968. E. J. W. Gibb Memorial, New Series, V.

Bedrosian, Robert, ed. *K'art'lis C'xovreba (The Georgian Chronicle).* New York: Sources of the Armenian Tradition, 1991.

Benjamin of Tudela. *The Itinerary of Benjamin of Tudela: Travels in the Middle Ages.* Trans. Marcus Nathan Adler. Malibu, CA: Joseph Simon/Pangloss Press, 1987.

Ben-Zvi, Itzhak. *The Exiled and the Redeemed.* Trans. Isaac A. Abbady. Philadelphia: The Jewish Publication Society of America, 1961.

Bezborodko, David. *An Insider's View of Jewish Pioneering in the Glass Industry.* Jerusalem: Gefen, 1987.

Birnbaum, Henrik. "On Jewish Life and Anti-Jewish Sentiments in Medieval Russia." In *Essays in Early Slavic Civilization,* ed. Henrik Birnbaum, pp. 215–245. Munich: Wilhelm Fink, 1981.

Bonnefoy, Yves, ed. *Asian Mythologies*. Trans. Gerald Honigsblum, et al. Chicago: University of Chicago Press, 1993.

Bowlus, Charles R. *Franks, Moravians, and Magyars: The
Struggle for the Middle Danube, 788–907*. Philadelphia:
University of Pennsylvania Press, 1995.

Comay, Joan. *The Diaspora Story: The Epic of the Jewish
People Among the Nations*. New York: Random House,
1980.

Czeglédy, Károly. "Pseudo-Zacharias Rhetor on the Nomads."
In *Studia Turcica*, ed. Lajos Munkái Ligeti, pp. 133–148.
Budapest: Akadémiai, 1971.

Dagoni, S. "When a Jewish Kingdom Ruled Southern Russia."
In *The Jewish People's Almanac*, ed. David C. Gross, pp.
430–431. New York: Hippocrene, 1994.

Davies, Norman. *God's Playground: A History of Poland*. Vol.
1. New York: Columbia University Press, 1982.

Dawson, Christopher, ed. *The Mongol Mission: Narratives and
Letters of the Franciscan Missionaries in Mongolia and
China in the Thirteenth and Fourteenth Centuries*. New
York: Sheed and Ward, 1955.

Dimitrov, Dimitur. *Prabulgarite po severnoto i zapadnoto
Chernomorie: kum vuprosa za tiakhnoto prisustvie i is-
toriya v dneshnite ruski zemi i roliata im pri obrazuvane-
to na bulgarskata durzhava*. Varna, Bulgaria: Georgi Bal-
akov, 1987.

Dunlop, Douglas Morton. *The History of the Jewish Khazars*.
New York: Schocken, 1967.

———. "The Khazars." In *The Dark Ages: Jews in Christian
Europe, 711–1096*, ed. Cecil Roth and I. H. Levine, pp.
325–356. New Brunswick, NJ: Rutgers University Press,
1966. World History of the Jewish People, second series,
vol. 2.

Eichhorn, David Max, ed. *Conversion to Judaism: A History
and Analysis*: New York: Ktav, 1965.

Erdélyi, István. "The Avars." In *Peoples That Vanished*, ed. P.
Puchkov, trans. Ye. Voronov, pp. 93–102. Moscow: Nauka,
1989.

Ettinger, Shmuel. "Kievan Russia." In *The Dark Ages: Jews in Christian Europe, 711–1096*, ed. Cecil Roth and I. H. Levine, pp. 319–324. New Brunswick, NJ: Rutgers University Press, 1966. World History of the Jewish People, second series, vol. 2.

———. "Jewish Participation in the Settlement of Ukraine in the Sixteenth and Seventeenth Century." In *Ukrainian-Jewish Relations in Historical Perspective*, ed. Howard Aster and Peter J. Potichnyj, pp. 23–30. Edmonton, Alberta, Canada: Canadian Institute of Ukrainian Studies Press, University of Alberta, 1990.

Fishberg, Maurice. *The Jews: A Study of Race and Environment.* London: Walter Scott, 1911.

Fodor, István. *In Search of a New Homeland: The Prehistory of the Hungarian People and the Conquest.* Trans. Helen Tarnoy. Gyoma, Hungary: Corvina, 1982.

Funch, Lars, and Krag, Helen Liesl. *The North Caucasus: Minorities at a Crossroads.* London: Minority Rights Group, 1994.

Gaster, Moses, ed. *The Chronicles of Jerahmeel.* New York: Ktav, 1971.

Gilbert, Martin. *Atlas of Russian History.* 2nd ed. New York: Oxford University Press, 1993.

———, ed. *The Illustrated Atlas of Jewish Civilization—4,000 Years of Jewish History.* New York: Macmillan, 1990.

Göckenjan, Hansgerd. *Hilfsvölker und Grenzwächter im mittelalterlichen Ungarn.* Wiesbaden, West Germany: Franz Steiner, 1972.

Godbey, Allen H. *The Lost Tribes, A Myth: Suggestions Toward Rewriting Hebrew History.* Durham, NC: Duke University Press, 1930.

Golb, Norman, and Pritsak, Omeljan. *Khazarian Hebrew Documents of the Tenth Century.* Ithaca, NY: Cornell University Press, 1982.

Golden, Peter Benjamin. *Khazar Studies: An Historico-Philological Inquiry into the Origins of the Khazars.* Vol. 1. Budapest: Akadémiai, 1980.

———. "The Turkic Peoples and Caucasia." In *Transcaucasia: Nationalism and Social Change*, ed. Ronald Grigor Suny, pp. 45–67. Ann Arbor, MI: University of Michigan, 1983.

———. *An Introduction to the History of the Turkic Peoples: Ethnogenesis and State Formation in Medieval and Early Modern Eurasia and the Middle East*. Wiesbaden, Germany: Otto Harrassowitz, 1992.

Goodman, Martin D. "Jewish Proselytizing in the First Century." In *The Jews Among Pagans and Christians in the Roman Empire*, ed. Judith Lieu, John North, and Tessa Rajak, pp. 53–78. London: Routledge, 1992.

———. "Proselytising in Rabbinic Judaism." In *Readings on Conversion to Judaism*, ed. Lawrence J. Epstein, pp. 33–45. Northvale, NJ: Jason Aronson, 1995.

Gow, Andrew Colin. *The Red Jews: Antisemitism in an Apocalyptic Age, 1200–1600*. Leiden, Netherlands: E. J. Brill, 1995.

Graetz, Heinrich Hirsch. *History of the Jews*. Vol. 3. Philadelphia: The Jewish Publication Society of America, 1896.

Grayzel, Solomon. *A History of the Jews*. New York: Meridian, 1984.

Greenbaum, Masha. *The Jews of Lithuania: A History of a Remarkable Community 1316–1945*. Jerusalem: Gefen, 1995.

Grousset, René. *The Empire of the Steppes: a History of Central Asia*. Trans. Naomi Waldorf. New Brunswick, NJ: Rutgers University Press, 1970.

Gubaroff, George V. *Cossacks and Their Land, in the Light of New Data*. Trans. John Nelson Washburn. Providence, RI: Cossack American National Alliance, 1985.

Gumilev, Lev Nikolaevich. *Ritmy Evrazii: epokhu i tsivilizatsii*. Moscow: Ekopros, 1993.

Györffy, György. *King Saint Stephen of Hungary*. Trans. Peter Doherty. New York: Columbia University Press, 1994. East European Monographs #403.

Hadas-Lebel, Mireille. *Flavius Josephus: Eyewitness to Rome's First-Century Conquest of Judea*. New York: Macmillan, 1993.

HaLevi, Yehuda. *The Kuzari: In Defense of the Despised Faith.* Trans. Nissan Daniel Korobkin. Northvale, NJ: Jason Aronson, 1998.

Halperin, Charles J. *Russia and the Golden Horde: The Mongol Impact on Medieval Russian History.* Bloomington, IN: Indiana University Press, 1985.

Hamm, Michael F. *Kiev: A Portrait, 1800–1917.* Princeton, NJ: Princeton University Press, 1993.

Harkavy, Abraham Elija. "Rab Sa'adyah Gaon al debar ha-Kuzarim." In *Semitic Studies in Memory of Rev. Dr. Alexander Kohut,* XXXV, ed. G. A. Kohut, pp. 244–247. Berlin: S. Calvary and Co., 1897.

Harshav, Benjamin. *The Meaning of Yiddish.* Los Angeles and Berkeley, CA: University of California Press, 1990.

Hitti, Philip Khuri. *History of the Arabs: From the Earliest Times to the Present.* 8th ed. New York: St. Martin's Press, 1963.

Hopkirk, Kathleen. *Central Asia: A Traveller's Companion.* London: John Murray, 1993.

Ilovaiskii, Dmitrii Ivanovich. *Razyskaniya o nachale rusi: vmiesto vvedeniya v russkuiu.* Moscow: Miller, 1882.

Irmukhanov, Beimbet Babiktievich. *Kazakstan: istoriko-publitsisticheskiy vzglyad.* Almaty, Kazakstan: Olke, 1996.

Josephus Flavius. *The Complete Works of Josephus.* Trans. William Whiston. Grand Rapids, MI: Kregel, 1981.

Kahle, Paul E. *The Cairo Geniza.* London: Oxford University Press, 1947.

Kaplan, Steve. *The Beta Israel (Falasha) in Ethiopia: From Earliest Times to the Twentieth Century.* New York: New York University Press, 1992.

Kasovich, Israel Isser. *The Eternal People: Holiday Sentiments on Jews and Judaism.* New York: The Jordan Publishing Co., 1929.

Katz, Zev. "The Jews in the Soviet Union." In *Handbook of Major Soviet Nationalities,* ed. Zev Katz, et al., pp. 355–389. New York: The Free Press, 1975.

Khass Hajib, Yusuf. *Wisdom of Royal Glory: A Turko-Islamic Mirror for Princes.* Trans. Robert Dankoff. Chicago: University of Chicago Press, 1983.

Khazanov, Anatoly Michailovich. *The Krymchaks: A Vanishing Group in the Soviet Union.* Jerusalem: The Marjorie Mayrock Center for Soviet and East European Research, The Hebrew University of Jerusalem, 1989.

King, Robert D. "Migration and Linguistics as Illustrated by Yiddish." In *Reconstructing Languages and Cultures,* ed. Edgar C. Polemé and Werner Winter, pp. 419–439. Berlin: Mouton de Gruyter, 1992.

Kirschbaum, Stanislav J. *A History of Slovakia: The Struggle for Survival.* New York: St. Martin's Press, 1995.

Klier, John Doyle. *Russia Gathers Her Jews: The Origins of the "Jewish Question" in Russia, 1772–1825.* DeKalb, IL: Northern Illinois University Press, 1986.

Kluchevsky, Vasilii Osipovich. *A History of Russia.* Vol. 1. Trans. C. J. Hogarth. New York: Russell and Russell, 1960.

Koestler, Arthur. *The Thirteenth Tribe: The Khazar Empire and Its Heritage.* New York: Random House, 1976.

Kosztolnyik, Z. J. *Five Eleventh Century Hungarian Kings: Their Policies and Their Relations with Rome.* New York: Columbia University Press, 1981. East European Monographs #79.

Kurinsky, Samuel V. *The Glassmakers: An Odyssey of the Jews—The First Three Thousand Years.* New York: Hippocrene, 1991.

Kwanten, Luc. *Imperial Nomads: A History of Central Asia.* Philadelphia: University of Pennsylvania Press, 1979.

Lang, David Marshall. *The Bulgarians: From Pagan Times to the Ottoman Conquest.* Boulder, CO: Westview Press, 1976.

Legg, Stuart. *The Heartland.* New York: Capricorn Books, 1971.

Lesley, Blanch. *The Sabres of Paradise.* New York: Carroll and Graf, 1960.

Litman, Jacob. *The Economic Role of Jews in Medieval Poland: The Contribution of Yitzhak Schipper.* Lanham,
MD: University Press of America, 1984.

Lubo-Lesnichenko, Evgenii Iosifovich. "The Huns, Third Century B.C. to Sixth Century A.D. " In *Nomads of Eurasia,*
ed. Vladimir Nikolaevich Basilov, trans. Mary Fleming
Zirin, pp. 41–53. Seattle: University of Washington Press,
1989.

Luciw, Jurij. *Sviatoslav the Conqueror: Creator of a Great
Kyivian Rus' Empire.* State College, PA: Slavia Library,
1986. Ukrainian Free Press Series Monographs #40.

Macartney, Carlile Aylmer. *The Magyars in the Ninth Century.*
Cambridge, England: Cambridge University Press, 1930.

Maenchen-Helfen, J. Otto. *The World of the Huns: Studies
in Their History and Culture.* Los Angeles and Berkeley,
CA: University of California Press, 1973.

Makkai, László. "The Hungarians' Prehistory, Their Conquest
of Hungary, and Their Raids to the West to 955." In *A
History of Hungary,* ed. Peter F. Sugar, pp. 8–14.
Bloomington, IN: Indiana University Press, 1990.

———. "The Foundation of the Hungarian Christian State,
950–1196." In *A History of Hungary,* ed. Peter F. Sugar, pp.
15–22. Bloomington, IN: Indiana University Press, 1990.

Mantran, Robert, ed. *Great Dates in Islamic History.* New York:
Facts on File, 1996.

Mayer, Egon. "Why Not Judaism?" In *Readings on Conversion
to Judaism,* ed. Lawrence J. Epstein, pp. 99–110.
Northvale, NJ: Jason Aronson, 1995.

Miller, Philip E., ed. *Karaite Separatism in Nineteenth-Century
Russia: Solomon Lutski's Epistle of Israel's Deliverance.*
Cincinnati: Hebrew Union College Press, 1993.

Minorsky, Vladimir Fedorovich. *Hudud al-`Alam (The Regions
of the World): A Persian Geography 372 A.D.–982 A.D.*
London: Messrs. Luzac and Co., 1937. E. J. W. Gibb Memorial, New Series, XI.

————. *A History of Sharvan and Darband in the 10th–11th Centuries*. Cambridge, England: W. Heffer and Sons, 1958.

Molé, Marijan, ed. *La légende de Zoroastre selon les textes pehlevis*. Paris: C. Klincksieck, 1967.

Nansen, Fridtjof. *Through the Caucasus to the Volga*. New York: W. W. Norton and Company, 1931.

Nicolle, David. *Medieval Warfare Source Book*. Vol. 2: Christian Europe and Its Neighbours. London: Arms and Armour Press, 1996.

Noonan, Thomas S. "Byzantium and the Khazars: a special relationship?" In *Byzantine Diplomacy: Papers from the Twenty-fourth Spring Symposium of Byzantine Studies, Cambridge, March 1990*, ed. Jonathan Shepard and Simon Franklin, pp. 109–132. Aldershot, England: Variorum, 1992.

Norwich, John Julius. *Byzantium: The Early Centuries*. New York: Alfred A. Knopf, 1989.

Oegema, Gerbern S. *The History of the Shield of David: The Birth of a Symbol*. Frankfurt am Main: Peter Lang, 1996.

Olson, James S., ed. *An Ethnohistorical Dictionary of the Russian and Soviet Empires*. Westport, CT: Greenwood Press, 1994.

Ostrogorsky, George. *History of the Byzantine State*. New Brunswick, NJ: Rutgers University Press, 1969.

Parker, William Henry. *An Historical Geography of Russia*. Chicago: Aldine, 1968.

Patai, Raphael. *The Jews of Hungary: History, Culture, Psychology*. Detroit: Wayne State University Press, 1996.

————, and Patai, Jennifer. *The Myth of the Jewish Race*. rev. ed. Detroit: Wayne State University Press, 1989.

Pauler, Gyula, and Szilágyi, Sandor. *A magyar honfoglalás kútföi*. Budapest: Nap, 1995.

Piechotka, Kazimierz, and Piechotka, Maria. *Wooden Synagogues*. Trans. Rulka Langer. Warsaw: Arkady, 1959.

Pinkus, Benjamin. *The Jews of the Soviet Union: The History of a National Minority*. Cambridge, England: Cambridge University Press, 1988.

Pletnyova, Svetlana Aleksandrovna. *Khazary*. Moscow: Nauka, 1986.

———. "The Polovtsy." In *Peoples That Vanished*, ed. P. Puchkov, trans. Ye. Voronov, pp. 21–33. Moscow: Nauka, 1989.

———. "The Khazars." In *Peoples That Vanished*, ed. P. Puchkov, trans. Ye. Voronov, pp. 49–60. Moscow: Nauka, 1989.

Posselt, Alfred H. *Geschichte des chazarisch-jüdischen Staates*. Vienna: Vereines zur Förderung und Pflege des Reformjudentums, 1982.

Prager, Dennis. "Judaism Must Seek Converts." In *Readings on Conversion to Judaism*, ed. Lawrence J. Epstein, pp. 79–97. Northvale, NJ: Jason Aronson, 1995.

Pritsak, Omeljan. *The Origin of Rus'*. Vol. 1. Cambridge, MA: Harvard Ukrainian Research Institute, Harvard University Press, 1981.

———. "The Pre-Ashkenazic Jews of Eastern Europe in Relation to the Khazars, the Rus' and the Lithuanians." In *Ukrainian-Jewish Relations in Historical Perspective*, ed. Howard Aster and Peter J. Potichnyj, pp. 3–21. Edmonton, Alberta, Canada: Canadian Institute of Ukrainian Studies Press, University of Alberta, 1990.

Riasanovsky, Alexander V., and Watson, William E., eds. *Readings in Russian History*. Vol. 1. Dubuque, IA: Kendall/Hunt, 1991.

Riasanovsky, Nicholas V. *A History of Russia*. 5th ed. New York: Oxford University Press, 1993.

Rorlich, Azade-Ayşe. *The Volga Tatars: A Profile in National Resilience*. Stanford, CA: Hoover Institution Press, Stanford University, 1986.

Rosenbloom, Joseph R. *Conversion to Judaism: From the Biblical Period to the Present*. Cincinnati: Hebrew Union College Press, 1978.

Roth, Cecil. *A Short History of the Jewish People*. London: Horovitz, 1969.

Rubin, Alexis P., ed. *Scattered Among the Nations: Documents Affecting Jewish History 49 to 1975*. Northvale, NJ: Jason Aronson, 1995.

Samuel, Maurice. *In Praise of Yiddish*. New York: Cowles, 1971.

Scheiber, Alexander (Sándor). *Jewish Inscriptions in Hungary from the 3rd Century to 1686*. Budapest: Akadémiai, 1983.

Schipper, Itzhak (Ignacy). "Dzieje gospodarcze Żydów Korony i Litwy w czasach przedrozbiorowych." In *Żydzi w Polsce Odrodzonej*, ed. A. Hafftka, Itzhak Schipper, and A. Tartakower, pp. 111–190. Warsaw, 1936.

―――. "Rozwój ludności Żydowskiej na ziemiach Dawnej Rzeczypospolitej." In *Żydzi w Polsce Odrodzonej*, ed. A. Hafftka, Itzhak Schipper, and A. Tartakower, pp. 21–36. Warsaw, 1936.

Schoenburg, Nancy and Schoenburg, Stuart. *Lithuanian Jewish Communities*. Northvale, NJ: Jason Aronson, 1996.

Shamir, Ilana, and Shavit, Shlomo, eds. *Encyclopedia of Jewish History: Events and Eras of the Jewish People*. New York: Facts on File, 1986.

Soldatova, Galina and Dement'eva, Irina. "Russians in the North Caucasian Republics." In *The New Russian Diaspora: Russian Minorities in the Former Soviet Republics*, ed. Emil Payin, et al., pp. 122–138. Armonk, NY: M. E. Sharpe, 1994.

Subtelny, Orest'. *Ukraine: A History*. Toronto: University of Toronto Press, 1988.

Tamir, Vicki. *Bulgaria and Her Jews: The History of a Dubious Symbiosis*. New York: Sepher-Hermon Press, 1979.

Tihany, Leslie Charles. *A History of Middle Europe: From the Earliest Times to the Age of the World Wars*. New Brunswick, NJ: Rutgers University Press, 1976.

Tóth, Sándor Laszló. "A nyolcadik törzs, (Hogyan lett magyar a kabar?)" In *Száz rejtely a magyar történelemböl*, ed. Ferenc Halmos, pp. 16–17. Budapest: Gesta, 1994.

Trigger, Bruce G. *A History of Archaeological Thought.* Cambridge, England: Cambridge University Press, 1989.

Ujvári, Péter, ed. *Magyar zsidó lexikon.* Budapest: Pallas, 1929.

Vainshtein, Sev'yan Izrailevich. "The Turkic Peoples, Sixth to Twelfth Centuries." In *Nomads of Eurasia*, ed. Vladimir Nikolaevich Basilov, trans. Mary Fleming Zirin, pp. 55–65. Seattle: University of Washington Press, 1989.

Vasiliev, Alexander Alexandrovich. *The Goths in the Crimea.* Cambridge, MA: The Mediaeval Academy of America, 1936.

Vernadsky, George. *A History of Russia.* Vol. 1: Ancient Russia. New Haven, CT: Yale University Press, 1948.

———. *A History of Russia.* Vol. 2: Kievan Russia. New Haven, CT: Yale University Press, 1948.

Wacholder, Ben Zion. "Attitudes Toward Proselytizing in the Classical Halakah." In *Readings on Conversion to Judaism*, ed. Lawrence J. Epstein, pp. 15–32. Northvale, NJ: Jason Aronson, 1995.

Walsh, Warren B. *Readings in Russian History.* Vol. 1. Syracuse, NY: Syracuse University Press, 1963.

Weinryb, Bernard Dov. *The Beginnings of East European Jewry in Legend and Historiography.* Leiden, Netherlands: E. J. Brill, 1962.

Wexler, Paul. *The Ashkenazic Jews: A Slavo-Turkic People in Search of a Jewish Identity.* Columbus, OH: Slavica, 1993.

———. *The Non-Jewish Origins of the Sephardic Jews.* Albany, NY: State University of New York Press, 1996.

Whittell, Giles. *Cadogan Guides—Central Asia.* London: Cadogan Books, 1996.

Wyszomirska (Werbart), Bozena. "Religion som enande politisk-social länk—exemplet: det Kazariska riket." In *Arkeologi och Religion: Rapport från arkeologidagarna 16–18 januari 1989*, ed. Lars Larsson and Bozena Wyszomirska, pp. 135–148. Lund, Sweden: University of Lund, 1989.

Yarmolinsky, Avrahm, ed. *The Poems, Prose, and Plays of*

Alexander Pushkin. New York: The Modern Library (Random House), 1964.

Zaprudnik, Jan. *Belarus: At a Crossroads in History.* Boulder, CO: Westview Press, 1993.

Zenkovsky, Serge A., ed. *Medieval Russia's Epics, Chronicles, and Tales.* New York: Meridian, 1974.

Zeynaloglu, Jahangir. *A Concise History of Azerbaijan.* Trans. Ferhad P. Abasov. Boston: F. P. Abasov, 1997.

Encyclopedia Entries

Golden, Peter Benjamin. "Turkic Languages." In *Encyclopedia of Asian History,* Vol. 4. New York: Charles Scribners' Sons, 1988.

Gottheil, Richard. "Adiabene." In *The Jewish Encyclopedia,* Vol. 1. New York: Ktav, 1901–1906.

Lipman, J. G. "Taman." In *The Jewish Encyclopedia,* Vol. 12. New York: Ktav, 1901–1906.

Rosenthal, Herman. "Chazars." In *The Jewish Encyclopedia,* Vol. 4. New York: Ktav, 1901–1906.

———. "Kiev." In *The Jewish Encyclopedia,* Vol. 7. New York: Ktav, 1901–1906.

Zajaczkowski, W. "The Karaites in Eastern Europe." In *Encyclopedia of Islam,* new ed., Vol. 4, ed. E. van Donzel, pp. 608–609. Leiden, Netherlands: E. J. Brill, 1993.

Zimonyi, István. "Kazárok." In *Korai magyar történeti lexikon (9–14. század),* ed. Gyula Kristó et al., pp. 336, 338. Budapest: Akadémiai, 1994.

INDEX

About the Author

Kevin Alan Brook, a resident of Connecticut whose Jewish ancestors immigrated to the United States from Ukraine, Belarus, Lithuania, and Poland, is the moderator of the Eastern European Jewish History (EEJH) discussion list on the Internet and maintains a popular website about the Khazars entitled "The Khazaria Info Center." He has been researching and writing about the history of the Khazars since 1993. Mr. Brook received his BS degree in Business Administration from Bryant College in Smithfield, Rhode Island. *The Jews of Khazaria* is Mr. Brook's first book.